# CONTEMPORARY POETRY AND POSTMODERNISM
## DIALOGUE AND ESTRANGEMENT

# Contemporary Poetry and Postmodernism

## Dialogue and Estrangement

Ian Gregson

*Lecturer in English*
*University of Wales, Bangor*

First published 1996 by
**MACMILLAN PRESS LTD**
Houndmills, Basingstoke, Hampshire RG21 6XS
and London
Companies and representatives
throughout the world

ISBN 0–333–65565–6 hardcover
ISBN 0–333–65566–4 paperback

A catalogue record for this book is available
from the British Library.

10   9   8   7   6   5   4   3   2   1
05   04   03   02   01   00   99   98   97   96

Printed and bound in Great Britain by
Antony Rowe Ltd, Chippenham, Wiltshire

---

Published in the United States of America 1996 by
ST. MARTIN'S PRESS, INC.,
Scholarly and Reference Division
175 Fifth Avenue, New York, N.Y. 10010

ISBN 0–312–15992–7 (cloth)
ISBN 0–312–15993–5 (paperback)

To Sue, Jean and Paul

# Contents

# Contents

# Acknowledgements

I make grateful acknowledgement for permission to reprint the following:

Extracts from "Mules", "Lunch with Pancho Villa", "Why Brownlee Left", "The Boundary Commission", "Cuba", "Immram", "Identities", "Elizabeth" "Good Friday, 1971, Driving Westward", "The More a Man Has the More a Man Wants" in *Selected Poems* by Paul Muldoon (Faber and Faber, 1986) copyright by Paul Muldoon, reprinted by permission of Faber and Faber Ltd.

Extracts from "A German Requiem", "In a Notebook", "Children in Exile", "Nest of Vampires", "A Vacant Possession", "Exempla", "The Fruit-Grower in War-Time", "South Parks Road", "Terminal Moraine", "The Pitt Rivers Museum, Oxford", "Chosun", "The Kingfisher's Boxing Gloves", "Letter to John Fuller", "Lines for Translation Into Any Language", and "A Staffordshire Murderer" in *The Memory of War and Children in Exile: Poems 1968–1983* by James Fenton, Penguin, 1994 copyright by James Fenton and "The Ballad of the Imam and the Shah" in *Out of Danger*, by James Fenton, Penguin, 1993 copyright by James Fenton, all reprinted by permission of Peters, Fraser and Dunlop.

Extracts from "Going Back", "In Focus", "Mornings After", "The Water Below", "The Soho Hospital for Women", "Clarendon Whatmough", "Blue Glass" and "Kilpeck" in *Selected Poems*, by Fleur Adcock (Oxford University Press, 1983) copyright by Fleur Adcock, reprinted by permission of Oxford University Press.

Extracts from "Glasgow Sonnets", "The Starlings in George Square", "One Cigarette", "The Unspoken", "The Second Life", "In Sobieski's Shield", "From the Video Box", "Cinquevalli", "Instamatic Poems", "Interferences" and "An Alphabet of Goddesses" in *Collected Poems*, by Edwin Morgan (Carcanet, 1990) copyright by Edwin Morgan, reprinted by permission of Carcanet Press.

Extracts from "City", "For Realism", "After Working", "Toyland", "Five Morning Poems", "If I Didn't", "The Thing About Joe Sullivan", "Staffordshire Red", "Handsworth Liberties", "Of the Empirical Self and for Me" in *Poems* by Roy Fisher (Oxford University Press, 1980) copyright by Roy Fisher, reprinted by permission of the author.

Extracts from "The Child at the Piano", "Moon Climbing", "Rilke's Feet", "Another Almost", "A Drive in the Country", "The Prose of Walking Back to China", "Anasphere: Le Torse Antique", "Definition", "In the Secret House", "A Road that is One in Many", "How to Listen to Birds", "The Armadillos" in *Selected Writings*, by Christopher Middleton (Carcanet, 1989), copyright by Christopher Middleton, reprinted by permission of Carcanet Press.

Extracts from "Ducks and Rabbits", "Zettel", "Address to the Reader from Pevensey Sluice", "Canzon", "The Garden of Proserpine" and "Richard II" in *Collected Poems and Translations* by Veronica Forrest-Thomson (London, Lewes, Berkeley: Allardyce, Barnett, Publishers, 1990). Copyright Jonathan Culler and the Estate of Veronica Forrest-Thomson 1990 and Copyright Allardyce, Barnett, Publishers, 1990. Reprinted by permission of Allardyce, Barnett, Publishers.

Extracts from "Dark Looks", "Cruelty Without Beauty", "Wherever You Are, Be Somewhere Else", "Well All Right", "A Shortened Set", "Stair Spirit", "Disintegrate Me" and "Laibach Lyrik" in *Mop Mop Georgette* by Denise Riley 1993 (Reality Street editions) copyright by Denise Riley, reprinted by permission of the author and Reality Street editions.

# Introduction

This book's division into two parts is meant to suggest comparisons and contrasts between "mainstream" poetry and kinds of modernist writing which have been regarded, or are still regarded, as outside that pale. Part of its point is to draw attention to the neglect which has been suffered by the three senior poets Roy Fisher, Christopher Middleton and, to a lesser extent Edwin Morgan who are discussed in the second section. However, I also wish to celebrate the exciting achievements of the mainstream and to redefine the nature of those achievements in what seem to me the most appropriate terms.

Most of the causes for the marginalising of Fisher, Middleton and Morgan have their sources in literary history rather than in what is happening currently. The careers of all three ought to have taken off in the early 60s when each of them started to produce their best work. Unfortunately for them that was a period of exceptional narrowness in the outlook of those in charge of the commanding heights of the poetic economy. In particular, a powerful prejudice was operating – thanks to the realist legacy of the Movement – against the Modernist tradition to which all three owed allegiance. In coining the term "retro-modernist" to describe these poets I am referring to this allegiance and also distinguishing them from postmodernists like John Ashbery – this is discussed in more detail in Chapter 8.

"Estrangement", then, refers to the way in which Fisher, Middleton and Morgan were (and to some extent still are) outsiders in British poetry. However, it also refers to what I take to be their most characteristic poetic strategy – their deployment of a relentless defamiliarising that is radically opposed to the consensual assumptions of the Movement. The realism of Larkin and the others depends upon a technique that implicitly, but consistently, refers to experiences and attitudes which are shared by poet and reader – it appeals, in other words, to a sense of familiarity. By contrast, the retro-modernism of Morgan, Fisher and Middleton wilfully, stubbornly, sometimes playfully but sometimes, also, austerely, insists on strangeness and difficulty. For this reason, it is the theorising of the Russian formalist Victor Shklovsky which provides the most fruitful access to their poetry. In his essay "Art as Technique"[1] he refers to the way in which "If we start to examine the general laws of perception, we see that as perception becomes habitual, it becomes automatic" (11). As an illustration of this he quotes a passage from Tolstoy's diary in which the novelist describes being unable to remember whether he had dusted a divan because the action of doing so had become so "habitual and unconscious" (12), and so, Shklovsky says, "life is reckoned as nothing":

> Habitualization devours works, clothes, furniture, one's wife, and the fear of war. "If the whole complex lives of many people go on unconsciously, then such lives are as if they had never been." And art exists that one may recover the sensation of life; it exists to make one feel things, to make the stone *stony*. The purpose of art is to impart the sensation of things as they are perceived and not as they are known. The technique of art is to make objects "unfamiliar", to make forms difficult, to increase the difficulty and length of perception because the process of perception is an aesthetic end in itself and must be prolonged. *Art is a way of experiencing the artfulness of an object; the object is not important.*
>
> (12)

Donald Davie has related this passage to Roy Fisher's description of himself as a "1920s Russian modernist" who subjects experience to "a slow-motion dismemberment"[2]. For in his repeated evocations of urban landscapes Fisher has used a wide range of techniques to overcome the way in which, through habit, those landscapes are perceptually erased. This has involved his poetry in a continual argument with realism whose project Fisher respects and whose techniques of detailed notation he deploys, but whose consensual assumptions he half-reluctantly but consistently deconstructs. What has especially concerned him is the way that the "real" changes according to the levels and kinds of subjectivity from which it is perceived: estrangement for Fisher is crucially achieved by moving from the hard clarity and objectivity of imagist techniques to effects which insinuate distortive states of mind and, beyond them, to effects which are sometimes painfully expressionist or wildly or playfully surrealist.

As Stan Smith points out, Christopher Middleton is similarly indebted to the theory of estrangement:

> This classical yet human distance is maintained by a deliberate employment of that "defamiliarisation" technique described by the Russian formalist Viktor Shklovsky (whom Middleton acknowledges on several occasions). The disjunctions, dislocations and unexpected collocations of his language, the experimental diversity of structure and theme, and a movement between extremes of abstrusity and explicitness, using the very opacity of his language to concentrate our gaze as if for the first time on familiar object and event, all enable Middleton to pursue that "defining of enigmas" which is for him the poetic vocation, exposing us to "the strangeness of being alive. . .the strangeness of living things outside oneself".[3]

This stress on strangeness is also evident in Edwin Morgan – even, paradoxically, in his Scottish nationalism. His scepticism about obsessively nationalist writing is one part of a generally centrifugal tendency in his outlook: he fears that self-consciously Scottish writing may distort experience, including Scottish experience, by artificially freezing it at a vanished historical moment and fencing it off from the rest of the world. This is anathema to him because one of his major concerns is that poetry should evolve strategies that enable it to cope with experience which is constantly unfixing the boundaries of the past. He worries, therefore, that a simplistic nationalism tries to impose fixed limits which misrepresent the shifting and elusive nature of the modern world. So he uses estrangement techniques partly in opposition to conservative nationalists who harp on the familiarity of the familiar. For those techniques suggest that a native place can only be thoroughly understood in the context of other places: they assume, too, that experience is radically unstable and that what is reassuringly fixed about familiar places and things is an illusion.

Inevitably, there is something self-consciously cerebral, even austerely so, about the rigorous application of estrangement techniques and this provides an important clue to why modernism has had a hard time in Britain where even many of the intellectuals are anti-intellectual. There is perhaps no more telling sign of the continuing effect of this than the immense popularity of the crudely anti-modernist poetry of Wendy Cope.

On the other hand, mainstream poets in Britain have consistently raided modernism and employed its techniques for their own ends – Larkin repeatedly used imagism and Audenesque montage while subordinating them to a dominantly realist context, thereby subjecting them to a kind of repressive tolerance. In the late 1940s and early 1950s he evolved a poetic whose first concern was to establish a consensus with his readers based on shared experience – but that this poetic evolved through a dialogue with modernism can be seen clearly in his most important poem "The Whitsun Weddings". This amounts to a realist rereading of *The Waste Land's* fertility metaphor. What does all that Jessie Weston stuff really mean to someone living in industrial mid-twentieth century England? Something like this: numerous couples heading on the same train towards their wedding nights in a London "spread out in the sun/ Its postal districts packed like squares of wheat," and then "A sense of falling, like an arrow shower/ Sent out of sight, somewhere becoming rain".

What characterises the generations after Larkin is a growing refusal to allow one stylistic idiom to dominate – modernist and realist techniques jostle with each other in their work, producing a greater open-endedness than in the poetry of the Movement, a sense of a plurality of voices. Douglas Dunn, for example, starts out in *Terry Street*[4] looking like a realist poet influenced by Larkin. However, even in that first book there are other influences at work which insist on the importance of narrative point of view – the centre of consciousness moves deliberately from the poet to the street's residents and back again in a way that subverts any single-minded sense of what "reality" is. There are even in *Terry Street* hints of a surreal element in Dunn's thinking and this acquires increasing importance later linked to a powerfully political consciousness which insists on opposing dominant ideologies with an exploration of how profoundly different the world looks when it is viewed from the margins, when the voices of the politically muted are allowed to speak.

This mingling of the real and the surreal in Douglas Dunn is an example of the tendency of post-Movement mainstream poets to deploy a stylistic "mélange". This is a postmodernist phenomenon to the extent that it self-consciously upsets expectations and destabilises any authoritative vision of the world, and the writing of these poets (Paul Muldoon, James Fenton, Craig Raine) is often playful, self-reflexive and parodic in the approved postmodernist way. However, once again the ability of the British to domesticate movements like this, to translate, assimilate and at the same time crucially alter them is in evidence. So where the work of thorough postmodernists is about the relentless deconstruction of the "real", there is in the work of even the most postmodernist of British poets a tendency to accord the real a residual respect and allow it a residual place.

Consequently, while recent mainstream British poetry has assimilated postmodernist concerns with self-reflexive fictiveness and with the way that language distorts and even constitutes the experiences it is supposed merely to describe, it has also persisted in believing in the reality of the political and moral issues it addresses. When it has evoked the postmodernist impossibility of speaking in a privileged voice it has tended, not to celebrate it as Ashbery's poems do, but to fret over it and struggle against it. This much at least the mainstream shares with Morgan, Fisher and Middleton who have retained a stubbornly pre-postmodernist resistance to pure fictiveness, and have persisted with a modernist anxiety over the boundaries of knowledge, with a modernist seriousness – even, at times, earnestness – about their explorations of the fragmentariness of being.

In mainstream poetry, however, there has been a tendency not so much to resist self-reflexive fictiveness as to incorporate it and deploy it as a technique alongside others. The stylistic "mélange" I referred to, though, is not mere eclecticism – it reflects a genuine concern to oppose single-minded visions of experience with a self-conscious emphasis on diversity and mutability. Much of the impetus for this is political, and arises from a post-Movement sensibility in British poetry which arises from cultural polyphony: where the Movement poetic assumed that writers and readers were white, English middle-class males, contemporary poetry is acutely aware of voices that insist on their differences from that model and draw attention to their class, gender, nationality or race. One of the most conspicuous characteristics of contemporary poetry, as a result, is the colloquial vividness and variety of its language, and this is not merely a question of mannerism but of something substantial and important, for

According to Bakhtin, each social group – each class, profession, generation, religion, region – has its own characteristic way of speaking, its own dialect. Each dialect reflects and embodies a set of values and a sense of shared experience. Because no two individuals ever entirely coincide in their experience or belong to precisely the same set of social groups, every act of understanding involves an act of translation and a negotiation of values. It is essentially a phenomenon of interrelation and interaction.[5]

Mikhail Bakhtin's theory of the "dialogic", consequently, is the key idea in the first section of the book, as Victor Shklovsky's "estrangement" is the key idea of the second. These two are generally regarded as the most important of the Russian formalist critics. The importance of the dialogic lies in its emphasis (as opposed to the single voice of traditional lyric poetry) on the interrelation and interaction of voices. There is a postmodernist element in this in the way it opposes the privileging of any one voice but there is an anti-postmodernist element also in the way it dwells on the felt authenticity of each voice, and in the political urgency of its championing of, as it were, the under-voices; so Bakhtin attacks the

centripetal forces in sociolinguistic and ideological life. . .[which] serve one and the same project of centralizing and unifying the European languages. The victory of one reigning language (dialect) over the others, the supplanting of languages, their enslavement, the process of illuminating them with the True Word, the incorporation of barbarians and lower social strata into a unitary language of culture and truth.[6]

What must be said in favour of mainstream poetry in the past fifteen years is that it has been self-consciously the opposite of an exclusive club. It has been an anti-establishment establishment which has placed the margins at the centre. Irish poets like Seamus Heaney and Paul Muldoon have been involved with a subtle but persistent critique of the values of the British heartland. Tony Harrison and Douglas Dunn[7] have declared themselves working-class "barbarians" dedicated to opposing the dominance of reigning languages. Their poetry assaults the "True Word" with a dialectical use of dialect – or rather a dialogical use since the argument is open-ended and without even a prospective synthesis. They oppose "Received Pronunciation" with the conviction that the way language is used is inevitably political and the imposition of one dialect on another is a form of censorship, a suppression of a value system as well as a voice. Similarly, women poets have been concerned to show the extent to which the "unitary language of culture and truth" actually imposes a masculinist vision on those, both men and women, who use it. In opposing this their poetry has evoked a subtle dialogue of genders which, while chary of essentialist simplifications, has explored the boundaries of the feminine and the masculine, and exposed the way that the "True Word" is a masculine monologue, a gendered monolith.

What is involved in this insistence on polyphony, however, is not mere pluralism. It is not a question of the bland tolerance of difference but of a profound sense that the self has no meaning except in interrelation with others, and that the lived experience of the self can only be expressed through determined efforts to evoke the otherness with which the self continuously interacts.

In the course of their dialogic projects these poets have evolved styles which are self-consciously, even confrontationally impure and unstable. Contemporary poetry has undergone what Bakhtin calls "novelisation" in the sense that, like the novel, it is not generically stable but self-consciously incorporates other generic elements and expectations, it is a hybrid form that cross-fertilises diverse languages. Sylvia Plath's comparison of the two genres is instructive here:

> If a poem is concentrated, a closed fist, then a novel is relaxed and expansive, an open hand: it has roads, detours, destinations; a heart line, a head line; morals and money come into it. Where the fist excludes and stuns, the open hand can touch and encompass a great deal in its travels.
>
> I have never put a toothbrush in a poem.
>
> I do not like to think of all the things, familiar, useful and worthy things, I have never put into a poem. I did, once, put a yew tree in. And that yew tree began, with astounding egotism, to manage and order the whole affair. It was not a yew tree by a church on a road past a house in a town where a certain woman lived. . .and so on, as it might have been, in a novel. Oh no. It stood squarely in the middle of my poem, manipulating its dark shades, the voices in the churchyard, the clouds, the birds, the tender melancholy with which I contemplated it – everything! I couldn't subdue it. And, in the end, my poem was a poem about a yew tree. That yew tree was just too proud to be a passing black mark in a novel.[8]

What Plath considers "poetic" is a concentrated kind of expression focused upon images. Her assumptions are Romantic in origin in their concern with a kind of Nature/Mind dialectic – the state of mind of the poet is involved with an ontological struggle with the objects of nature in which the end of struggle is a kind of synthesis, a transcendant tying up of loose ends. Her own most characteristic version of this is an expressionism in which a powerful state of mind imposes itself so much on what surrounds it that everything is perceived in the terms of that state of mind. In "Parliament Hill Fields"[9], for example, the poet's preoccupation with a miscarriage makes the "spindling rivulets" she refers to a displaced equivalent of the dwindling of amniotic fluid. In her hands, then, the Nature/ Mind dialectic is resolved in favour of Mind: the yew tree takes over the poem because it becomes the displaced equivalent of the poet's all-consuming point of view. Paradoxically, Plath's famous onto-logical insecurity results in her psyche spilling over onto everything.

For this reason, Plath's own poetry is very much the opposite of novelistic expression. In the use her work makes of the poetic image "all activity – the dynamics of the images-as-word – is completely exhausted by the play between the word (with all its aspects) and the object (in all its aspects)". (*D.I.*, 278)

A Plath poem is a rarefied kind of expression, a "closed fist" which "excludes and stuns" – the yew tree is removed from its daily context and deployed in a way that draws upon all its tradi-tional symbolic associations which are newly focused by Plath's particular ontological concerns. It is their "egotism" which gives her poems their power; the way they narrow down, "manage and order the whole affair" creates a singular and uniquely Plathian "world" with its characteristically skewed and obsessive vision. The point about the lack of toothbrushes in this world is that they are objects which have a social rather than an ontological meaning and are excluded because of their lack of expressionistic clout.

So it is partly what is excluded from Plath's poems that accounts for their strange force – they are bizarrely pure lyrics. By contrast, the poetry of Paul Muldoon, James Fenton, Craig Raine, Fleur Adcock and Carol Ann Duffy refers itself to an altogether different tradition where the emphasis is on the dialogic rather than the dialectic, on the juxtaposition of worlds rather than the refining of a single world. In their poems synthesis is avoided in favour of an open-ended argument which preserves a vivid and untidy lack of reconciliation. This tradition goes back at least to Byron's *Don Juan* (which delib-erately deploys images for their social rather than their symbolic meaning), and also includes, most prominently, Robert Browning,

George Meredith's *Modern Love* and early T.S. Eliot. In these novelised poets there is an "open hand" rather than a "closed fist", there are "roads, detours, destinations". Their work resembles that of the novelist to the extent that its images are not primarily concerned (in Bakhtin's terms) with the play between the word and the object; in them, as in the work of novelists, the yew tree may well stand "by a church on a road past a house in a town where a certain woman lived":

> the object reveals first of all precisely the socially heteroglot multiplicity of its names, definitions and value judgements. Instead of the virginal fullness and inexhaustibility of the object itself, the prose writer confronts a multitude of routes, roads and paths that have been laid down in the object by social consciousness. Along with the internal contradictions inside the object itself, the prose writer witnesses as well the unfolding of social heteroglossia *surrounding* the object, the Tower-of-Babel mixing of languages that goes on around any object; the dialectics of the object are interwoven with the social dialogue surrounding it. For the prose writer, the object is the focal point of heteroglot voices among which his own voice must also sound, these voices create the background necessary for his own voice.
>
> (*D.I.*, 278)

Estrangement and the dialogic are not mutually exclusive. There are dialogic elements in the poets in my second section, especially in Edwin Morgan, and the poets in my first section, especially Craig Raine, all defamiliarise their material in one way or another. My focus on each as key terms is meant merely to draw attention to what is most characteristic in the two generations: estrangement in the retro-modernist, anti-Movement poets, the dialogic in the post-Movement poets with their hesitations between realism, modernism and postmodernism. Where the former work constantly at evoking strangeness, the latter tend to arbitrate between strangeness and familiarity, which is evoked both as a realist resource and as a device for opposing hierarchy and authoritarianism. In this they are calling upon what Bakhtin calls the carnivalesque, which is partly about "familiarisation":

> All *distance* between people is suspended, and a special carnival category goes into effect: *free and familiar contact among people*

. . .Linked with famiarization is a third category of the carnival sense of the world: *carnivalistic mésalliances*. A free and familiar attitude spreads over everything: over all values, thoughts, phenomena and things. All things that were once self-enclosed, disunified, distanced from one another by a noncarnivalistic hierarchical world view are drawn into carnivalistic contacts and combinations. Carnival brings together, unifies, weds and combines the sacred with the profane, the lofty with the low, the great with the insignificant, the wise with the stupid.[10]

So, while there is an emphasis on detachment, cool analysis and dissection or dismemberment in the estrangement poets, there is a contrary tendency in the dialogic poets towards a promiscuous mingling of materials, an enjoyment of hybrid forms and images, a conflating of voices and perspectives. In the "Martian" poets there is a constant reference back to the familiar in the dialogue between, in particular, the domestic and the exotic, and the sacred and the profane – there is an "humane" retrieval of the unfamiliar, its reinstalment in the familiar. Similarly, in the self-consciously hybrid forms of Paul Muldoon, there is a combining of materials which bring diverse images, languages and genres into familiar contact with each other.

The diversity of mainstream poetry at the moment makes it exciting and vigorous. Current and recent editors of a number of magazines have, through their broad-mindedness, encouraged a fascinating range of writing – Peter Forbes at *Poetry Review*, Alan Jenkins at the *TLS*, Karl Miller at the *London Review of Books*, Michael Schmidt at *PNReview*, Robert Crawford at *Verse*. Because of this the distinction between "mainstream" writing and the rest is increasingly difficult to maintain: when a stream is as broad as this it can, at any time, incorporate its tributaries. For this reason it ought to be all the easier, now, to accord Fisher, Middleton and Morgan the recognition they deserve. Moreover, despite the current strength of mainstream poetry there is still much it could learn from these senior figures. For the dialogic writing I have been describing has tended to call upon linguistic ready-mades, upon pre-existent forms, and mingled them. By contrast, the retro-modernists have been immensely fertile in their invention of new forms – they have been restlessly experimental in a way that only James Fenton has been in the mainstream. Most of what they have discovered in the course of their experiments remains to be absorbed by other poets. Moreover, there have been few poets in the mainstream who can match their intellectual rigour – their insistence on using poetry as a medium in which to say the most philosophically difficult things that can be said in expressive writing. By contrast with that much mainstream poetry seems unambitious, even, at times, philistine. It seems to me that if there could be a *rapprochement* between these two kinds of writing it would produce poetry of immense interest and power.

# Part I
## Dialogue

# 1

# "But Who Is Speaking": "Novelisation" in the Poetry of Craig Raine

In an essay published in 1978, John Osborne[1] lamented the dismissiveness with which Craig Raine's first book *The Onion Memory*[2] had been greeted by reviewers. He pointed out that they had failed to take account of the extent to which Raine was in a postmodernist tradition stretching back to Wallace Stevens, the Joyce of *Finnegan's Wake*, international surrealists like Lorca, Dali and Breton, and including, more recently, figures like Philip Roth, Kurt Vonnegut, Angela Carter and David Hockney. In these artists, he said, "the intense Modernist quest for a sense of the real is subordinated to, or abandoned in favour of, an aesthetic of the fictive" (54). Osborne pointed out that Raine, like all postmodernists, draws attention to the "ludic, fabulatory structure" (53) of his work. In answer to reviewers like Julian Symons and Derek Mahon, who took this as merely self-conscious and flippant smartness, he demonstrated how such self-reflexiveness works (albeit playfully and wittily) to reveal "the fact that our sense of the real is dependent upon our perceptual equipment, and that the said equipment is fanciful and capricious" (60) and that "all sentient beings are at the centre of their own universe but at the periphery of everyone else's" (61).

Osborne was amongst the first to discern the effects of postmodernism on contemporary British poetry. His essay on Raine preceded *The Penguin Book of Contemporary British Poetry*[3] by four years; in their introduction to that influential anthology Andrew Motion and Blake Morrison declared that "the poets included here do represent a departure, one which may be said to exhibit something of the spirit of postmodernism" (20) and described this departure as involving

a preference for metaphor and poetic bizzarrerie to metonymy and plain speech. . .[and] a renewed interest in narrative – that is,

15

in describing the details and complexities of (often dramatic) incidents, as well as in registering the difficulties and strategies
involved in retailing them. It manifests, in other words, a preoccupation with relativism – and this represents a radical departure
from the empirical mode which was conspicuous, largely because
of Philip Larkin's example, in British Poetry of the 1950s and 60s.

(12)

The introduction of postmodernism as a concept into the understanding of contemporary British poetry has helped Raine's poetry
to be more widely appreciated. Osborne's essay on Raine is still in
many ways the best (though the one by Alan Robinson[4] deals with
more recent material and contains much useful close analysis).
However, while Raine is a postmodernist in the general ways that
Osborne and Motion/Morrison describe, it should be said that this
(anyway deeply problematic) concept is unhelpful when it comes
to describing some aspects of his work, and that others actually run
counter to it. For instance, he is certainly not as postmodernist as
John Ashbery whose assimilation of surrealism has led him endlessly to deconstruct himself and to question the reality of what he
has said, is saying and will say. Ashbery's poetic contexts continually dissolve: by contrast Raine's poems usually have a single iden-
tifiable setting. In Raine the postmodernist impulse struggles with
a realist impulse to mirror the world in all its complexity; as he says
in his essay "Poetry Today":

> All good literature aspires to the condition of life. We know that
> words are only words, but this doesn't mean we shouldn't spend
> our lives arranging words and choosing words and coining words
> so that we are denied by our own illusion of life. Joseph Conrad's
> preface to *The Nigger of the "Narcissus"* states the tasks of the
> writer simply and movingly. It is "to make you hear, to make
> you feel – it is, before all, to make you see. That – and no more,
> and it is everything." Every serious artist believes this.[5]

In Ashbery, by contrast, the mirrors distort and multiply to infinity
– he is not interested in deceiving us with the illusion of life but in
drawing our attention to the deception.

Nonetheless, that phrase "deceived by our own illusion of life"
does indicate that Raine is a postmodernist of sorts – he is aware
that such verisimilitude is deceptive and his poems do keep ludically

pointing this out. One way of defining his postmodernism would be to refer to the kind of visual art which is the most accurate analogue for his poems; where for Ashbery this would be the surrealism of de Chirico, Magritte and Dali, for Raine it would be the analytical cubism of Picasso and Braque. His poems typically view and review their subjects from different angles, as Raine himself has said:

> By using fractured images [Picasso had] broken the rule of the fixed viewpoint: the equivalent in poetry might be to mix your metaphors. At the same time, the most successful of his cubist pictures were those that depicted something so familiar (like the human face) that one could distort a great deal without losing the fundamental sense of it. By analogy, I thought subjects like a butcher or a barber could be bombarded with images from a thousand different directions without destroying the unity of impression.[6]

So where Ashbery's surrealism involves endless defamiliarisation, Raine relies on an underpinning of the familiar and this explains the greater stability of his poems (moreover, his concern with "unity of impression" runs counter to the tendency towards fragmentation in postmodernism).

The cubist analogy is an important clue to the nature and extent of Raine's postmodernism, which consists largely of the ludic multiplying of perspectives upon a stabilised subject-matter. Raine characteristically describes how a scene or object looks from one viewpoint (or assumes a consensual view of that scene or object) and then undercuts that view with a radically different one. "In the Mortuary"[7] for example, starts by describing a corpse in impersonal, merely physical terms, it is "the usual woman" reified by death – "two terra cotta nipples/like patches from a cycle kit" and so on, until the last four lines imagine someone who had been intimate with the woman, someone who would see her as a person and not a thing:

> Somewhere else, not here, someone
> knows her hair is parted wrongly
> and cares about the cobwebs
> in the corners of her body

What Raine does here is to start with the unfamiliar – the grotesque alienness of a corpse – and then introduce the familiar paradoxically as a shock; the closing viewpoint is the one we accept as
the customary way of thinking about human beings. This, too, is
characteristic. For although Raine appears to be concerned above
all to "defamiliarise" his material it is more accurate to say that he
sets up a dialogue between the unfamiliar and the familiar – and
that the implicit and sometimes explicit presence of the familiar is
crucial. For this reason he is a more conservative poet than Ashbery
(and this says a good deal, too, about the difference between the
British and American poetic establishments).

Nonetheless, the juxtaposition of viewpoints in Raine's work does
make it much more unstable than that of the poets of the generations preceding his. Given his interest in this it is not surprising that
he has more recently begun to write dramatic works like his libretto
*The Electrification of the Soviet Union*[8] and his play *"1953"*[9] in which
the clashing of points of view can be given theatrical form. Raine
has always mistrusted lyric selfhood, his poems constantly imply it
is claustrophobic and distortive: the form of these dramatic works
averts those dangers in advance. In *"1953"* Princess Ira explicitly
voices Raine's mistrust – she is grateful to Orestes because his love
for her allowed her a kind of self-escape:

> what I wanted was release
> from the thought of being me. Little me.
> Like someone in one room
> without a change of clean clothes, I stank
> of me.

What are more important in the end (even to her) than the princess's view of herself are the "different views of Ira" (35) held by
Orestes and Vittorio – the one in love with her, the other, despite
his pledge to marry her, not.

Dramatic dialogue could be placed alongside cubism as an analogue for Raine's poetic strategies – a single scene, multiple viewpoints. Ultimately, however, the dialogue between individuals which
occurs in drama is insufficient for these purposes – for what Raine
does is to juxtapose "worlds" rather than individuals. So the dramatic world of *"1953"* is in dialogue with several other dramatic
worlds – with Racine's *Andromaque*, on which it is based, and with
the actual events of the Second World War and its aftermath – for

it imagines those events radically altered by the victory of Germany and Italy.

In other words, the premise of *"1953"* is that the present can only be fully understood in the perspectives of the past and of other possible versions of the present. The way that Racine's Achilles and his son Pyrrhus become Raine's Mussolini and his son Vittorio indicates the difference between modern views of war and heroes and that of the seventeenth century – this means that Raine's heroes cannot acquire the tragic status that Racine's have. That there are also similarities, however, is more interesting – it reveals that officially outmoded views of heroism popularly survive and, given changed circumstances, can easily recrudesce. Ira's love for Vittorio has a perverted aspect fuelled by her awed sense of him as a great general:

> History will fix his stature, find he was
> the chief of all the chiefs of staff.
> And envied accordingly.
>
> (86)

Similarly, our complacent sense of post-war history is disturbed by the play's exploration of what might have been:

> You'd believe me if you'd seen the Thames
> infuse and brighten with the blood
> of all the bodies bobbing there like teabags.
>
> (12)

So, too, the play's depiction of a world ruled by fascists – and the implications of that for the emotional lives of individuals – defamiliarises our experience of the triumph of liberal democracy.

What is involved here, then, is larger than dialogue. It resembles what Mikhail Bakhtin calls the "dialogic". This differentiates *"1953"* from what the Soviet critic calls "pure drama", which

> strives towards a unitary language, one that is individualized merely through dramatic personae who speak it. Dramatic dialogue is determined by a collision between individuals who exist within the limits of a single world and a single unitary language.[10]

Unitariness is replaced in Raine's play by the multiplying of worlds. It is in this that Raine's postmodernism can be most accurately discerned – that his poems and dramas work as Brian McHale has described postmodernist novels working:

> Baxtin has shown us how dialogue among discourses is a staple of all polyphonic novels. Postmodernist fiction, by heightening the polyphonic structure and sharpening the dialogue in various ways, foregrounds the ontological dimension of the confrontation among discourses, thus achieving a polyphony of *worlds*.[11]

So, where the Derridean concepts of deconstruction, decentring, supplementarity and free play work well for discussing Ashbery, for Raine the Bakhtinian concepts of the dialogic, of heteroglossia and the carnivalesque are more appropriate. Implied here are radically different views of subjectivity – behind Ashbery's view lies the influence of the surreal which undermines any stable sense of social context. Raine's postmodernism has the surrealist strand removed and, like Bakhtin, Raine regards subjectivity as socially constituted (and inseparable, therefore, from intersubjecivity): "Each person's inner world and thought has its stabilised *social audience* that comprises the environment in which reasons, motives, values and so on are fashioned."[12] So Bakhtin sees subjectivities defining each other by the way they interact in socially and historically defined contexts, so that, as in Raine's view of cubism, the unfamiliar, however bizarre, is comprehended finally by the familiar.

Behind Raine's work then, there is a more specific influence at work than that of postmodernism. I mean the influence of what Bakhtin has called "novelisation"; the novel's influence on other genres, he says, is to make them

> more free and flexible, their language renews itself by incorporating extraliterary heteroglossia and the "novelistic" layers of literary language, they become dialogised, permeated with laughter, irony, humour, elements of self-parody and finally – this is the most important thing – the novel inserts into these other genres an indeterminacy, a certain semantic openendedness, a living contact with unfinished, still-evolving contemporary reality.
>
> (*D.I.*, 7)

The novel's influence is evident, for instance, in the effects of romantic irony in Byron's *Don Juan*, of multiple perspective in

Browning's *The Ring and the Book*, of free indirect speech in Eliot's *The Waste Land*. But that influence has never been more pervasive than it is currently – for instance, in the narrative effects of poets as diverse as James Fenton, Carol Ann Duffy, Selima Hill, Iain Sinclair and Glyn Maxwell, and in the "dialogic" concern with language and power in Tony Harrison and Douglas Dunn.

However, Craig Raine's sensibility seems to me the most profoundly novelised in contemporary British poetry. As Peter Forbes has pointed out[13], Raine often refers to novelists in his essays and epigraphs; he himself has said that the "writer I most admire is Joyce: I take *Ulysses* everywhere with me in case I get knocked down by a bus" (*Viewpoints*, 179) and that it is "amazing what you can learn from prose" (Forbes, 9).

This, though, is merely circumstantial evidence and it is likely that the novelistic characteristics of Raine's work have also been learned from other novelised poets; the process has been at work for over two hundred years. Whatever their source, however, Raine's poems are strongly marked by those "dialogic" forms of writing which Bakhtin regards as characteristic of the novel. Certainly his "Martian" poetic insists on the necessity of dialogic ways of seeing – that the self cannot be understood by itself, that it requires another to comprehend it:

> one can speak of the absolute need of man for the other, for the other's activity of seeing, holding, putting together and unifying, which alone can bring into being the externally finished personality; if someone else does not do it, this personality will have no existence.[14]

For this reason Raine consistently introduces alien viewpoints in order to correct, freshen or enrich familiar ones. His sense of the "dialogic" produces an affinity with Dostoevsky as described by Bakhtin, who says the novelist saw

> many and varied things where others saw one and the same thing. Where others saw a single thought, he was able to find and feel out two thoughts, a bifurcation; where others saw a single quality, he discovered in it the presence of a second and contradictory quality. . .In every voice he could hear two contending voices, in every expression a crack, and the readiness to go over immediately to another contradictory expression; in every gesture he detected confidence and lack of confidence simultaneously;

he perceived the profound ambiguity, even multiple ambiguity of every phenomenon. But none of these contradictions ever became dialectical, they were never set in motion along a temporal path or in an evolving sequence: they were, rather, spread out in one plane, as standing alongside or opposite one another, as consonant but not merging. . .as an eternal harmony of unmerged voices or as their unceasing and irreconcilable quarrel. Dostoevsky's visualising power was locked in place at the moment diversity revealed itself – and remained there, organizing and shaping this diversity in the cross section of a given moment.[15]

This description of the "dialogic" in Dostoevsky works equally well when applied to these effects in Craig Raine – although the brilliance of Raine's imagery has drawn attention away from this more important aspect of his work. In fact his images are almost always rendered, implicitly or explicitly, as perceived by a particular consciousness which bifurcates and so surprises several meanings in those images. He is not interested in imagist objectivity but with how differently objects appear when viewed from different states of mind. In this he resembles James Joyce whose methods, as Raine has pointed out, "involved not only parallels. . .but also *parallax* – the same story seen from an entirely different point of view" (*Haydn*, 390). Where imagism employs "superposition" of objects – placing them on top of one another to evoke them by visual comparison and contrast[16] – Raine's poems may be said to employ "superposition" of consciousnesses.

Several such superpositions recur in his work – most importantly of various kinds of innocent consciousness on top of more familiar, more sophisticated ones. Sometimes the innocents are children, as for example in "The Butcher" (*Onion*, 2), "Listen with Mother" (*Martian*, 3) and "In Modern Dress"[17]; less often they are non-Western outsiders, as in "In the Kalahari Desert" (*Martian* 8–10), "Gauguin" and "Inca" (*Rich*, 30 and 34–35); and on one famous occasion the innocent is a Martian:

Caxtons are mechanical birds with many wings
and some are treasured for their markings –

they cause the eyes to melt
or the body to shriek without pain.

> I have never seen one fly, but
> sometimes they perch on the hand.
>
> (*Martian*, 1)

The crucial feature of poems like this is that they are never confined within the innocent's perspective – instead, that perspective interacts with the more familiar one. Charles Forceville misses this point when he complains that "the poet has not consistently shown the world from the Martian's point of view"[18]. For the poem employs the novelistic method of indirect free speech, where the novelist's words paraphrase the speech or thought of the character, so that what may appear to be one voice is actually two; as Bakhtin says, indirect discourse

> is used mainly for reporting the internal speech, thoughts and experiences of a character. It treats the speech to be reported very freely; it abbreviates it, often only highlighting its themes and dominants. . .Authorial intonation easily and freely ripples over its fluid structure.
>
> (*Marxism*, 133)

It is important in this context that the lines I have quoted are the ones that open Raine's second book and so provide its keynote – for they self-reflexively draw attention to their own presence in a book and so to their own activity of representation. In particular, "mechanical birds" are an artificial version of an organism, just as free indirect speech is an artificial voice. All of this implies an author speaking at the same time as a character – a dialogue between Craig Raine and his Martian.

Raine's comments on the artistic representation of children are relevant here. In "At a Slight Angle to the Universe" (*Haydn*, 454–457) he stresses that, although Wordsworth apparently presents the world-view of his idiot boy, it is actually "the author's own" (455) and that Dickens is the real source of "Pip's slight angle to the universe in *Great Expectations*" (454). The innocent eye of the child is paired with the knowing eye of the author to create the stereoscopic vision of art. Raine's poem, similarly, is a dialogue between its author's language – which a Martian would not be able to speak – and its character's perspective, so that the poem wavers, in a complex, disorienting way, between the familiar and the unfamiliar. The argument between language and perspective reveals how much perspective is determined by linguistic expectations, so the poem reveals how we "read" the world and how our reading varies with our experience of other worlds and other texts. It is not an accident, then, that the poem opens with a reference to books and ends with a reference to how

> At night, when all the colours die
> they hide in pairs
>
> and read about themselves
> in colour, with their eyelids shut.
>                                     (2)

The Martian moves from objective texts to (as it were) subjective ones and, in between, reveals through his skewed version of English how we move between the two.

What appears to be one voice in "A Martian", then, turns out to be two which are "consonant but not merging" so that the poem indicates "the profound ambiguity, even multiple ambiguity of every phenomenon" (*Dostoevsky*, 30). Elsewhere, this dialogic quality is more explicit. In "The Butcher" (*Onion*, 2), as John Osborne has pointed out:

> That we are observing the scene from a child's diminutive view-point is suggested by the theatrical larger-than-lifeness of the butcher; yet the brilliance of the verbal pyrotechnics so clearly exceeds a child's inventive capacity that we deduce the presiding consciousness to be that of an adult engaged in retrospection.
>                                     (63)

Similarly, "A Cemetery in Co Durham" (*Onion*, 30) suggests that where death is concerned social pressure wants to impose a properly "mature" attitude – so "YOUNG CHILDREN ARE NOT ALLOWED WITHOUT SUPERVISION" and "CHILDREN IN ARMS ARE NOT ADMITTED/ TO FUNERALS". However, the childlike imagery of the poem, deployed like free indirect thought, unnervingly suggests that death reduces adults to children by overwhelming their self-control. An inappropriate childish humour threatens the decorum of mourning:

The stones line up in corrugated rows
like a game of *Dover Patrol*
and the ground is full of pencil boxes.

The bereaved pray, or conduct an imaginary conversation with the dead, but the poem's atheism insists they are merely conducting a monologue:

Untidy as a nursery floor, with toys
and little furniture, it is a good place
to come and talk like a child to yourself –
no one is listening.

The poem subverts the imagined conversation by insinuating its own dialogue between adulthood and childhood – what the adults are doing here is reverting to the fantasy talk of a child in its solitary play.

So the superposition, in poems like this, of an innocent perspective on top of a more familiar, mature point of view enacts the disorienting return of a forgotten freshness. Chronology is implied – vivid earliness, humdrum lateness, the two coinciding through association of ideas or memory. There is an assumption that the two usually exist separately, which is how the humdrum is *kept* humdrum. The superposition of the Martian, or the non-Western exotic, on the familiar works from similar premises – usually the Martian lives on Mars, but somehow now he finds himself here. In this case it is not time which is crossed, but space – but once again the implication is that the two normally exist separately.

However, there are other superpositions in Raine's work where it is implied that the two perspectives co-exist. "Anno Domini" (*Onion*, 70–84) for example, is a dialogue between the religious and the secular, and the assumption is that these are different states of mind that always exist side by side and interpret the same experiences in different ways. The sequence resembles the paintings of Stanley Spencer, of whom Raine has written:

For him, the ordinary was more numinous than the conventionally visionary. This world constantly imposes itself on the otherwordly so that, for example, Christ and the twelve apostles are metamorphosed by Spencer's imagination: "I want to paint J.C. &

Co. like a football team, don'tcha know, sitting there in two rows
with their arms folded like this, and looking tough."

(Haydn, 107–108)

The central figure of "Anno Domini" is a modern faith-healer, based
on Raine's father[19], but it "takes as its structural basis the life of
Christ" (*Viewpoints*, 183). However, the religious outlook is not
validated by the way that Biblical references enter the poem's
modern settings – "Anno Domini" preserves its semantic open-
endedness by maintaining a balance between blasphemy and mysticism. For instance, in section VII, "Sunblest Bread and Two
Tail-Ends of Cod", the figure who enters near the end and behaves
like Christ feeding the five thousand has a mock-mysteriousness
bestowed on him which at the same time asks a larger question –
not so much about spiritual meaning as about meaning in poems:

> "Who wants to join my gang? Who wants
> to suck a lion-tamer?" (Me, mister, me.)
>
> But who is speaking?
> Who holds the Extra-Strong Mint like a host?
>
> Who is feeding five thousand kids
> from a bottomless paper bag?

This appears to make a gesture towards an ambiguity which is
easily and comically resolved (is it about the mystical hearing of
voices? – no). But in fact by so doing it asks a question about voices
in poetry which is very relevant for Raine's work as a whole. Whose
voice speaks in a poem? Raine himself says of this sequence "it's
also about poetry. . .it's about my father, but it's more or less about
the imagination" (*Viewpoints*, 183).

The controlling metaphor of the sequence compares poetic transformation with Christ's miracles. But by drawing attention to the
question of who is speaking, section VII indicates that the kind of
poetic transformation that comes about is determined by whose
eyes the reader is seeing through. The religious/secular dialogue
lays particular stress on whether an experience should be interpreted in one of those two ways. Many of the sections could be
interpreted as "epiphanies" in either a Christian or a Joycean sense
depending on who is speaking – do they hint at the presence of
God, or at transcendent but still human spots of time that require
authorial expression to achieve their full meaning? But in section

VII this dialogue has, momentarily at least, only an exemplary status, as Raine refers more broadly to his poetic as a whole; this section hints that that poetic is concerned with the multitude of dialogues that constitute the human experience of the world.

Such dialogic elements can be said to be the product of novelisation. However, there is a distinct difference in the effect they make in poetry as compared with their effect in the novel. In particular the greater succinctness of poetry and the way its rhythms foreground images and metaphors inevitably produce more of the mysteriousness that "Sunblest Bread" evokes. As a less social form than the novel, poetry imposes less pressure to define context and this can produce ambiguities that would be unavailable in narrative prose; the question of who is speaking in a poem can be left unresolved in a way that would breach novelistic decorum (though such ambiguities *are* available to short story writers).

So "Flying to Belfast, 1977" (*Martian*, 32–33) can be said to be literally equivocal. It demonstrates again Raine's ability to hear in every voice "two contending voices, in every expression a crack, and the readiness to go over immediately to another contradictory expression"(*Dostoevsky*, 30). Firstly, there is some question whether the "I" in the poem is the prospective bride, or the implied author who imagines her – their voices are joined, anyway, in the indirect free thought of which the poem is constituted. More importantly (though it may be this first question that generates the second) there is doubt whether Belfast should be regarded in personal and domestic terms, as the scene of the bride's marriage, or in social and political ones, as the scene of civil strife which can threaten her domestic tranquillity.

In this way the poem conflates two kinds of fear. The first is intimate and associated with the excitement of a rite of passage; its sexual element is linked in a Freudian way to the fear of flying ("It was possible to laugh/ as the engines whistled to the boil"). The second is wholly negative but unignorable: the way it casts its shadow is suggested by how it insinuates itself into the same images as the first. The image of boiling which hints at sexual climax in terms of the first fear, hints at an explosion in terms of the second. This is why, at the end of the poem, the bride is "only half afraid"

> ...of an empty house
>
> with its curtains boiling
> from the bedroom window

Similarly, the lines "And then Belfast below, a radio/ with its back ripped off" work at one level to reinforce the domestic view of the city – its small, self-contained appearance from the air makes it seem cosy. However, this image, too, equivocates – for the IRA rip the backs off radios in order to turn them into bombs. The line "everything was wired up" reinforces this reading and also sums up the poem by suggesting that the intimate and the social are inextricably bound up with each other.

In this way, Raine, as a novelised poet, opens up each object in his poems to unfold what Bakhtin calls the "social heteroglossia surrounding the object, the Tower-of-Babel mixing of languages that goes on around any object" for "the dialectics of the object are interwoven with the social dialogue surrounding it. . .[so] the object is the focal point for heterglot voices among which his own voice must also sound, [and] these voices create the background necessary for his own voice" (*D.I.*, 278). Raine himself has written in favour of "Babylonish Dialects" (*Haydn*, 87–92) and of "a vernacular invigorated by the wierd poetry of the city, or of aeronautics and space travel" (*Haydn*, 86). Much of the humour in his poetry comes from the incongruous mingling of "heteroglossia", of languages normally kept separate from one another – as, for instance, in the unmiraculous transformation of five loaves and two fishes into "Sunblest Bread and Two Tail-Ends of Cod". Sometimes, too, this effect can be deeply serious, as when Raine borrows the "expression from Timothy Mo's fine novel *Sour Sweet* – to 'wipe someone's face', meaning to kill someone" (*Rich*, 11) and places it in the Anglo-Saxon context of "Wulf and Eadwacer" (*Rich*, 27).

What is most significant about this mingling of voices, however, is that it implies the juxtaposing of diverse voices with the author's own. This concern became more explicit in *Rich*. In the title poem the woman the poet is in love with "cannot ever know/ the extent of her riches" (15) – for this her vision must be joined with the verbal art of the author, the "keeper of the dictionary" (17). Human vision and the world, and the texts that represent them, conduct metaphorical conversations that mutually enrich each other:

> And there, beyond the books
> on the windowsill, her floods,
> transforming the world
>
> like the eye in love.

(16)

A similar mingling occurs in "In Modern Dress" (18–20) which likens a child and Sir Walter Raleigh as discoverers of new worlds who "ponder the potato/ in its natural state/ for the very first time". What is important, however, is that the poet and the reader both re-enact these discoveries by watching the child. Moreover, the fact that the poet is "author/ of this toga'd tribune"

> who plays his part
> to an audience of two
>
> repeating my words

wittily reveals that, as well as being the poet's biological creation, the child has become a character in a fiction: author, character and reader are enriched by the way that perspectives and voices mingle in the authorial speech of the poem.

In *The Electrification of the Soviet Union* there are literally characters "repeating [Raine's] words". This is an opera but its debt to the novel is obvious – Raine's libretto is based on Pasternak's novella *The Last Summer*. Moreover, as the "Production Note" indicates, "There is a table at downstage right, where Pasternak sits, writing the action that the audience sees" (18) and Pasternak's version of his younger self, Serezha, is the central figure. So three authors are in conversation with each other – one implied (Raine), one dramatised (Pasternak), and one prospective (Serezha). In a sense the opera takes this prospectiveness as its central theme – in showing Serezha in the process of becoming Pasternak, it shows how authors assimilate the voices of others, for Pasternak is writing all the parts, not just Serezha's. So Serezha is dramatised in the attempt – which is simultaneously that of the lover and of the novelist – to extend his sympathetic understanding to Anna. He is also shown metaphorically trying on his sister's political voice and simultaneously subverting it:

> NATASHA
> He stands for everything new
> he isn't a dreamer like you.
> The time for you dreamers is past,
> the new world has woken at last:
> all power
> is ours;
> the people have spoken at last.

SEREZHA
(*clapping ironically, improvises an instant parody*)
I look forward to meeting Lemokh,
but first forty winks in the sack.
This old brain has been on the train
this old brain is feeling the strain,
this old brain
(*comic pause for inspiration*)
has migraine,
(*speaks the next line*)
This old brain wants to lie down.

(30)

This dialogic subversion of revolutionary language is very significant from the Bakhtinian point of view – for the dialogical principle
was invented against the background of monological Stalinism. What
Serezha is doing here is very much in the spirit of the plea for
polyphony. And Bakhtin's implied protest against the turning of
citizens into voiceless objects is voiced by Pasternak in the opening
song:

Love has been put off today,
phone-calls are cut off today:
to wives and to brothers
and countless sweet others,
the party has nothing to say.

The iron comrade comes to life.
His best friend is a gun.
The sharpened sickle is his wife,
the hammer is his son.

(22)

It is not true, then, that Craig Raine "elevates image-making to the
supreme structural principle of his work"[20]: instead the supreme
structural principle is the interaction of points of view. The thinking behind this is that it is consciousness which brings images to
life. As Bakhtin says:

As soon as consciousness appears in the world. . .the world (being) changes radically. The stone remains stone and the sun

remains sun, but the event of being in its (unattainable) whole becomes altogether other because, on the stage of earthly being, for the first time, a new and decisive character in the event makes his entrance: the witness and the judge. And the sun, which retains its physical identity, becomes other, through the act of consciousness that the witness and judge have of it. It has ceased just being, to begin to be in itself and for itself (these categories appear for the first time) and for the other, because it is reflected in the consciousness of another witness and judge: in this, it has changed radically, become richer and transformed.

(Quoted in Todorov, 97)

This idea of a human fiat, an original act of consciousness, lies behind many of Raine's poems, which try to retrieve it through the effects of "innocent" perspective I have discussed. But the importance of this for Raine, as for Bakhtin, is that the original act leads to further acts of consciousness, which interact – consciousness and the world become "richer and transformed" through the multiplying of otherness. It is this which *Rich* repeatedly refers to: at the start of that book the perspectives of love and childhood enrich the world; at the end the perspectives of death and apocalypse impoverish it (but also recall former riches).

This concern with otherness has nothing to do then with "alienation", the word Edward Larrissy repetitively applies to it[21], for Raine, like Bakhtin "speaks of alterity, which is a condition friendly to man, rather than alienation, which is the same structural situation but has been perceived from Marx to Sartre as hostile".[22]

This is not merely a technique but an important insight – the self and the world alter constantly so that we can be sure of neither. Such uncertainty is most surprising where the self is concerned, but, "A man never coincides with himself. One cannot apply to him the formula of identity A = A" (*Dostoevsky*, 59). Some states of mind make this more obvious than others, as Orestes finds in "*1953*":

> . . .I can't explain,
> but I was next to myself. Yes? Watching Orestes
> as if Orestes was insane.
> And I felt sorry. I felt sorry for myself.
> Except my hands. They frightened me.
> I recognized them, but they weren't mine any more.

> They were just hands. Completely free.
> And they wanted to burst Vittorio's eyes.
>
> (43–44)

This renews the cliché "to be beside yourself" and discovers within it the knowledge of the alterity of the self – that jealousy can render it unrecognisable. But Raine's poetic insists that it is not only such powerful feelings that produce these effects – in "A Free Translation", too, hands become unfamiliar to their owner, but in this case only because the domestic scene is playfully re-oriented by Eastern references: "I observe my hands/ under the kitchen tap/ as if they belonged/ to Marco Polo" (*Rich*, 36).

Through this emphasis on alterity Raine's poems are consistently disconcerting – largely because they take doubt as their premise. Raine's sympathies clearly lie with Elizabeth Bishop, rather than Marianne Moore, when he says that Bishop "is more sceptical, even of herself" and that

> her underlying attitude is different from [Moore's] transposed Deism, which is founded on a general confidence that she does not share – a belief in rules and explanations, in finality. Her own world is less confidently certain. Explanations, knowledge are less forthcoming. Her poetic manner is provisional.
>
> (*Haydn*, 331)

This is also true of Raine. His poems characteristically avoid the feeling of closure, their manner is often deliberately awkward, angular, and they often employ ellipsis like a shrug of the shoulders. His manner, too, is provisional because he wishes to insist on "incompleteness, becoming, ambiguity, indefinability, non-canonicalism – indeed all that jolts us out of our normal expectations and epistemological complacency" (Clark and Holquist, 312). Interestingly, though, Clark and Holquist are describing here what Bakhtin saw in the "carnival spirit". And it is clear that there is in Raine something like a satirical impulse to undermine monological ways of thinking which is linked to elements in his work of the "carnivalesque". Such elements, "were over thousands of years transposed into literature, particularly into the dialogic line of development in novelistic prose":

> A free and familiar attitude spreads over everything: over all values, thoughts, phenomena, and things. All things that were

once self-enclosed, disunified, distanced from one another by a noncarnivalistic worldview are drawn into carnivalistic contacts and combinations. Carnival brings together, unifies, weds and combines the sacred with the profane, the lofty with the low, the great with the insignificant, the wise with the stupid. "Connected with this is. . .a whole system of carnivalistic debasings and bringings down to earth, carnivalistic obscenities linked with the reproductive power of the earth and the body, carnivalistic parodies on sacred texts and sayings, etc." (*Dostoevsky*, 124).

So "A Walk in the Country" (*Rich*, 67–69) is a literal bringing down to earth of Canto XIV of Dante's *Inferno*, two lines of which are quoted as its epigraph. The fire, which in the Dante symbolises God's anger, becomes burning stubble which makes the graveyard seem "ringed with fire/ and somehow forbidden". It is linked, therefore, with both death and rebirth, for the fields will later be replanted. Perhaps for this reason the lines Raine has isolated in his epigraph refer to what is unavailable to the damned of Canto XIV, refer to that Lethe which lies "fuor di questa fossa/ la dove vanno l'anime a lavarsi" ("beyond this abyss where minds go to cleanse themselves"[23]). In "A Walk in the Country" this cleansing is represented (earthily enough) by the sewage farm and where in the Dante the fire represents only punishment (for the sinners in Canto XIV have insulted God and cannot be redeemed), in Raine's poem it combines destruction with the possibility of renewal, and such composite images are present throughout:

> . . .here is a man
> gardening a grave
> methodically,
> lost in the rituals
>
> of growth

This substitutes the burning desert of Canto XIV – "una landa/ che dal suo letto ogni pianta rimove" (180) – with the "essence of carnival [which] lies in change, in death-rebirth, in destructive-creative time; carnivalistic images are basically ambivalent" (Todorov, 79). In this way "A Walk in the Country" parodies and subverts a sacred text: its fire is like that of carnival rather than that of the *Inferno*:

Deeply ambivalent also is the image of *fire* in carnival. It is a fire that simultaneously destroys and renews the world. In European carnivals there was almost always a special structure...called "hell", and at the close of carnival this "hell" was triumphantly set on fire (sometimes this carnival "hell" was ambivalently linked with a horn of plenty).

So while Craig Raine can be described in general terms as a postmodernist, then, these Bakhtinian concepts – heteroglossia, the dialogic, the carnivalesque – work to describe his poems and plays in more specific ways. What is particularly appropriate about them is that they suggest an equivocation between stability and instability rather than the endless instabilities which are the premise of the most radical postmodernists like John Ashbery and, in Britain, figures like John Ash and, in his more recent work, Paul Muldoon. In particular, that element which seems most characteristically postmodernist in Raine – his playfulness and wit, even in the face of solemn subject-matter – is most accurately defined by reference to the carnivalesque.

It is this notion writ large which lies behind Raine's most recent book *History: The Home Movie*[24] to the extent that it places the stuff of conventional history in the background and focuses on private and intimate moments often involving the body in its most grotesquely pressing moments. This indicates that the carnivalesque has a traditional aspect as well as a postmodernist one – it places him in the company of satirists who have subverted human pretensions. This is what is involved when hierarchy and decorum are repeatedly covered in confusion by his metaphors, which embarrass them with strange bedfellows; when sacredness of all kinds is disconcerted by proximity to profanity of all kinds; when Martians and children keep pointing out that the king is naked, that people have genitalia and anuses, that they reproduce and die; when the surprising, the grotesque and the bizarre are repeatedly used to unsettle expectations and celebrate creative freedom. What they suggest, in the end, is that Raine is, in the broadest sense, a comic writer – he calls human values into question in order to reveal which are worth affirming.

So there is a characteristic dialogic premise behind *History* – it assumes that the history that is familiar is public and surprises that with the private so that the relationship between the two is interrogated. Paradoxically the family is introduced, therefore, as the unfamiliar as Raine recounts fragments of the lives of his most recent ancestors and those of his wife, Ann Pasternak Slater, against the background of events like the Russian revolution and two World Wars.

The blurb's description of this book as "a novel" is accurate, then, in the sense that it continuously suggests the crossing-over of points of view, and dwells on the novelistic stuff of the everyday as the vivid context of the intimate. So the title of "1919: Back from the Front" (29–35) punningly suggests a date regarded from an unfamiliar angle and delivers on this promise by registering the impact of the end of war with self-conscious earthiness. The poet's great-grandmother is depicted sighing over a copy of *Alice's Adventures in Wonderland* and implicitly grieving – the book belonged to her daughter Alice who died four years earlier. Characteristically, though, any solemnity is diffused by Raine's (and Carroll's) habit of turning things back to front, which can become one textual way of suggesting a child's vision. This is confirmed by her toddler turning shy and disappearing under her skirt "like old Stanhope Hicks/ the Studio Photographer".

Photography as an analogy continually suggests itself in Martian poems but, unlike in imagist ones, is always present to be modified – here because this is a "home movie" and so concerned with movement and change, but also because its realist aspect is both crucially important and continuously open to question. This photographic reference leads to two contrasting stills. The first arises from grief but mingles it with the taut apprehension that characterises the rest of "Back from the Front": Queenie puts the book down carefully "as if she could see a child/ poised and precious/ at a fifth-floor window,/ and dare not shout". The second employs its cropped stasis to evoke a moment as it turns momentous with her husband's homecoming: "Henry. Silent, smiling, handsome,/ and framed by the frame/ of the sitting-room door."

What already makes these images other than simply photographic, though, is that they are both coloured by Queenie's angle of vision. Then, in a characteristically "novelised" way, Henry becomes the centre of consciousness so that the domestic scene is visited by the larger history with which this section is concerned. This becomes explicit when Henry "finds the regimental photograph" and Queenie "watches while he marks/ the faces of the dead". But its implicit presence is more important in superposing his experience of war with his reacquaintance with his wife and family, and his sense of "Home" is therefore not merely renewed but radically reappraised. So this section dwells lovingly on mundane domestic objects – but also tensely. The rigidity of the static images I referred to is taken up and repeated in the imagery that follows which clusters around hardness and frozenness:

> A line of willow pollards
> have ceased to be themselves,
>
> stony as the faceless emperors
> on the Sheldonian wall.
> But the cricket square is pale
>
> with care and attention,
> adhesive plaster removed.
> The patient sight-screens
>
> survive like polar ice-caps,
> and at this world's omphalos
> an abandoned iron castor.
>
> "Home", he whispers to Queenie,
> watching his youngest lurch
> on sturdy statuesque limbs.

Flesh here keeps turning into stone or metal. But the more Henry settles in the more the tension is resolved – or, rather, is melted sexually away. This is signalled first in his desire being likened to "a thick tile of honey", an image precariously poised between solid and liquid, but it takes control when Henry is said to have "waited too long/ to touch the wetness/ he has wanted all day" – so that the previous images of hardness and dryness are retrospectively adjusted. What is important above all, though, is the way that "Back from the Front" – with the carnivalesque inflections that character-ise *History* as a whole – sees the domestic backside of history from the "front" side of political history (the ending of war) so that the back and the front are placed in dialogue with each other. They marry here in a brief tentative agreement reached through sex:

> "You're a good-hearted man,"
> she says, and eases him over
> onto his side, suddenly easy herself.

It is this side – the physical and intimate – that Raine harps on, but the conventional tug in the direction of political history ensures that, throughout the poem as a whole, there is continually an evocative equivocation between the two.

What makes Bakhtinian concepts especially useful when applied to recent mainstream British poetry is that they reveal the extent to which it has broken with the tradition of the Movement, whose poetic Andrew Crozier accurately defines in terms of an

> authoritative self, discoursing in a world of banal, empirically derived objects and relations, [which] depends on its employ-ment of metaphor and simile for poetic vitality. These figures are conceptually subordinate to the empirical reality of self and objects, yet they constitute the nature of the poem.[25]

Crozier's point is proven by the extent to which Larkin, for exam-ple, repeatedly starts his poems by painstakingly notating self-con-sciously mundane parts of the "real" world in a way which not only establishes a stable, apparently objective setting, but implicitly constructs a speaker who observes and responds in a reliable way. The result is that a firm but unspoken sense of self is established – an essentially realist self whose coherence is unquestioned.

"The Whitsun Weddings"[26] can be read partly as an argument against the modernist deconstruction of the self which Eliot achieved in *The Waste Land*. Where Eliot's poem dwells metaphorically on imagery of sterility, Larkin's insists – in a spirit of humane revision-ism – on the possibility of fertility, both literal and metaphorical, in individual human lives. In this process the "reality" of those lives and of the (by implication particular) individuals who live them is asserted in opposition to Eliot's ontological mistrust.

Crozier is wrong, however, to insist that such "a poetics of ob-jects, sites and moments" (205) was still dominant at the time when he wrote, and that in Craig Raine "the Larkin-Hughes-Heaney canon extended itself in the late seventies". (230)

One of the principal characteristics of the Martian poetic is the way it systematically undermines the authority of the self by rest-lessly enacting the vulnerability of its knowledge. Both Larkin and Raine refer to what Crozier calls "banal, empirically derived objects". However, in Larkin these evoke a familiarity meant to reassure the reader that the self in the poem resembles his or her own. By contrast banal objects have a habit in Raine's poems of transforming themselves – they disorient the reader with the spectacle of reliability bewildering itself – so that all continuity and coherence is removed from any self that might be observing them. The "Martian" who speaks Raine's most famous poem is, in a sense, an anti-self, a creature made entirely of English words who can only speak in paraphrase, or a hybrid voice that combines character and implied author.

So Craig Raine replaces the ontological stability so self-consciously constructed by Movement poets with ontological doubt. In this he resembles other novelised poets, like Paul Muldoon and James Fenton, who first came to prominence in the late seventies. Fenton's narrative poems contain characters with as little ontological substance as those in postmodernist novels. And Muldoon, as I shall argue in my next chapter, harps on hybrid imagery and deploys hybrid forms (like parody and the juxtaposition of diverse generic elements) in order radically to call into question the whole nature of identity.

# 2

# "The Best of Both Worlds": the Hybrid Constructions of Paul Muldoon

The notion of hybrid form is a crucial one in Paul Muldoon's work. As a biological analogy this appears most explicitly in the early "Mules"[1] and the more recent "Cauliflowers"[2]. In the earlier poem, "the best of both worlds" refers primarily to earth and heaven: the mare has "feet of clay" but also a "star burned in [her] brow"; "Parsons' jackass" is a beast of burden but the "cross" he used to carry draws attention also to the fact that there is "a dark stripe running down the back of an ass, crossed by another at the shoulders. The tradition is that this cross was communicated to the creature when our Lord rode on the back of an ass in His triumphant entry into Jerusalem."[3] So the hybrid nature of mules is related metaphorically to the idea of a mix of the earthly and the heavenly, which are also combined, by implication, in the sexual act which is the central event of the poem. The idea of birth which follows from this act in this way acquires epiphanic associations, especially in the pun on "Dropped" which relates the Above to the Below and leads to the closing metaphor:

> We might yet claim that it sprang from earth
> Were it not for the afterbirth
> Trailed like some fine, silk parachute,
> That we would know from what heights it fell.

This is reminiscent of the Platonic idea, which was important to William Blake, of the descent from heaven into birth – except that the imagery and the fact the birth is that of a mule makes it earthier, more grotesque. The afterbirth-as-parachute is itself a hybrid of earth and heaven; its combination of the bodily and the transcendent relates it to a key Bakhtinian concept:

Bakhtin writes that the function of the "carnival-grotesque" is to "consecrate inventive freedom, to permit the combination of a variety of different elements and their rapprochement, to liberate from the prevailing point of view of the world, from conventions and established truths, from clichés, from all that is humdrum and universally accepted."[4]

Behind this concept is the idea of a kind of subversive miscegenation which is a key value in Bakhtin's thought because it is regarded as healthy and creative. It is connected in this way with Bakhtin's linguistic concern with "hybrid" forms like parody and free indirect speech where two or more languages, as it were, intermarry:

in parody two languages are crossed with each other, as well as two styles, two linguistic points of view, and in the final analysis two speaking subjects. . .every parody is an intentional dialogized hybrid. Within it, languages and styles actively and mutually illuminate one another.[5]

Elements of parody and the carnival-grotesque have become increasingly important in Muldoon's work so that his treatment of the Troubles in Northern Ireland in "The More a Man Has the More a Man Wants" (85–109), for example, mocks the official and journalistic language normally used to describe them in a way that borders on bad taste.

However, the idea of the hybrid does seem to be Muldoon's premise and analogy for all this. "Mules" is concerned, not just with a biological metaphor for a hybrid of earth and heaven, but with the way languages and perspectives mingle and, in a sense, reproduce. This is especially evident in the way the pronoun "they" is used so that it can refer primarily to the Muldoon's mare and the Parsons' jackass but also to Mr. Muldoon and Mr. Parsons who, through their sympathetic identification with the coupling of mare and ass, become themselves hybrids of animal and human, having "the best of both worlds", being "neither one thing or the other":

> It was as though they had shuddered
> To think, of their gaunt, sexless foal
> Dropped tonight in the cowshed.

The cliché about shuddering to think is dismantled by the line ending here, so that it conjures up, not merely awe mixed with revulsion, but the imagining of sexual climax. The pun as a device is itself a marrying of meanings, and it is one of Muldoon's favourite effects – there is another in "I watched Sam Parsons and my quick father/ Tense for the punch below their belts", this time referring to a sense of something illegitimate in this sexual act and that their involvement in it is voyeuristic and a bit perverse and cruel. But if the men are voyeuristic, what about the poet who is looking back at himself ("I watched") looking at the voyeurs? The double perspective in the latter, and the implied but crucial gap between the two, is similar to that in some of Craig Raine's poems and I have discussed its effects in my chapter on Raine. In "Mules", though, this is doubled again with the overlapping of the perspectives of the animals and their owners in the use of "they" and "their".

The controlling metaphor of the hybrid in "Mules", then, works not just thematically but self-reflexively to refer to the way that the act of creation that made the poem involved the bastard mingling of languages and perspectives. The numerous references in Muldoon's poems to his father, and his concern with the epic theme of the search for the lost father – especially in "Immram" (58–67) – suggest that there is something self-reflexive in this also, that the poem is created in the process of recreating the figure who created the poet. Stated like this the theme may sound po-faced and masculinist, but it is treated with characteristic irony by Muldoon, and in such playful and fictive ways, that the search for authenticity, or male "authority", which it implies, is self-consciously subverted. Muldoon's hybrid constructions work in this context to insist that any search for a pure origin is a simplification – just as, in "Mules", they draw upon but ultimately mock the Platonic idea of the soul's heavenly origin.

Of course, the concern with origins is especially fraught for a poet in Northern Ireland. It may be that Muldoon's eponymous mules are, at one level, an analogy for the mix of Irish and British, Catholic and Protestant, that combine in the culture there. However, the use of the sexual act and its offspring as a metaphor for this is much more explicit in Seamus Heaney's "Act of Union"[6]. The contrast between the methods of the poets is most obvious here where their subject-matter to some extent converges. Heaney's pun on "union" is in deadly earnest and is pursued throughout the poem single-mindedly through his characteristic references to landscape ("a bog-burst,/ A gash breaking open the ferny bed"). These references suggest an intense response to nature in its violent and sexual aspects which is reminiscent of D.H. Lawrence and Ted Hughes – in particular with their interest in evoking a Nietzschean will to power whose presence in nature reflects that in human beings, especially men:

> And I am still imperially
> Male, leaving you with the pain,
> The rending process in the colony,
> The battering ram, the boom burst from within.

Although maleness is being abhorred in this passage, it is actually being taken much more seriously than it ever is in Muldoon's references to fathers – it acquires a perversely glamorous aura of cruelty and power. This could never happen in Muldoon's insistently ironic structures which involve the juxtaposition of jarringly different kinds of language. Heaney's "Act of Union" is about the mating of England and Ireland but its language is a nervous thoroughbred. This is partly because Heaney's intentions are thoroughly political in a way Muldoon's never are – in fact, Muldoon, asked in an interview what his politics were, replied "I don't think it matters. I don't think it's of any interest. . .It doesn't matter where I stand politically, with a small 'p' in terms of Irish politics. My opinion about what should happen in Northern ireland is no more valuable than yours."[7]

The eroticised landscape of "The Act of Union" is cognate with Heaney's archeological concerns in that it operates like a myth that aetiologically unearths the origins of present circumstances. Just as the "bog people" poems provide ancient analogues and explanations for the present political circumstances in Ireland, the "act of union" between England and Ireland reveals how the past gave birth to the present. By contrast, Muldoon is uninterested in explanations and revelations. The act of union to him produces something more like the couple in "Whim"[8] who get stuck together during intercourse and are "manhandled on to a stretcher/ Like the last of an endangered species" – the union is grotesque, clumsy, unstable, awkward. More importantly, it is unnatural, and this too marks an important contrast between Heaney and Muldoon – the older poet's political meditations constantly refer to landscape and sex in a way that tends, mystically, to make the political situation seem like a product of nature.[9] By contrast, Muldoon's self-consciously hybrid constructions emphasise human agency which has efficiently erased all trace of whatever was "natural" in origin. Moreover, although Muldoon shares Heaney's rural background, he does not share his awed yet anxious respect for nature, and has grown increasingly cosmopolitan and urbane (he now lives in America and teaches at Princeton University). Instead he shares with the hero of "Why Brownlee Left" (51) a profound restlessness that is not content with content – with "two acres of barley,/ One of potatoes, four bullocks,/ A milker, a slated farmhouse."

His poems express this restlessness in the form of self-conscious instability, a rejection of explanation and revelation and a love of the unexplained and unexplainable. The most important form this takes in his early work is a questioning of the boundaries of personal identity, and two poems show these concerns most explicitly. "Identities" (12) describes a marriage of convenience that takes place in fraught political circumstances: the merging of identities this involves occurs as a result of a series of external pressures and of mere chance, so that the fragility of selfhood is stressed. The gratuitous, that is to say non-narrative, detail with which the hotel is descibed, "pink and goodish for the tourist/ Quarter" draws attention to a surprise that such a building looms so large for them as the place where they "happened" to meet. The poem ends in bewilderment:

> I have been wandering since, back up the streams
> That had once flowed simply one into the other,
> One taking the other's name.

The last line appears to be a simple metaphorical reflection of the act of marriage but it is qualified by the preceding two. To go "back up the streams" suggests that search for a source which will become an important theme in Muldoon's work – but here as elsewhere it is a baffled search. And the penultimate line introduces some complexity paradoxically with the words "once" and "simply". It may be that the streams have dried up which would symbolise the infertility of the marriage; it is more likely, though, that the shift has occurred in the speaker's mind – that the confluence of the streams had once seemed simple but has acquired more disturbing connotations for him after his own experience of combined identities.

Where "Identities" is about fortuitous merging, "The Boundary Commission" (48) is about gratuitous division, describing a village "where the border ran/ Down the middle of the street,/ With the butcher and baker in different states". Where "Identities" refers to

the meeting of waters, the later poem refers to them coming to a
halt, to a shower of rain that

> Had stopped so cleanly across Golightly's lane
> It might have been a wall of glass
> That had toppled over. He stood there, for ages,
> To wonder which side, if any, he should be on.

It is not an accident that both these key poems describe political
circumstances – this indicates that, while Muldoon does not identify himself with sectarian concerns, he is profoundly aware of the
extent to which personal identity is influenced by what is happening in the state. But what this poem stresses is a belief that the
choosing of sides is bizarrely artificial. The shower of rain that stops
as abruptly as a boundary works like magic realist satire – it fan-
tastically defamiliarises the drawing of boundaries so that it is revealed as unnatural, monstrous even. The dilemma referred to at
the end surreally reflects the impossibility of making a genuine
choice, and "if any" paradoxically enforces the fact that, willy nilly,
you will find yourself on one side or the other.

The shower that stops like a wall in "The Boundary Commission" is the antithesis of the belief expressed, implicitly or explicitly
throughout Muldoon's work, in the inevitably hybrid nature of
experience. Everywhere he opposes the idea of the clear-cut divid-
ing line and insists on overlap and merging. In "Cuba" (47), for
example, Muldoon's father combines, with apparent (and comic)
gratuitousness his anxiety over the missiles crisis with that over his
daughter's chastity. What are connected concerns for Mr. Muldoon,
however, are contrasted in the end – enmity in the political with
tenderness in the private world, as the daughter confesses that a
boy had touched her but implicitly rebukes the priest's question as
to whether the touch was immodest: "'He brushed against me,
Father. Very gently.'"

In "Lunch with Pancho Villa" (19–21) it is the worlds of politics
and poetry which are juxtaposed, and so raise the question of what
is "real". Villa scolds the poet speaker for writing rondeaux while
people are being killed and pours scorn on stock poetic imagery –
"stars and horses, pigs and trees". This appears to be a politician's
view of poetry, but there is some question whether or not it is a
poet's view of a politician's view, for in the second section the
speaker refers to "a mild invention" – which may describe the poem
as a whole. The volumes he attributes to Villa seem to have been

invented by the poet – though the whole question of hybrids is introduced here again because Villa is described as their "co-author" and the poet later wishes he was "their other co-author". In a sense co-authorship is the subject of the poem, which suggests the way that the world and experience are created as an unstable mixture of points of view, of multiple "authors". This is a political point in the widest sense. The question of whose point of view prevails, whose voice is heard mirrors in personal experience what happens in the state.

This question is placed in the foreground in literature and especially in the choice of narrative voice in the novel. It is also acute, though, in novelised poets like Muldoon who, in "Lunch with Pancho Villa" deliberately undermines the reliability of his speaker. Historical objectivity is dismissed as an impossibility – Pancho Villa's truculent question, "'When are you going to tell the truth?'" is undermined with the insistence that "there's no such book, so far as I know,/ As *How it Happened Here*". Instead, there are only points of view:

> But where (I wonder myself) do I stand,
> In relation to a table and chair,
> The quince-tree I forgot to mention,
> That suburban street, the door, the yard –
> All made up as I went along
> As things that people live among.

The doubt about where he stands is both aesthetic and political and calls into question the status of the images that follow it: are they merely poetic images, on the lines of the stars, horses, pigs and trees scorned by Villa, or are they items from the scene-setting of historical writing? Perhaps the most accurate way to think of them is as the product of a kind of co-authorship between the pamphleteer and the poet – they are bits of the real world but they are also made up as the poet "went along". In this way they indicate simultaneously that poetry is an imaginary garden that contains real toads and that history writing focuses on real toads but places them in the imaginary garden of their author's political point of view.

The question of where Muldoon's speakers stand is fundamental and is reflected in his interest in telling stories in his poems, an interest which was present from the start:

I'm very interested in the narrative, the story, and in wanting almost to write novels in the poem. I like to think that a whole society is informing the lines of a poem, that every detail is accurate. And I'm interested in the dramatic persona. I like using different characters to present different views of the world.[10]

So, in Muldoon's earliest poems, there is often a very close focus on a particular incident which acquires significance largely from the implication that it has divergent meanings for its participants. In "Elizabeth" (13–14) a husband describes the extreme fear caused in his wife by a flock of birds flying over their farmhouse, and the poem's meaning arises in the gaps between the fear and its source and the husband's state of mind and the wife's. The real cause of the fear remains enigmatic in a way that suggests the difficulty men and women have in understanding each other. It is probably connected to pregnancy – but whether the state itself or desire for, or fear of, or incapacity for is unclear: anyway the husband's references to his "promised children" and, in the last line, to a time when his wife will "seem thinner" point to this. What this mostly does, however, is to evoke a masculine sense of awe in the face of the feminine – here Muldoon's interest in the extreme "écriture feminine" of Mebdh McGuckian whom he anthologised very substantially in his *Faber Book of Contemporary Irish Poetry*[11] – seems relevant. As in McGuckian's poems there are essentialist premises behind "Elizabeth" – a sense that masculine and feminine sensibilities are radically different, and the mysterious power that the birds acquire arises from somewhere deep in a woman's mind. However, Muldoon's poem is in many ways *less* sexist in its implications than those of McGuckian which tend to confirm what men most complacently think about women: that they are dreamy, irrational, mystical, maternal, domestic, garrulous, a bit exasperating (but also, admittedly, mysterious and beautiful). Where McGuckian's poems employ a single, privileged, feminine voice, "Elizabeth" is self-consciously a baffled masculine vision of a woman. The man is as apprehensive of his wife as she is of the birds – he regards her as potentially destructive, and changeable, connecting her with hurricanes that have "the name of a girl" and later referring to her by troubled variants on her name ("Lizzie and Liz and plain Beth") and suggesting she is a danger to herself and others:

> You hold yourself as your own captive;
> My promised children are in your hands,
> Hostaged by you in your father's old house.

Muldoon has referred to this kind of effect as "ventriloquism" (*Viewpoints*, 134) and insisted "we mustn't take anything at face value, not even the man who is presenting things at face value" (*Viewpoints*, 135). "Good Friday, 1971. Driving Westward" (9–10) refers to these points almost explicitly – its own ventriloquism contrasts with the authority of John Donne's voice in "Good Friday, 1613. Riding Westward". There is a struggle in the Donne poem – "Pleasure or business" makes him travel westwards on the very day when his "soul's form bends towards the east". However, his struggle is resolved as the poem progresses by his determination to fix his mind's eye on its proper object. The difference between the two poems, then, is the difference between dialectic and dialogue – there is a solution, however hard-won, to the the problem in Donne's poem, but none to that in Muldoon's. Instead of the sophisticated certainties of the Platonic Christian tradition there are the sophisticated uncertainties of late 20th century relativism and perspectivism.

The first line provides a clue to this in the way it questions the goodness of Good Friday which, after all, involved a death (whether or not Muldoon's poem involves a death is its crucial mystery – as the cause of the wife's fear was crucial in "Elizabeth"). Characteristically, though, the word is introduced in a punning phrase; "good going" trivialises the idea of goodness with a sense of ease, and "going along with" adds to this with connotations of merely going for a ride, complacently taking a direction dictated by another. Then, "going along with the sun" introduces an effect which is crucial in this poem which consistently humanises the non-human.

The latter is a stock effect in poems but Muldoon questions it in this one by associating it with a facile belief that the world corresponds with one's own view of it. Throughout, there is a sense that the speaker is too confident in his interpretations and, once, literally too sanguine: "Letterkenny had just then laid/ Open its heart and we passed as new blood/ Back into the grey flesh of Donegal." To some extent what Muldoon is doing in this way is to deconstruct the anthropomorphism of the poetry of moralised landscape (of which "Good Friday, 1613" is an early and oblique example). Doubts arise because of the insistence with which the effect is used, because of a kind of alarming facility in the fluent rhythm – especially in the way it leaps from an unpunctuated line at the end of each stanza (as it were, without looking) into the next – and the way it is joined by another kind of poetic effect, that of a generalising reference that conflates time and place (and its landmarks) too readily, as in

"I moved through morning towards the sea", and "life was changing down for the sharp bends". At the start of the third stanza, this
is combined with a further effect which has also been implicit all
along – that use of montage which juxtaposes social activities and
which is associated with Auden, though here (since travel through
a landscape is involved) it may be closer to the Larkin of "The
Whitsun Weddings". So he says, "A whole country was fresh after
the night"

> Though people were still fighting for the last
> Dreams and changing their faces where I paused
> To read the first edition of the truth.

Montage pretends to be objective but Muldoon casts doubt on that
by ventriloquising it, by juxtaposing it with the subjective effects I
have referred to, and by insinuating into its characteristically panop-
tic scope a kind of imagery which implies knowledge an observer
could not have, especially that of dreams. In this way, the omnis-
cience which is a premise of montage is called into question, and
this is reinforced by the reference to newspapers which suggests
that, later in the day, "the truth" will be different.

However, these doubts are only an undercurrent and it takes the
introduction of another perspective really to call into question the
speaker's fluent confidence. As in "Elizabeth" it is a woman's state
of mind which is juxtaposed with that of the masculine speaker in
"Good Friday, 1971" and once again the question of what really
happened is left open. What is clear is that the man's poetic generalisations are undermined by the apparent smallness, in his version, of what becomes, through the woman's dialogic intervention,
the central event in the poem, when "she thought we had hit something big/ But I had seen nothing, perhaps a stick/ Lying across
the road". In a sense this rebukes the monologic confidence of poetry
itself (or perhaps more specifically a masculine poetic tradition that
too easily assimilates Nature and Mind) by stepping to one side
of it and seeing it from a fresh angle. Instead of moving, as loco-
descriptive poems characteristically do, from description to argument, this one moves from description to narrative. Moreover, this
narrative ensures that instead of there being consonance between
premise and conclusion, there is dissonance and an inconclusive-
ness that argues with the over-confident premises.

Although Muldoon speaks of "wanting almost to write novels in the poem" (*Viewpoints*, 133) "Elizabeth" and "Good Friday, 1971" more closely resemble short stories. They both contain only two characters and they both centre upon a single incident which functions like an epiphany. However, in writing the sequence "Armageddon, Armageddon" (35–41) Muldoon seems to have learned how to introduce more characters and how to move quickly between scenes. So, by the time he came to write "Immram" (58–67) he could construct a poem which was novelistic in its scope, though its source is closer to epic:

> "Immram" means "voyage tale". Under the influence of the *Navigatio Sancti Brendani* the earlier forms of voyage tales were given a Christian veneer. One of the best known of them is "Immram Mael Duin" (another is the "Voyage of Bran", which partly explains a small joke in an earlier poem), in which the hero sets out to avenge his father's death, goes through many fabulous adventures, and at the end discovers an old hermit sitting on a rock – who turns out to be a Howard Hughes figure in my version – who tells him that he should turn the other cheek. Swift was very likely aware of the genre, and Tennyson has a dreadful version of it. I've tried to write a version which gives it a contemporary setting, because one of the few genres in which the heroic mode is possible is the thriller. Apart from that, I like Chandler a great deal; I think he's a very good writer, a good stylist. Byron is knocking around there too.
>
> (*Viewpoints*, 139)

This use of the "voyage tale" suggests a search on Muldoon's part for his Irish origins – especially since the hero of the principal model, Mael Duin, has a prototype of his name. This is echoed at the thematic level by the speaker's search for his lost father. If this were the case, Muldoon's concerns would resemble those of Heaney who, in a poem like "Broagh" (*NSP*, 25) delves for an authentic Irishness through the combination of Irish place and Irish word in a way that suggests a search (in both language and landscape) for "roots": the Irish word "Broagh" is a shibboleth that distinguishes between natives and strangers who find its "last/ gh. . ./difficult to manage".

Despite his apolitical stance it does seem clear that Muldoon sympathises with Heaney's nostalgia for a lost Irishness and its connected abhorrence of a British imperialism which suppressed and violated that Irishness. The title poem of *Meeting the British*[12] is, for Muldoon, a surprisingly savage indictment of the colonizing of native Americans who are clearly an analogue for the Irish: "They gave us six fishhooks/ and two blankets embroidered with small-pox". However, it is as though Muldoon usually takes all this for granted and is more interested in exploring the complex contemporary ramifications than in protesting about the violent imperialist roots. So the event described in "Meeting The British" becomes one of the premises of *Madoc* but is almost lost there in an immense thicket of epistemological roots and branches, and in the earlier poem itself is already connected with Muldoon's characteristic imagery of merging:

> We met the British in the dead of winter.
> The sky was lavender
>
> and the snow lavender-blue.
> I could hear, far below,
>
> the sound of two streams coming together
> (both were frozen over)
>
> and, no less strange,
> myself calling out in French

This confluence of streams is reminiscent of that at the end of "Identities" (12) and once again there is no sense of Wordsworthian unity in the merging – instead there is sinister deadlock compounded by a surreal disturbance that, despite being frozen, they are not silent. Clearly, though, whatever sound they make, they do not speak with a Wordsworthian "one voice" and the (again surreal) idea of the red Indian speaker "calling out in French" enforces the sense of something bizarre and involuntary. Sky and snow are almost merged by reflecting each other – but, again, not quite, the one being "lavender", the other "lavender-blue" and the (again incomplete) intermingling of nature and culture is suggested later as this imagery is picked up in the direct speech of Colonel Henry Bouquet (whose name suggests flowers and scent):

> As for the unusual
> scent when the Colonel shook out his hand-
> kerchief: *C'est la lavande,*
> *une fleur mauve comme le ciel.*

The indignation in the poem's last line – which seems so powerful on a first reading – gets increasingly swamped in re-readings by a sense of the complexity of the event and its implied consequences. Perhaps most symptomatic of this is the poem's self-reflexivity – it calls its own medium into question by dwelling on voices and languages. So the "British" in the title are also French, and the manner in which nature and culture are confounded in the "lavender" imagery and the name "bouquet" raises important questions about how language structures experience.

It is from this perspective, then, that the search for origins in "Immram" is most accurately seen: while that search has powerful psychological motives (echoed in archetypal patterns and imagery) it is doomed to fail because the *point* of origin has bewilderingly ramified, and its implied sense of a full single presence has been lost or endlessly fragmented. So the speaker's search for his father is ridiculed as early as the first stanza:

> "Your old man was an ass-hole.
> That makes an ass-hole out of you."
> My grand-father hailed from New York State.
> My grandmother was part Cree.
> This must be some new strain in my pedigree.
>
> (58)

Muldoon's concern with hybrids is taken one ludic step further here – the speaker's ancestry is not only mixed, it contains a sort of absence in the place of the full phallic presence of his father. Later, he is described as a "mule"; but at the start he seems to have disappeared up his own backside and genetically transmitted the same tendency to his son. This is an absence that is, as it were, present throughout – the son may possibly be on his father's trail but that trail is all that is left and it is unstable – his father fled from "alias to alias" (66) – tenuous, mostly purposeless, morally ambiguous at best.

This hybrid imagery is echoed in the hybrid style. What "Immram" does is to conduct a dialogue with epic which – like James Joyce's *Ulysses* – draws upon its resources at the same time as revealing its inadequacies for modern subject-matter and in this way defining that subject-matter by contrast with that of the older genre. Katerina Clark and Michael Holquist succinctly summarise the way that Bakhtin defined epic – a necessarily partial definition since his interest lay in how the novel superseded the older form:

The time of epic is not chronological, it is rather a world of beginnings and peak times in the national history, a world of firsts and bests. Epics are not simply set in a time that has receded, for epic time is best perceived as a value. What was in the past is automatically considered to be better, bigger, stronger or more beautiful. In epic, someone is speaking about a past that is to him inaccessible, and he adopts the reverent point of view of a descendant. In its style, tone, and manner of expression, epic discourse is far removed from the discourse of a contemporary addressed to other contemporaries...It is impossible to change, to rethink, or to reevaluate anything in epic time, for it is finished, conclusive and immutable. It exists in a world without relativity or any gradual, purely temporal progressions that might connect it with the present where people constantly rethink, change and reevaluate.[13]

What are implicit in this definition are the opposite qualities which Bakhtin associates with the novel – broadly, the dialogic and the carnivalesque. It is these qualities which Muldoon uses to subvert the monologic nature of the epic voyage tale. So, while it is a poem spoken by a "descendant" and, partly at least, about "a past that is to him inaccessible", his point of view is far from "reverent" and the narrative is far from "immutable" – instead it is endlessly open to reevaluation and change, and endlessly relative. His claim to be "telling this exactly as it happened" (58) is constantly undermined by the way scenes and characters dissolve into each other and carry with them unstable intertextual residues – especially from "Immram Mael Duin", Raymond Chandler, Byron and Shakespeare's *The Tempest*: "My poem takes the episodes and motifs of the original and twists them around, sometimes out of all recognition. At one stage, for instance, a confrontation with a white cat becomes a confrontation with a black cat". (*Viewpoints*, 139)

What is most important in subverting the speaker's authority, however, is the way his voice is called into question by the use of parody. Stylistically, "Immram" is a hybrid of epic and the Chandleresque novel. Muldoon is interested in what the two share in common, what he calls "the heroic mode" (*Viewpoints*, 139) and, connected with this, their sense of purpose – the quest in epic, the search for a solution in the detective story. Both genres focus on actions and events and claim to describe them objectively. However, the paradoxical effect of merging them is to evoke unheroic purposelessness, and to call their objectivity into question by dwelling on the way they are composed out of language and stock literary effects. The generic instability of "Immram" unsettles expectations and cuts off both the speaker and the reader from the reassurances that are singly offered by epic and detective story, and so suggests a restless refusal on the part of experience itself to be too easily packaged. One key effect here is the way the, as it were, wateriness of the voyage tale is partly denied by the landlocked nature of the detective story but, nonetheless, keeps surreally infiltrating itself, as Edna Longley has pointed out, in

> "Foster's pool-hall", "Which brought me round to the Atlantic Club" (possibly a poetic school of *immram*-writers by analogy with "The Country Club"), "the wild, blue yonder", "that old Deep Water Baptist mission"[14].

Puns like these are linguistic amphibians and they are combined throughout the poem with other characteristic Muldoon effects which are like genetic mutations of conventional poetic devices. Its ten-line stanza, for example, is a bastard form of Byron's ottava rima, and the half-rhymes they contain ("hat-band"/"happened"; "treble"/ "highball"; "syringe"/"strange": "guru"/"Bureau") do not so much clinch ideas as force a double-take that reassesses them.

The way the setting of "Immram" hesitates between sea and land is roughly equivalent to the way it hesitates between the solidity of the "real world" and the deliquessence of dream or hallucination, sometimes explicitly drug-induced. Individual images within each scene loom up with vivid particularity but the scenes are linked by a problematic series of "dissolves" and each scene is itself vulnerable to undergoing a "sea-change":

> I did a breast-stroke through the carpet,
> Went under once, only to surface
> Alongside the raft of a banquet-table –
> A whole roast pig, its mouth fixed on an apple.

In these lines it is as though "ventriloquism" itself is being called into question. The "hard-boiled" Chandleresque tone is maintained and the reference to swimming might be one more of its hyperboles but is too surreal for that and questions the reality of the setting too subversively. Generically, it is, to quote "Mules", "neither one thing or the other" (34) and, as such, calls profoundly into question the stability of the structures that we use to perceive and understand reality.

It is strange, then, that at the centre of this complex fictive web sits a real person, Howard Hughes, the figure with whom the poem ends:

> He was huddled on an old orthopaedic mattress,
> The makings of a skeleton,
> Naked but for a pair of drawstring shorts.
> His hair was waistlength, as was his beard.
> He was covered in bedsores.
> He raised one talon.
> "I forgive you," he croaked. "And I forget.
> On your way out, you tell that bastard
> To bring me a dish of ice-cream.
> I want Baskin-Robbins banana-nut ice-cream."
>
> (67)

After the relentless intertextuality and fabulatory self-reflexiveness of the main body of the poem, its shift into this documentary register and realist notation is the biggest shock that it delivers. What this does is to dispel any sense (monolithic in its own anti-realist way) that "everything is fiction": it insists that literature is a compound of truth and invention. So the person described in this stanza is at the same time a real and a fictive person: "One of the things that set me off was this vision of an old hermit who's visited every day by an otter bringing him a loaf of bread and a jug of ale, which I treat in terms of Hughes' penchant for Baskin-Robbins banana-nut ice-cream." (*Viewpoints*, 140)

It is this hybrid of the fictive and the real which provides the most important clue to Muldoon's most recent work. So "Bechbretha" (*MB*, 18–20) combines references to Merlyn Rees and Enoch Powell with stories, of varying levels of credibility, about bees. And "7, Middagh Street" (*MB*, 36–59) presents versions of W.H. Auden, Benjamin Britten, and Salvador Dali, amongst others, saying and doing things that combine history with fantasy.

However, this combination is much more disturbing in "The More a Man Has the More a Man Wants" (85–109), where detailed references to terrorist killings have a self-consciously problematic relationship with a shockingly adulterous mixture of materials. One way of discussing this might be to refer, as Clair Wills does in discussing "Sushi" (*MB*, 34–35) to the "assertion of absolute relativity between all found objects" which "may in certain contexts be read as a utopian project which breaks down hierarchical barriers (the 'essence' of post-modernism)"[15] – though clearly, in this context, the project is far from utopian. On the contrary, Muldoon's poem seems to employ this relativity as a shock tactic which suggests alarm at the way the post-modern condition tends to break down *moral* hierarchical barriers at the same time as political and aesthetic ones. In other words, although elsewhere in Muldoon's work the notion of the hybrid is celebrated and welcomed – which may well suggest that Muldoon has a postmodernist sensibility – here it seems to be examined quizzically and anxiously at arm's length.

What is perhaps most shocking about the poem is its unventriloquial nature. Responsibility for the poem's vision is not shifted, as in "Immram" and elsewhere onto an unreliable first person narrator. Instead, this poem has an omniscient, third-person narration which suggests that it is the implied author himself who sees things like this. Perhaps this is Muldoon's equivalent of the way that Heaney, in his "bog people" poems implicates himself in the sectarian killings, confessing that he would "have cast. . ./the stones of silence" and

> would connive
> in civilized outrage
> yet understand the exact
> and tribal, intimate revenge.
> (*NSP*, 72)

Certainly, "The More a Man Has" seems self-consciously to present a characteristic Muldoon voice – almost at times as though parodying itself – in a way that seems to worry about that voice's lack of appropriate respect, or its inability to come up with the correct poetic response:

> Once the local councillor straps
> himself into the safety belt
> of his Citroen
> and skids up the ramp

> from the municipal car park
> he upsets the delicate balance
> of a mercury-tilt
> boobytrap.
> Once they collect his smithereens
> he doesn't quite add up.
> They're shy of a foot, and a calf
> which stems
> from his left shoe like a severely
> pruned-back shrub.

Heaney carefully weighs and defines his response. By contrast, all emotion seems to have drained from these lines so that they raise the whole question of response – that of the poet to the killing, and the reader to the poem. By analogy with minimalism, they provide so little guidance to the reader that they implicitly ask what it is possible to say or feel about an event of this kind. In this manner they draw attention to how second-hand, or mediated, post-modern responses are – knowledge of these killings is largely transmitted through the media and accompanied by characteristic media rhetoric. Given how those media transform their material and collapse its hierarchies by flattening it (in Wills' paradoxical phrase) into "absolute relativity", it becomes impossible to respond in the appropriate ways morally and emotionally. At one point, a terrorist and an arms dealer get conflated with transcendentalist philosophers:

> On the Staten Island ferry
> two men are dickering
> over the price
> of a shipment of Armalites,
> as Henry Thoreau was wont to quibble
> with Ralph Waldo Emerson.

So, throughout the poem, events of alarmingly different moral status are described in the same disorientingly light-headed style. Alice repeats the same sentence when referring to her dealings first with a penis " 'Oh, I'm not particular as to size' " (96) and then with a stick of gelignite (99). Gallogly, the poem's central character, is presented as a lovable rogue whether engaged in terrorist activities or simply stealing a milk van:

He had given the milkman a playful
rabbit punch.
When he stepped on the gas
he flooded the street
with broken glass.
He is trying to keep a low profile.

(87)

In tracing Gallogly's activities, "The More a Man Has" acquires,
like "Immram", a picaresque quality – but here it is surreally at
odds with its subject-matter so that style and content refuse to fit,
and form an unstable compound. This is a deeply troubling poem
because it uses postmodernist techniques self-consciously to invoke
what postmodernism's critics consider its lack of moral responsibility and so raises the whole question of what such responsibility
means – here using the word in its connection, also, both politically
and aesthetically, with "response". In some ways, this poem explores at greater length the questions raised in "Lunch with Pancho
Villa" (19–21) about poetry and politics, representation and the "real"
but it does so much more uncomfortably because it treats its subject
with relentless objectivity and so with an apparent heartlessness
that questions its readers, in a *tu quoque* way, about how feelingly
*they* react.


It is a key characteristic of the hybrid of "truth" and fiction in
Muldoon's recent work that, through it, both become a problem –
they face up to and question one another. *Madoc* explores the problem in great detail, and polyphonically, by placing real historical
figures – most importantly Coleridge and Southey – into a merely
hypothetical history haunted by both mythical explanations and
philosophical interpretations. For this reason, this long poem's closest affinity is with what Linda Hutcheon has called the "historiographic metafiction" of some postmodernist novels:

Recent postmodern readings of both history and realist fiction
have focused more on what the two modes of writing share than
on how they differ. They have both been seen to derive their
force more from verisimilitude than from any objective truth;
they are both identified as linguistic constructs, highly conven-
tionalized in their narrative forms, and not at all transparent,

either in terms of language or structure; and they appear to be equally intertextual, deploying the texts of the past within their own complex textuality. But these are also the implied teachings of what I would like to call postmodern "historiographic meta-fiction" – novels that are intensely self-reflexive but that also both re-introduce historical context into metafiction and problematize the entire question of historical knowledge.[16]

That there has been a sense of something like this almost from the start in Muldoon's work is evident from the way he uses it in conjunction with the idea, almost his signature, of the hybrid – though here, in "Cauliflowers" (10–11) the analogy takes a more sophisticated and postmodern form, as his epigraph describes: "Plants that glow in the dark have been developed through gene-splicing, in which light-producing bacteria from the mouths of fish are introduced to cabbage, carrots and potatoes."

So this poem prefigures the compound of the fictive and the historiographic which constitutes *Madoc* as a whole with a compound of the fictive and the autobiographical. In the Coleridgean terms which are appropriate to the subject-matter of this long poem, "Cauliflowers" employs the memory and the fancy to link ideas together through association. Muldoon, like the Coleridge of the "conversation" poems, describes himself in a particular setting and evokes the way that scenes from his past arise in his mind linked by images and verbal patterns. In a motel in Oregon he listens "to lovers/ repeatedly going down/ on each other in the next room" and remembers his father and uncle taking cauliflowers to market. However, in Muldoon's case the links seem capricious and this is part of their point – they are achieved largely through puns which echo through the poem through its use of a bastardised – because assonantal – sestina form. Rather than suggesting an "organic" link, as Coleridge does, between one association and another, this suggests merely personal obsession: the same words ("light", "pipe", "cauliflowers", "going down") crop up again and again in different contexts with altered meanings – but with the implication that the poet cannot free himself from a vicious associative circle.

As a result, there is no final sense, in Muldoon's poem, of Coleridge's "esemplastic" imagination working all the separate materials into a transcendant unity. Instead, those materials are spliced together in a way that leaves all the joins still visible. And there is a further sense that the act of splicing – which the human mind seems compelled to perform – is distortive, and almost, at times, gratuitously so. It forms hybrids that make cauliflowers glow in the dark. Here, of course, the Romantic and the postmodernist are poles apart – the former aiming to equate the natural and the aesthetic, the latter insisting on their absolute incompatibility. A postmodernist text is one that keeps declaring itself to be a construct of vegetable and fish: it collapses natural hierarchies, so that the barriers even between forms of life are broken down.

So the way that the memory and the fancy transform the autobiographical material in "Cauliflowers" uses Muldoon's personal history synecdochically to suggest how, in Hutcheon's terms, the historiographic metafiction of *Madoc* insists on "verisimilitude" rather than "objective truth", insists on itself as a "linguistic construct" with an intertextual relation to historical and literary texts.

The most important way this intertextuality is signalled in the main body of the poem is in how each section is named after a philosopher – "Duns Scotus", "Locke", "Saussure", "Bachelard", "Bakhtin" etc. It is not that these sections are "about" these specific thinkers. Instead these names suggest the whole history of Western thought and thereby that "the world" is indistinguishable from human interpretations of it. The specific importance of this for *Madoc* is that the poem centres around the discovery of the "New World" but the presence of these names insists on how it is inevitably perceived in old ways – they work like a reference grid on the map of the new land.

Connected with this there are two Western motifs which Muldoon suggests are especially important for the way the New World was, and is perceived – the search for origins, and the dream of utopia. These are linked in the poem through the figure of Southey who himself wrote an epic called *Madoc* and who, with Coleridge, fantasised about the founding of a "Pantisocratic" community on the banks of the Susquehanna. Southey's poem tells the story of

a Welsh prince who supposedly set sail for America in the twelfth century, found land, returned to Wales and supposedly set sail again to be heard from no more. The story of the descendants of Madoc, that mythical tribe of Welsh Indians, living somewhere in the American hinterland, was. . .well-known at the court of Elizabeth; and Sir Walter Raleigh was commissioned to write it down, confirming the prior "claim" of the English to the "New World" against that of Spain.[17]

This dubious story has to be read to some extent in the context of other poems by Muldoon – especially of his scepticism about the search for origins in "Immram" and his reference to native Americans in "Meeting the British" (there has been a suggestion that these Welsh indians were themselves deliberately killed off with small-pox[18]). On the one hand it is clear that Muldoon does not take this story at face value but on the other there are hints in the poem that he does take seriously its significance at a mythical level. Origins are not a simple matter – as soon as the natives were encountered by Europeans they were changed, if only by being perceived differ-ently (as the name "red indians" itself indicates). The idea that they might already be British (Welsh) before they met the British is a witty analogy for this. On the other hand, the imperialist way *in which* they were changed is treated with sophisticated but nonethe-less bitter satire by Muldoon and represented by how violent im-agery constantly erupts into the poem.

So there is a sense in which *Madoc* is an oblique elegy – some-thing already prefigured at a personal level in "Cauliflowers" where the vicious associative circle I referred to centres on the death of Muldoon's father and uncle – "All gone out of the world of light./ All gone down/ the original pipe" (11). The Pantisocratic dreams of Coleridge and Southey are mocked throughout with the implica-tion that they amounted to one more scheme by Europeans to trans-form the New World in their own image – another series of texts (this time hypothetical) to add to the dense intertextuality which would, as it were, make red Indians call out in French. All of this is characteristically muted in keeping with Muldoon's apolitical stance – he refuses to simplify, and political statements are difficult to make in the face of the postmodern problem, as Hutcheon puts it, of "the entire question of historical knowledge". But as in "The More a Man Has", there are suggestions in *Madoc*, despite its obvi-ous postmodernist characteristics, of a final mistrust of the post-modern, even of a kind of nostalgia which Jean-François Lyotard regards as the antithesis of the postmodern[19]. It suggests the end-lessly hybrid nature of experience but also worries about it and the way it can connive politically with those whose texts are most privi-leged, and allow oppressors to speak, in the end too unproble-matically, with "forked tongue".

# 3

# James Fenton: Expert at Cross-Fertilisation

Much of James Fenton's distinctiveness arises from how thoroughly he is a social poet and the restless inventiveness he has deployed in finding techniques, forms and varieties of language for the writing of social poetry. The variousness of his work is the product of a kind of self-effacement that looks outwards at the complex variousness of society which is reflected in the multiplicity of languages it uses. Consequently, one of the most prominent features of his work is its self-conscious exploration of heteroglossia. Nancy Glazener's account of Bakhtin's concept is helpful here:

> Bakhtin derives the heteroglossia of literary discourses – their multiplicity and their tendentious interaction – ultimately from the stratification of social life, in which different social groups create distinctive discourses from their common language; as a result, the meaning of a word is always a function of its torque, of its being turned to incommensurate purposes by speakers who use it in different discourses. Likewise, these discourses, products of discrete but inextricable social formations, depend so much on their interrelationship for their intelligibility that they are ultimately significant only in relation to the entire complex of language use. Discourses cannot be tailored semantically to the expressive intentions of an individual without betraying the social fabric from which they have been cut.[1]

The expressive intentions of individuals – which are the traditional subject of poetry – always carry with them, when they are present in Fenton's work, the sense that they cannot be regarded accurately in isolation, that their shape, texture and cloth have been determined by their contextual fabric.

Fenton's own explicit emphasis is on the social context of poetry, as evidenced in his theory of the poetries of "extrinsic" and "intrinsic" interest:

> It is pretended that we either do or should read a poem in pursuit
> of its pure merit, but this is a narrow pursuit, and impossible.
> Our interest in a poem changes when we learn that it was written
> by Henry the Eighth, for instance. Nor is there anything wrong
> in reading poetry for its *interest*, though it be heresy to say so.[2]

This dismissal of "purity" and defence of "extrinsic interest" is also
a defense of the occasional in poetry – Fenton goes on to show how
much more interest there is in the quatrain "In the corner *one* –/ I
spy Love!/ In the corner *None*,/ I spy Love" when the reader knows
it is by Coleridge. Then he shows how "Butchered to Make a Dutch-
man's Holiday" is interesting largely because it was written by
"Breaker" Morant on the eve of his execution, and because of "the
awful authenticity of the voice".

"Extrinsic interest" arises from our biographical interest in the
poet; "intrinsic interest" relates to bits of the "real world" observed
by the poet, the term

> is supposed to help in identifying those works of art which de-
> rive a part of their charge from, for instance, facts which are in
> themselves interesting. If, say, I had been in Romania last Christ-
> mas, and had therefore witnessed some of the major events, and
> had a clear view of what happened, and you asked me, and as an
> answer I sang you a ballad containing all the details of what was
> actually said and done during the trial of Nicolae and Elena, this
> would (what a dreadful fantasy) count as an intrinsically interest-
> ing poem. The critical things that might be said of it ("He has
> revived the street-ballad", etc) would pale into insignificance in
> the light of the facts themselves.
>
> > ("Ars Poetica", 13 May 1990, 18)

Implicit behind Fenton's championing of both "extrinsic" and
"intrinsic" interest is a dissatisfaction with the traditional lyric and
its single "pure" voice: the former draws attention to the biographical and social context in which the poet speaks, and the latter brings
that context into the poem's foreground. Another way of putting
this would be to say that Fenton wants to introduce objective kinds
of writing into his poetry alongside more conventional subjective
ones – and sometimes almost to the exclusion of subjective ones.

One form this takes connects Fenton with a kind of "avant garde"
writing to which he might otherwise seem vehemently opposed:

Much poetry has been inspired by the *curious*, a passage from a book or newspaper, the thing that stays in the mind leaving the poet wondering, "There is *that*. . .but what can I do with it?"

In a found poem, the poet has answered this question by saying "Don't do anything with it; just bung it on the page". Found poetry is fun, but it does not get us very far; in a way, it becomes repetitive, saying "Look at this, isn't it curious, or fun or horrible, or mysterious". It is an ostensive gesture.

So the big question is: given the intrinsically interesting *donné*, what do I do with it?

("Ars Poetica", 13 May 1990, 18)

Section V of Fenton's *The Memory of War and Children in Exile*[3] contains variations on the found poem. The first of these, a quotation from Erasmus Darwin, helps to explain the ones that follow: "The general design of the following sheets is to inlist Imagination under the banner of Science". Darwin, too, seems to have believed in "intrinsic interest": "The matter must be interesting from its sublimity, beauty, or novelty: this is the scientific part; and the art consists in bringing these distinctly before the eye". So "Exempla" (73–80) begins with a rigorously factual account of the habits and sense-perceptions of frogs: "A frog hunts on land by vision. He escapes/ Enemies mainly by seeing them" etc. Fenton is closer here than he would like to think to the minimalist writers whose work he attacked in his piece "Reductio ad Absurdum":

The obvious fault, as with so much imagist and projectivist verse, is the banality of the aesthetic stance. Pay attention to things! says the poet, they are so amazingly *thingy*. The phenomenal world. . . it's *phenomenal*! A Williams poem from 1919 reads: "Lo the leaves/ Upon the new autumn grass –/ Look at them well. . .!"

("Ars Poetica", 18 March 1990, 20)

In fact, Fenton's "Exempla" do ask the same implicit questions as poems like "The Red Wheelbarrow" by William Carlos Williams – minimalist questions about the boundaries of the aesthetic, about how objects (or animals) acquire human meaning and get transformed by art.

To be fair to Fenton, though, these poems have more affinities with those of Marianne Moore than of Williams – they share her syllabic technique and her concern to emulate scientific rigour. As his discussion of the found poem indicates, he wants to take the *donné* as a starting-point and he is less preoccupied than Williams with aesthetic philosophy. A clue to Fenton's thinking here is an early poem by his friend and mentor, John Fuller, whose "Objet Trouvé: Piazza San Marco"[4] refers to a religious relic, "St Mark's personal foot" and reflects that "The object made the most of little/ And challenged our aesthetic sense/ With a luxurious reticence." Fuller's rhyming couplets and elegant discursiveness transform the object's foundness in the process of discussing it. The oxymoron "luxurious reticence" acknowledges minimalism but has already leapt beyond it. Fenton's aims are similar and there is a further link here to Auden (Fuller's mentor) whose "In Praise of Limestone" uses the influence of Marianne Moore as a stylistic starting-point from which to place physical science in a human and social context, which means that his focus is on the register and terminology as much as on the imagery. So the power of the quotation from Lyell's *Principles of Geology*, which concludes "Exempla", arises from the heteroglossia it contains, from the way it shifts from one language into another so that history suddenly seems to infiltrate geology:

This terminal point remains usually unchanged from year to year, although every part of the ice is in motion, because the liquefaction by heat is just sufficient to balance the onward movement of the glacier, which may be compared to an endless file of soldiers, pouring into the breach, and shot down as soon as they advance.
(80)

The shock here comes from a simultaneous sense that the simile is physically accurate and in its way as rigorous as the geological language that precedes it – but that it introduces a vivid emotional charge that is inappropriate and gratuitous. The way it affects our sense of Lyell is ambiguous. It may make us think his eye is so much on the glacier it causes him to lapse into an absent-minded heartlessness. Or it may make us admire him for feeling so strongly about glaciers that they made him think of this emotive image – to admire him as Fenton does Craig Raine:

When a poet looks at his wife and thinks of a tomato, one may feel that he lacks feeling. But when he further shows that his feeling for tomatoes is more deeply affectionate and more sexually alert than most poets' feelings for their first girlfriends, one is obliged to think again. Obliged to *feel* again.[5]

Fenton is referring here to the dialogic double-take that the Martian poetic causes the reader through its juxtaposing of perspectives. Something similar is caused by the juxtaposing of languages in the Lyell passage. But this can also be seen as a small-scale version of what happens generally in these elaborated found poems which self-consciously place non-literary kinds of writing in a literary context. By so doing they suggest the insufficiencies of the literary and insist on the importance of multiple points of view, a point which is made self-reflexively in the passage on the frog by its emphasis on the limitations of that amphibian's sense organs – "He will starve to death surrounded by food/ If it is not moving": "His sex life is conducted by sound and touch"; "He does remember a living/ Thing provided it stays within/ His field of vision and he is not distracted". The register is different but the framing of these lines in a poetic form inevitably makes them recall beast fable so that human pretensions are by implication debunked as they are, for example, by those of the cock in Chaucer's "The Nun's Priest's Tale" – also an "exemplum". A similarly cautionary effect is achieved by the fragmentariness of "Exempla" and the randomness of its montage technique – both stress the impossibility of a fully comprehending vision.

The linguistic juxtaposition of the beast fable and the scientific paper draws attention to differences ("Imagination" versus "Science", "Poetry" versus "Prose") but also to similarities – both are about attempts to establish a just orientation of the human to the natural. The dialogue between the two keeps the poem generically unstable and unsettles easy assumptions which might too readily assimilate the natural into the human. The other poems in this group appear less radical in their form and language but the way they are placed after "Exempla" (which is also the title of the whole section) suggests that they are meant to be read in the light of lessons learned from this opening poem. "The Fruit-Grower in War-Time" is closest to "Exempla" in its deployment of a scientific register, but here the warnings are more explicitly ecological – "We must observe the fruit-grower with caution". His use of "arsenate of lead" as an insecticide is made to acquire apocalyptic associations because it makes us compare ourselves "to the last idiot heirs/ Of some Roman province, still for the/ Sake of form eating off lead platters". "South

Parks Road" refers to "Blossom and/ Birdlime on windscreens and
a drain spluttering/ Froth under the laburnums" and so evokes an
undercurrent below the apparent glamour and ease of, as it were,
Oxford's *human* life. "Things are unhappy" and

> . . .I hear a voice from a garden hut
> Relating the case history of a chimpanzee
> Which, faced with an elementary learning problem of
> Peanut-here or peanut-there, chose knowingly
> To administer itself
>
> A lethal electric shock, in pique at being used
> As a guinea pig.

"South Parks Road" clearly emerges from Fenton's experiences
as a student in experimental psychology – but it is "A Terminal
Moraine" and "The Pitt-Rivers Museum, Oxford" that deal directly
with subjective responses and formative experiences. The former
refers to the Romantic dialectic of Nature and Mind and evokes
those moments when the two are joined in a transcendent synthesis
– "in the deep/ Of the night, when I am alone, I landscape my sleep
and I become a thing/ Of caves and hollows, mouths where the
winds sing". However, the poem's title refers back to the Lyell
quotation and so insinuates a post-Romantic questioning of Nature,
a geological doubt. So, in the end, "A Terminal Moraine" suggests,
not the certainties of dialectic, but the uncertainties of dialogue and
a longing for human society rather than the solitary communion
with landscape – "when a car is on the road I hear/ My heart beat
faster as it changes gear".

Geology functions in "A Terminal Moraine" as a reminder of the
alienness of Nature which persists despite the anthropomorphic
tendencies of poetry. "The Pitt-Rivers Museum, Oxford" refers to
anthropology in order to explore how the human defines itself by
the way it structures its understanding of the natural world – especially the way it treasures *objets trouvés*, or fashions natural objects,
in order to express its fantasies or calm its fears. The bizarre exhibits in the museum serve as reminders of the collective childhood of
the race and these are linked to memories of more contemporary
individual childhoods in a way that suggests the persistence of
superstitious wishes and fears. The exhibits constitute an archaeology of human attempts to communicate with, and thereby order

the unknown but the museum works like a poem desperately trying to order incongruous juxtapositions coherently and meaningfully, to transcend its "found" nature. In the end coherence is achieved in the poem only through the expression of the desire for order which arises as a response to fantasy and fear. Those collective feelings are focused on an individual child "entering the forbidden/ Woods of his lonely playtime" imagining "what tortures the savages had prepared/ For him there". The desire to ward off the unknown, on the other hand, is focused on the child's father who is responsible for the placard that reads "TAKE NOTICE/ MEN-TRAPS AND SPRING-GUNS ARE SET ON THESE PREMISES". Human attempts to calm fears, then, are not inadequate and comically irrelevant, they are often in themselves a source of added self-inflicted danger.

One poem which might well have appeared in the "Exempla" section but does not is "Chosun" (51–54) which includes, according to Fenton's notes, material drawn from books and a magazine about Korea. This material's "intrinsic interest" arises largely from the way it suggests a very foreign culture trying to order its experiences:

There were large people, overflowing people, reciprocal people,
Immortal, cross-legged, perforated, hoary,
Among beautiful clouds, summer prefecture, breathing peace,
    perennial hemp,
There were sorcerers, deep-eyed, mulberry and pear, without
    entrails.

The poem continues in this vein for four pages and is reminiscent of a passage quoted from a "certain Chinese encyclopaedia" by Borges which declares that

animals are divided into: a) belonging to the Emperor, b) embalmed, c) tame, d) sucking pigs, e) sirens, f) fabulous, g) stray dogs, h) included in the present classification, i) frenzied, j) innumerable, k) drawn with a very fine camelhair brush, l) *etcetera*, m) having just broken the water pitcher, n) that from a long way off look like flies.[6]

As Michel Foucault points out:

In the wonderment of this taxonomy, the thing we apprehend in one great leap, the thing that, by means of the fable, is demonstrated as the exotic charm of another system of thought, is the limitation of our own, the stark impossibility of thinking *that*.

(xv)

So the point about the foreign structure of thought outlined in "Chosun" is its dialogic relationship with that of the West – that others can regard the world so differently calls into question our own way of regarding it. Or, more radically still, it draws attention to the fragility, in general, of human orderings of the world. This is frightening in a similar way to the ending of "The Pitt-Rivers Museum" – if the way we regard the world is as open to question as this then perhaps even our fears are over-confident. Except that "Chosun" is frightening in, as it were, a more systematic way. "The Pitt-Rivers Museum" threatens order with incongruity, but as Foucault points out:

there is a worse kind of disorder than that of the *incongruous*, the linking together of things that are inappropriate; I mean the disorder in which fragments of a large number of possible orders glitter separately in the dimension, without law or geometry, of the *heteroclite*; and that word should be taken in its most literal, etymological sense: in such a state, things are "laid", "placed", "arranged" in sites so very different from one another that it is impossible to find a place of residence for them, to define a *common locus* beneath them all. . .*Heterotopias* are disturbing, probably because they secretly undermine language, because they make it impossible to name this *and* that, because they shatter or tangle common names, because they destroy "syntax" in advance, and not only the syntax with which we construct sentences but also that less apparent syntax which causes words and things (next to and also opposite one another) to "hold together".

(xvii–xviii)

Fenton's struggles to find a meaningful way to use the "found object" self-consciously collapse in "Chosun". Where Fuller, in his "Objet Trouvé" falls back upon Christian thinking to give epiphanic significance to St. Mark's foot – "Mark rose upwards through the air/ Out of his feet left standing there" (Fuller, 27) – Fenton's poem insists on the post-Christian difficulty of finding a larger meaning for individual experiences. What seems the bizarre arbitrariness of Chosunese taxonomy deconstructs the whole endeavour of connecting materials to achieve coherent forms. Moreover, as Foucault points out, that arbitrariness also disconcerts language by calling into question the way that syntax connects discrete phenomena.

Fenton, to judge by his public pronouncements, is robustly sceptical about this kind of post-structuralist thinking. In "Obviousness", for example, he says: "The world is full of poems which speak of, for instance, the essentially self-referential nature of language, or the deliquessence of meaning, or some other piece of pseudo-philosophy. But this stuff becomes tiresome" ("Ars Poetica" 25th November, 1990, 37). Nonetheless, there is a sense in which he is an experimental poet whose self-conscious exploration of heteroglossia asks restless questions about how and what language represents. He may praise "up-front rhythms, fauvist brushstrokes, bright rather than shrinking rhymes" (25th November, 1990, 37) and sometimes write like that himself, but equally characteristic are lines like:

> . . .Wallworth
> described the fungus as possessing
> a pezizaform hairy sporochodium
> with a flattened powdery surface layer
> of globose, vesiculate, hyaline conidia.
>
> (77)

What makes "Chosun" so radical is that it makes heteroglossia collide with what Foucault calls "heterotopia": the linguistic representation of otherness encounters an experiential otherness so extreme that it subverts representation itself.

A similar effect is achieved, despite appearances, by Fenton's nonsense poems. In form and tone these resemble the light verse which Fenton praises in "Obviousness" and which he practices, in collaboration with John Fuller, in *Partingtime Hall*. However, this is misleading. In light verse like "Nuns" (*Partingtime*, 20–21) there is complete consonance between the robust manner and the implicit confidence of the world-view on the one hand, and the poetic technique on the other. This is a limerick and so assumes a high level of consensus between the author (or speaker) and the reader (or hearer) – this is confirmed by the way that the best jokes are the most hackneyed:

The organ was busy at Lauds
And neighboring nuns drove in hordes
To hear settings of psalms
By Chopin and Brahms
And to come at the very first chords.

The notorious crudity of the oral form is matched by the self-conscious crudity of the subject-matter. The only thing that does not match is the high-brow nature of some of the references ("late Henry James", "opera seria") but these are treated dismissively and anyway work as a formal joke – the authors are more sophisticated than the form they are currently employing.

Despite their surface similarities with this kind of writing, Fenton's nonsense poems work in an almost opposite way. For example, the confidence inspired by the formal elegance of "The Kingfisher's Boxing Gloves" (96–99) is surreally at odds with its refusal to acquire much more than local meaning. Structurally, it pretends to be a kind of Audenesque montage – one of those poems where society is evoked, and its ills diagnosed, by placing one kind of activity on top of another. This effect, combined with the insistent rhymes (ABABABAB) makes the confidence trick especially plausible. But when the lack of coherence is perceived these effects actually enhance the feeling of comic hollowness. The disparity between form and content produces an effect analogous to that produced by what Bakhtin calls the "double voice" of parody – which, to some extent, is what the poem is. Yet, by being the opposite of the poetry it pretends to be, it calls that poetry into question: by being radically "open" where both Audenesque montage and light verse are "closed", it suggests that the confidence of those forms is itself a kind of trick:

The cicerone is unknown to flap,
The sort of chap who never makes a slip.
He can provide the only useful map.
He tells the men how much and when to tip.
He buys the sort of rope that will not snap
On the descent. He tells you where to grip.
That it's the thirteenth step that springs the trap.
That smugglers sweat along the upper lip.

(97)

Repeatedly the poem pretends to define a topography but its efforts succeed only, as Foucault puts it, in arranging things "in sites so very different from one another that it is impossible to find. . .a *common locus* beneath them all" (Foucault NB). Or the common locus is "The Empire of the Senseless" – the title Fenton gives to the nonsense section of *The Memory of War*. Instead, then, of a topography the poem evokes a "heterotopia" and so destroys the "syntax" of both words and things: these are connected in such dubious ways that the whole enterprise of connecting is ridiculed.

Described in this way, Fenton's poems are made to seem radically experimental. This conflicts with the reactionary tone of his pronouncements on poetry – but it is that tone which is misleading. The poems *are* experimental, and all the more so because they carry out their experiments, often, in a variety of traditional forms. The significance of Fenton's nonsense poems is in the way they show him testing the furthest boundaries of sense in order to discover how to make poems *make* sense in a way that is fresh but which still calls upon the tried resources of poetry. Together with his found poems they subject the genre to extreme (though playful) pressure in order to discover what it is still possible to say.

Tested like this poetry is opened up to contain elements that might seem profoundly foreign to it. I have referred already to the scientific registers which are employed in "Exempla": even more characteristic, however, is the way that journalistic writing is accommodated, albeit in a changed form. What is involved here again is extreme pressure – but this time that of the urgency of critical, often dangerous, political events. This kind of writing arouses extrinsic interest in the sense that the presence of the poet himself is strongly implied, like that of "Breaker" Morant, or of Wilfred Owen whose "legendary status derives in great measure from his having been a combatant: about what fighting is like, he can speak with irreplaceable authority" ("Ars Poetica" 2nd September, 1990, 24). Fenton implicitly claims this authority in his poems, and explicitly in his journalism which continually refers to his personal responses and condemns the kind of reporting that misses things out because it is afraid to imply that the reporter "had been present at the events [he is] describing"[8]. The pressure that is exerted as a result is simultaneously on the poet and the poem. Fenton as both journalist and poet, despite or because of the danger, makes himself experience, at first hand, the most important events of his time:

> Those who actually set out to see the fall of a city (as opposed to those to whom this calamity merely happens) or those who choose to go to the front line, are obviously asking themselves to what extent they are cowards. But the tests they set themselves – there is a dead body, can you bear to look at it? – are nothing in comparison with the tests that are sprung on them. It is not the obvious tests that matter (do you go to pieces in a mortar attack?) but the unexpected ones (here is a man on the run, seeking your help – can you face him honestly?).
>
> (*Wrong Places*, 103)

What this curiously resembles is the Extremist project that Fenton has famously attacked in his "Letter to John Fuller" (53–59). As poet-journalist Fenton is, above all, urgent – he takes existential risks in order to express in poetry the anguished mess of late twentieth century global politics. And yet the word "urgent" arouses in him a public-school reflex:

> For a poet to heave into view –
>   To be *emergent* –
> He must whine, as if he wants the loo,
>   "Please sir, I'm *urgent*."
>
> (69)

Urgency is *infra dig* and unEnglish. Perhaps for this reason Fenton avoids the confessional mode which is employed by Extremist poets like Lowell, Berryman and Plath and writes his journalistic poems mostly in an impersonal way, concentrating on arousing "intrinsic" rather than "extrinsic" interest.

The extrinsic element is nonetheless present because the poems inevitably have an intertextual relationship with the journalism where his own presence in the scene is emphasised. That presence foregrounds questions of interpretation and requires him to draw a self-portrait which involves focusing upon the bizarreness of being in "all the wrong places" in the first place. A process of self-discovery occurs at the same time as the discovery of places and events and he sometimes deliberately draws attention to the strangeness, in retrospect, of how he behaved, and the quirkiness of his subjective responses. So he describes himself, during the fall of Saigon, hitching a lift on a tank as it was about to drive into the grounds of Thieu's palace:

> The tank slowed down and a North Vietnamese soldier in green jumped off the back, and went at me with his gun, as if to hit me. . .I held out my hand abruptly, indicated the back of the tank. I remember worrying, as I climbed on, that I might touch something very hot. Then, as the soldier told me to keep my head down, I idiotically produced my passport, which they dismissed scornfully.
>
> (*Wrong Places*, 85–86)

What this also indicates is that, while there is a kind of authority associated with the author's presence in the scene, there is also a questionableness. Fenton's explicit reference, in his public pronouncements, to authority once again indicates how in those contexts he appears conservative and realist in his outlook. His actual practice, as both poet and journalist, is much less conservative, and more postmodernist than realist. As well as detailing his subjective responses, he refers to lapses of memory – "I wish I could remember it all better" (*Wrong Places*, 200) – and to the way the mechanics of writing transforms its subject-matter. So, writing about the events in the Philippines in the 1980s, Fenton says at one point that there is "one thing missing" (161) from his account. When he first says this he is talking specifically about not having met the NPA. Having met them, however, he still feels his account is incomplete: speaking to his friend Fred he says,

> "I'd like just one more thing."
> "One more thing?" said Fred. "What sort of thing?"
> "That's it. I don't know. Just one more thing to round it off."
> (175)

Here in Fenton's text, then, is a portrait of Fenton producing that text, searching for material that will make it whole. Failing to find it leaves the text open at this point, self-consciously incomplete – although this is clearly a question, partly, of authorial choice. There are obviously options available to Fenton – the addition of further analysis, for example, or deviation into more personal responses – which might solve his problem at an aesthetic level. Refusing to take those options amounts to choosing incompleteness and the pages that follow show why. For the "one more thing" turns out to be the "snap revolution" that occurred at this point.

In this way, then, actual events solve Fenton's aesthetic problem. Incompleteness in the text had mirrored incompleteness, as it were, in the Philippines: political completeness facilitates completeness in the text. But the problem posed by the desire for "one more thing" continues to draw attention to the textual nature of what Fenton is doing, so that even when the revolution rounds his text off its roundness is still in question.

All of this is important to Fenton's poetic practice because it is impossible not to read his poems about Asia without the extrinsic sense of his activities as a journalist affecting that reading. And there is clearly an interaction, anyway, between the two kinds of writing which works in a way analogous to that in which Auden used, as Fenton says, "the language of prose to find words and grammar for his poetry":

> When Auden took to prose for his poetic purposes, he tended to work on a much larger scale, using the journal, the letter, the prize-giving speech, the sermon as his forms. He was an expert at cross-fertilisation.
>
> ("Ars Poetica", 8th July 1990, 31)

Fenton's poems are also cross-fertilised – in "Exempla" by the scientific paper; in "Cambodia" (23), "In a Notebook" (24–25), "Dead Soldiers" (26–28), "Wind" (40), "Lines for Translation into Any Language" (29) and most of the poems in *Out of Danger*[9] by reportage.

That Fenton has one eye on language in these poems is evident from the way "In a Notebook" is divided into two halves which pretend to be jottings made before and after a war. These two halves reflect each other but as though in a distorting mirror. Some lines are repeated exactly but acquire different meanings by being shuffled out of their original context. Others are subtly changed, so that "wishing", in "And I sat drinking bitter coffee wishing" has, at first, a direct object in the lines that follow it, which have conditional verbs – "wishing/ The tide would turn to bring me to my senses/ After the pleasant war and the evasive answers". In the second version, "wishing" is more generalised and more like regret, and the verbs that follow it are in the past tense – "wishing – /And the tide turned and brought me to my senses./ The pleasant war brought the unpleasant answers." The title's reference to a notebook and the conditional mode employed in the first section both suggest incompleteness – the need for "one thing more". In the second section this (the war) has happened but the air of incompleteness still prevails in the repeated phrase "I'm afraid" which refers both to the fear caused by war and to a blander, more conventional anxiety about not fully knowing.

This blandness is a characteristic resource for Fenton, who likes to open a gap between the manner and register of his war poems on the one hand and their violent content on the other. "I'm afraid", on one level, has the assured personal style of light verse. The distance between that level and genuine fear is like that between the literal meaning of the "Dead Soldiers" in the poem of that name and its use as a nickname for empty bottles which sums up the elegantly conspicuous consumption and supercilious callousness of "the mad Norodoms" whose "lunch on the battlefield" includes "frogs' legs", "pregnant turtles" and Napoleon brandy. There is a similar disparity between the functional brusqueness of the phrasebook register of "Lines for Translation Into Any Language" (29) and the actual content of the lines – "5. That night the city was attacked with rockets", for example.

So, while Fenton assumes that the "obviousness" he regards as a poetic goal is incompatible with a concern with "the essentially self-referential nature of language" ("Ars Poetica", 25th November, 1990, 37) his own poems manage to combine something close to both. The self-referential element is never the main subject of the poem – it functions as a way of facilitating the cross-fertilising of one language by another, of allowing, for example, the poetic and the journalistic to form an unstable hybrid. In this way "Children in Exile" (30–37) describes young refugees from Cambodia adapting themselves to the West and does so partly by evoking their attempts to master Western registers, referring to "Grammars, vocabularies, the Khao-i-dang hedge dictionary,/ The future perfect, subjunctive moods and gloom", to "Too many words on the lookout for too many meanings./ Too many syllables for the tongue to frame". This is, as it were, *obvious* self-referentiality. These lines reflect the way that poems negotiate their subject-matter – but their main function is to draw upon this self-reflexive element to demonstrate the part that language plays in negotiating new experiences. As such they are part of the poem's repeated references to education, which constitute its controlling metaphor. The child exiles must

learn about the West but, by showing them in the process of learning, the poem draws upon traditional poetic resources – it uses the
capacity of the child's innocent eye (even more innocent here because the eye is also foreign) to defamiliarise adult ways of seeing.
Such resources are drawn upon by Wordsworth and, more recently,
by Craig Raine (whom Fenton was the first to call "Martian" in the
now accepted sense).

However, Fenton complicates this poetic resource by drawing,
also, upon journalistic ones, which enable him to introduce information about Cambodian politics and so provide "intrinsic interest".
The gap is bridged by a metaphor which suggests that the children
are the products of a radically different "educational system" from
the one they are about to experience, they are "Students of calamity,
graduates of famine":

> Who have settled here perforce in a strange country,
> > Who are not even certain where they are.
> They have learnt much. There is much more to learn.
> Each heart bears a diploma like a scar –
>
> A red seal, always hot, always solid,
> > Stamped with the figure of an overseer,
> A lethal boy who has learnt to despatch with a mattock,
> Who rules a village with sharp leaves and fear.
>
> > > > > > > > > > > > > > (30)

The "university of life" cliché is very close here but is renewed by
both journalistic metonymy (the "lethal boy", the "mattock" and
"sharp leaves") and poetic metaphor (the "red seal"). The children
are suffering from a radical disorientation which makes them think
of themselves as living in a place that is an unstable compound of
where they are and where they were – a frightening heterotopia;
they are afraid the Italian woods will contain "tigers, snakes and
malaria" (31). This disorientation is reflected by the way the poetic
and the journalistic clash with each other, by the gap between the
"diploma" and the "overseer". The instability that results is figured
also in the "red seal" being always (and impossibly) both "hot" and
"solid"; the instability of their lives has paradoxically become a
fixture.

The cruelty and political chaos of the children's origins is transcended in "Children in Exile" by a final emphasis on their resilience and their ability to learn and adjust which opens up a Martian
richness for them in the West. The poems in *Out of Danger* are much

more thoroughly pessimistic, even desperate. "Blood and Lead" (34) and "Jerusalem" (18–21) both dwell on the way that violence perpetuates itself; "The Milkfish Gatherers" (14–17) details the routine cruelty which the eponymous fishermen inflict on their prey; "Here Come the Drum Majorettes" (65–68) is sardonically, and yet at the same time almost deliriously, obsessed with sordid attitudes and behaviour, especially of a sexual kind. Perhaps most successful in this volume, however, are two poems in which Fenton may be said – as he imagined might be said of a poet who constructed a poem about the events in Rumania at the end of 1989 – to have "revived the street ballad" ("Ars Poetica", 13 May 1990, 18). Fenton would say, however, that the important thing in "The Ballad of the Imam and the Shah" (35–38) was its "intrinsic interest":

> And so the Shah was forced to flee abroad.
> The Imam was the ruler in his place.
> He started killing everyone he could
> To make up for the years of his disgrace.
> And when there were no enemies at home
> He sent his men to Babylon to fight.
> And when he'd lost an army in that way
> He knew what God was telling him was right.
>
> (36)

The plodding rhythm and loud rhyming in this passage make what would otherwise be a journalistic register both more and less than that. They make what is being said seem *too* simple so that "Obviousness" becomes an ambiguous quality as the point where the simple shades into the simplistic is explored. Fenton is in favour of obviousness but here it is deployed ironically to indicate the dangerous simplifications of the "Imam". There is again a minimalist effect – a "reductio ad absurdam" that rebounds satirically on the Ayatollah whose thoughts are wittled down to an incriminating free indirect speech.

Minimalism in this poem and "The Ballad of the Shrieking Man" – their deliberate paring down of poetic effects – works with the reductiveness of a newspaper cartoon where the implicit point is that political complexity is being travestied by self-conscious crudity. The light verse manner seems alarmingly insufficient for the subject-matter and the gap between them produces an effect of black humour akin to that in a drawing by Georg Grosz. Moreover, as these poems progress the consensual stability which underlies light

verse, which is taken for granted in its outlook, increasingly collapses under the influence of their italicised choruses whose manic
repetitions and hectic rhythms suggest that language itself is out of
control. What begins, in the Iranian poem, as a chorus suggesting
how one thing leads to another, "From felony to felony to crime"
(35) gathers increasing pace from more insistent rhyming. Now the
very urgency and importance of what is being said starts alarmingly to undermine what is being said, starts to garble it, starts to
push the words away from meaning towards mere sound. So what
started out pretending to be light verse veers towards nonsense,
towards "The Kingdom of the Senseless" in which cause and effect
are multiplied into a baffling infinity: "From felony/ to robbery/ to
calumny/ to rivalry/ to tyranny/ to dynasty/ to villainy/ to policy/
to heresy/ to clerisy/ to litany/ to fallacy/ to poverty/ to agony/
to malady/ to misery" (37).

This disintegration of meaning appears personified in "The Ballad of the Shrieking Man" in the form of a speaker of the italicised
choruses who resembles the mentally disturbed derelicts who haunt
city streets, but who carries resonances also of literary figures (both
writers and characters) whose pronouncements tread the line
between madness and visionary truth. This street ballad, like its
Iranian counterpart, is structured as a dialogue between a commonsense story-telling register – "And it was Monday and the town/
Was working in a kind of peace" (43) – and a litany that verges on
a rant:

> Arms are mad
> And legs are mad
> And all the spaces in between.
> The horror spleen that bursts its sack
> The horror purple as it lunges through
> The lung
> The bung
> The jumping-bean
> The I-think-you-know-what-you-think-I-mean
> Are up in arms against the state
> And all the body will disintegrate.
>
> (45)

The words "mad" and "horror" recur in these choruses like epithets
that transfer themselves on an epidemic scale – how much they

belong where they are placed rather than in the mind of the character who places them there is the poem's central question. That is to say, is it the shrieking men or the world which is mad? In this particular chorus, once the line "The I-think-you-know. . ." is disentangled it suggests only subjective knowledge of the meaning of an "I" who may be either the poet or the tramp. And the tenor and vehicle of the body politic metaphor are jumbled to such an extent that the disintegration on which it terminates may be either personal or political.


The furthest reaches of Fenton's experimentation – his testing of how much poetry can be reduced before it becomes absurd, and how far it can be pushed before it becomes nonsense or shrieking (and his enjoyment when it topples over these boundaries) – are interesting in themselves but also because his most substantial poetic achievements are more fully understood when seen in the context of these experiments. The boundaries of what can be said are also implicitly the boundaries of what can be experienced – ultimately they are also the boundaries between being and nothingness, and it is these boundaries which are implied in "A German Requiem", "Prison Island", "Nest of Vampires", "A Vacant Possession" and "A Staffordshire Murderer".

In "A German Requiem" (11–19) this is obvious enough from the insistence of negative constructions and the way the minimal pared-down style reflects how the Nazis and the Second World War pared down Germany: "It is not what they built. It is what they knocked down./ It is not the houses. It is the spaces between the houses" (11). Being itself has been reduced to the point where people are "bent figures" (14) and become equated with their furniture or clothes – "boiled shirts", "a leering waistcoat" (13) – a funeral and a wedding become interchangeable (12) and a smile is so attenuated it is "Like a breeze with enough strength to carry one dry leaf/ Over two pavingstones" (19). Most memorable of these images, though, is the one that resembles a "found poem", which refers to how because "so many had died, so many and at such speed/. . .They unscrewed the name-plates from the shattered doorways" and used them like headstones:

"Doctor Gliedschirm, skin specialist, surgeries 14–16 hours or by
   appointment."

Professor Sargagnal was buried with four degrees, two associate
  memberships
And instructions to tradesmen to use the back entrance.
Your uncle's grave informed you that he lived on the third floor,
  left.
You were asked please to ring, and he would come down in the
  lift
To which one needed a key. . .

(16)

It is important that Fenton allows the "foundness" of this to remain
partly intact – characteristically that quality imports alien language
into the poetic text and that is appropriate because it evokes the
alienness of this language in a cemetery and indicates the gap between a name-plate and a headstone register. The element of
minimalism in it is also effective because it self-reflexively suggests
that there is also here an existential *"reductio ad absurdam"* – that life
itself has been reduced so grotesquely that it is haunted by surreal
black humour.

In Fenton's narrative poems, too, this reductiveness is crucial
because their centres of consciousness hover on the boundary of
being and nothingness. A clue to this is in "The Skip" (55–57) which
provides a light verse, and therefore robustly explicit, version of
that treatment of the self which is implicit in, for example, "A Vacant
Possession" – a treatment that suggests that selves can be swapped.
The speaker throws his life on a skip, then someone comes and
takes it, then the speaker takes theirs, dries it by the stove, tries it
on and finds it fits "like a glove" (56). If selves adhere as little to
their owners as this it is not surprising that the centres of consciousness in the narrative poems are shadowy and constantly in doubt
– are possibly, and in "Prison Island" certainly, ghosts – "The guards
ignored me. I realised I too was dead" (42).

However, the most radical ontological questioning in these poems arises from the way they mingle languages. Cross-fertilising is
effected in the poems I discussed earlier between poetry and science and poetry and journalism – here the effect of "novelisation"
is all the more obvious because the cross-fertilising is with the novel.
As Alan Robinson has pointed out:

> Fenton's work appears analogous to John Fowles' novels in its
> generic incorporation but simultaneous parody of the narrative

structures of such popular forms as the romance, thriller and detective novel. Such conventional material is a useful semantic
shorthand, but its hackneyed blatancy destabilises the aesthetic
distance, preventing the reader from comfortably locating the text
within a single comprehensible framework.[10]

These poems, then, are parodic hybrids – they speak with several
voices at once. The way this works is exemplified in the way that
Fenton modulates from "found" writing in the lines I quote from
"A German Requiem" into a free indirect speech that paraphrases
that register and so mingles the "found" voice with that of the
author. Then there is a further step into a second person narration
which still refers to the displaced name-plates: "Your uncle's grave
informed you that he lived on the third floor, left", with a pun on
"lived" that would have been impossible in the "found" form.

Clearly Fenton enjoys the surreal jolts these shifts in perspective
cause and to this extent he is, as Alan Robinson insists, a postmodernist "self-consciously deconstructing any pretensions to the
formal coherence of Modernist poetry" (15). Robinson is right, too,
to refer to "a process of generic redefinition" at work but simplifies
when he says this "gleefully adopts uncertainty as its structural
principle" (15). What this ignores is the extent to which "Nest of
Vampires" (44–46) and "A Vacant Possession" (47–49) are socially
and historically bounded, how meticulously they evoke an upper-
middle class milieu. In fact, one reason why the self appears so
tenuous in these poems is because it is more or less suffocated by
its surroundings which are notated in such detail. Nonetheless, there
is not much question about the accent in which that self speaks:

> "Where's that wretched boy?" I'm going now
> And soon I am going to find out.
>
> (46)

For this reason the Bakhtinian stress on "the heteroglossia of literary discourses" and their derivation "ultimately from the stratifica-
tion of social life, in which different social groups create distinctive
discourses from their common language" (Glazener, 109) seems to
me much more helpful for discussing Fenton than Robinson's
Derridean emphasis on uncertainty. For uncertainty is present in
"Nest Of Vampires" and "A Vacant Possession" for specific reasons: their generic instability evokes the ontological insecurity not

so much of individuals as of a country and a social group, the post-imperial bafflement of the English upper-classes. A clue to this is given early on in "Nest of Vampires" in the reference to "pictures/ Depicting Tivoli, an imperial/ Family in its humiliation" (44). The evocation of this is oblique but that is partly because, as Fenton has said

> Englishness, for a poet, is almost a taboo subject. Britishness is altogether out. Whereas an American poet may speak to, or on behalf of, his nation, this is hard for an English poet, now that it is not clear what his nation is...When the war was over, the sense of Britishness, or Englishness, remained embattled. Many people preferred not to think about it, or go on about it, for fear of being taken for jingoists or reactionaries.
>
> ("Ars Poetica", 10 June 1990, 18)

Moreover, there is a sense in which the obliqueness is itself an English characteristic related to a buttoned-up refusal to speak openly about problems of an emotional or financial kind (both of which are hinted at). Nonetheless, the way both poems describe families vacating large houses suggests that both these institutions are employed synecdochically in the novel to refer to wider social themes – here a sense of terminal decline as the "cold sets in" (37).

So the poems express a post-war sense of the loss of a settled social and political role – especially, perhaps, as perceived in adults by a child growing up (as Fenton did) in that period. The centres of consciousness struggle surreally with genre and adopt melodramatic imagery in an attempt to express the sense of dark forces at work under an apparently still surface.

These suppressed forces are even more evident in "A Staffordshire Murderer" (58–61), which depicts archaeological depths of violence lying under the apparent calm of the countryside. The poem employs multiple registers: psychological – "Every fear is a desire"; pedagogic – "You may learn now what you ought to know"; geographical – "Large parts of Staffordshire have been undermined"; commercial – "we are offered on the easiest terms"; historical – "They say that Cromwell played ping-pong with the cathedral" etc. Most importantly, though, it mingles two genres, the detective story and the topographical poem, so that landscape is interrogated for clues. This means that natural objects – a traditional poetic subject

– are dialogically subverted by a bizarre shift in perspective which regards Nature itself as though it were a murder suspect:

> The cowparsley is so high that the van cannot be seen
> From the road. The bubbles rise in the warm canal.
> Below the lock-gates you can hear mallards.
>
> (60)

The effect is to call language itself into question, or even to undermine it like a landscape:

> Large parts of Staffordshire have been undermined.
> The trees are in it up to their necks. Fish
> Nest in their branches.
>
> (59)

Just as guilt is punningly attributed to the trees in these lines, expectations are reversed repeatedly – fear is desire, death is like sex, a murderer is like a lover. There is again, then, radical uncertainty in this poem. However, what makes it one of Fenton's most powerful works is the way it pushes topography to the verge of "heterotopia" but keeps it tottering on that verge, so that its subject remains recognisably English – but in a way that radically (but playfully) questions Englishness. What prevents it being thoroughly postmodernist in an Ashbery vein is the coherent (if interrogated) sense of place that it builds up. This means that it is certainly about England but that at the same time it disconcerts presuppositions about the country as a paragon of civilised peace in contrast to the places described in Fenton's journalistic poems. Its closeness to heterotopia and its deployment of heteroglossia upset a familiar landscape with a frightening otherness.

# 4

# "Your Voice Speaking in my Poems": Polyphony in Fleur Adcock

Fleur Adcock was born and spent her first five years in New Zealand, but her family moved to England in 1939 and spent the war years there. She has written that her father "seems to have no concept of 'home'"[1] so that they moved around obsessively and in "seven and a half years I attended eleven English schools, with a New Zealand one at each end to make it thirteen" (R.B., 5). Moving back to New Zealand in 1947

> I lost my much derided English accent and, after a time, some of my sense of cultural displacement. I learned to live with an almost permanent sense of free floating, unfocused nostalgia, and with the combination of crushed humility and confident arrogance that comes from not quite belonging. It is no bad thing to be an outsider, if one wants to see places and events clearly enough to write about them. At any rate an outsider seemed to be what, after so much practice at it, I had become.
>
> (R.B., 12)

This feeling of being an outsider was later reinforced when (after reading Classics at Victoria University, Wellington) she emigrated to Britain in 1963:

> I had never intended to be a New Zealander, and it was not until I was back in England that I found I had become one. I experienced culture shock for the second time in my life, but now it was accompanied by excitement and a sense of the world opening out instead of closing in. Gradually and inevitably I adapted, until I reached a state in which New Zealanders of the new nationalistic breed now scorn me as a Pom. Fair enough: the country of

84

my birth feels deeply foreign to me after more than twenty years away from it.[2]

The broad theme of cultural displacement is a constant one in Adcock's work and her poems repeatedly dwell on her experience of rootlessness. Geography is important in itself in this respect but, as I shall show, it can also be regarded synecdochically – the physical displacements she has experienced can be seen as analogues for other, more complex psychological displacements which raise questions about identity. The crucial form this takes in her work is in the shift from one perspective to another, or others. In particular, especially in her recent work, this has involved the juxtaposition of masculine and feminine points of view for effects of comparison and contrast.

However, the best way to start this discussion is to refer to Adcock's poems about the emotional effects of straightforwardly physical displacement. "Going Back"[3] approaches this theme via the Wordsworthian concern with the return in which objects familiar from the past are regarded from the perspective of the present. As in Wordsworth this collision of different angles of vision baffles the familiar objects – by being interrogated for what they meant and what, if anything, they still mean they acquire (despite, or almost because of their ordinariness) a disorienting vividness. This is registered in the second stanza by the way such objects stretch the third line to an extraordinary nineteen syllables (when the average is about half that) – "a wall with blackboards; a gate where I swung, the wind bleak in the telegraph wires". As in Wordsworth, too, such images are rendered with a careful, loving detail which suggests a need to derive comfort from them, a reassurance of the reality of the past and present and a meaningful continuity between them; at the same time the suggestion of such a need implies anxiety – the fear of loss and of insignificance.

Like Wordsworth, too, Adcock reflects on the way that the past remains present in the poet's mind – or rather a version of it, questionable because the extent of its subjectivity is unknown. "In Focus" (75–76) takes as its premise images seen on the edge of waking; a

> . . .close-up of granular earthy dust,
> fragments of chaff and grit, a triangular
> splinter of glass, a rusty metal washer
> on rough concrete under a wooden step.

These lines are characteristic of the way Adcock allows in the rough edges of experience and the care with which she notates contingent details in order to resist the feeling that meaning is being too easily imposed on her subjects. The staccato rhythm and fricative sound accentuate the sense of sharp focus; the hard objects, juxtaposed, define each other by contrast of size, shape and material, and are framed between the concrete and step so that this passage seems at first to employ imagism of the most starkly objective and precise kind.

However, these images are transformed, by the context, from fragments of the real world into a dream version of a place from Adcock's past. They are "Not a memory" but, as it were, a revision by the unconscious mind of a scene from childhood:

> Not a memory. But the caption told me
> I was at Grange Farm, seven years old,
> in the back yard, kneeling outside the shed
> with some obscure seven-year-old's motive,
> seeing as once, I must believe, I saw:
> sharply; concentrating as once I did.

The presentation of the objects appears direct but the photographic analogy referred to in the poem's title indicates that it is filtered through a medium. Beyond the objective frame of concrete and wood there is a subjective one of childlike (and kneeling) angle of vision (hence the closeness to the ground) buried childlike interpretation (the "obscure seven-year-old's motive") and adult dream.

This is Wordsworthian to the extent that it is set in the problematic ground between a carefully rendered scene and the poet's changing mind. Where it differs is in the introduction, within the same poem, of perspectives radically different from that of the poet, so that the central concern is not with the dialectic of Nature and Mind but with the dialogue of minds. So the poem introduces the inhabitants of Grange Farm at the time where Adcock's dream memory originates: Uncle George and his wife and the daughter they now live with in Melton Mowbray. These three and the poet herself "all went out together in the car/ to see the old place" but it is through the eyes of the aunt (who, is "not well" according to her husband, and "doesn't talk" and who, according to her daughter, is suffering from "Premature senility") that this return is seen:

> . . .Auntie sitting
> straight-backed, dignified, mute,
> perhaps a little puzzled as we churned
> through splattering clay lanes, between wet hedges
>
> to Grange Farm again: to a square house,
> small, bleak, and surrounded by mud

Or rather this is Adcock trying to imagine what the aunt sees. From this point of view the sense of loss – of fallings from us, vanishings – is more powerfully rendered than it could possibly be from that simply of the poet. For what is implied is the attempt to understand the extent of what has been lost by someone whose adult life is associated with this place – that there is even a question of whether or not the aunt can now feel this loss, of whether even the memory has been lost, makes this all the more poignant. In this context, the extreme partialness of Adcock's memory of Grange Farm in the opening lines paradoxically acquires an added significance as its triviality is fully revealed: her "close-up" of "a patch of ground" now suggests how radically one person's apprehension of an experience can trivialise another's.

However, a further revision of the close-up is effected by the way the last two stanzas find intimations of mortality in the themes of memory and loss referred to earlier:

> I find it easiest to imagine dying
> as like the gradual running down of a film,
> the brain still flickering when the heart and blood
> have halted, and the last few frames
> lingering. Then where the projector jams
> is where we go, or are, or are no longer.

So the images Adcock saw on the edge of sleep become, in retrospect, the prototypes of images she imagines may be seen on the edge of death. The last stanza hints that this aunt and uncle are now dead and hopes that what they saw as they died was "something better than mud and silence/ or than my minute study of a patch of ground". The poem ends with this hope which wants to insert Adcock's own transformation of her "close-up": that is, to extend to them the way, in the third stanza, she "let the whole scene open out" to become one of relaxed plenitude ("the strolling chickens, the pear trees next to the yard,/ the barn full of white cats, the loaded haycart"). This hope juxtaposes death with images of a fertility which is powerfully asserted by its presence in the last line so that it becomes like an after-image of the whole poem – "sunny ploughland, pastures, the scented orchard". This fertility is all the more vivid because it is summoned up so precariously. These were images flickering on the edge of darkness. More than this, though, they may not have occurred at all – they are only the poet's hope of what occurred in minds quite other than her own.

The Wordsworthian theme of the return is radically altered in Adcock's poems, then, because they lack that reassurance of a powerful and commanding ego which characterises the work of the Romantic poet. It is true that Wordsworth's poems contain anxieties about loss, change and death but these occur in the context of a single mind whose development is charted in immense detail. By contrast, Adcock's personal and poetic identity seems repeatedly in question and her attempts to define it through meditating on her family background and places associated with it only increase this feeling. The places change: revisiting her school in "Going Back" she finds "Broken windows, grassy silence, all the children gone away,/ and classrooms turned into barns for storing hay" (94). And family members die. So the attempt to define an identity seems especially desperate in "My Father"[4] in which the poet describes a visit to Hulme, in Manchester – where her father grew up – just after he had died (though this was unknown to her at the time). What she finds is a "rubbled/ wasteland, a walled-off dereliction" – "It's nowhere now". But, having heard of his death, she is determined to establish a connection – convinced in the face of a modern city's complex impersonality ("the net/ of close-meshed streets", "motorways and high-rise") that

> There must be roads that I can walk along
> and know they walked there, even if their houses
> have vanished like the cobble-stones – that throng
>
> of Adcocks, Eggingtons, Joynsons, Lamberts, Listers.
> I'll go to look for where they were born and bred.
> I'll go next month; we'll both go, I and my sister.
> We'll tell him about it, when he stops being dead.

The last line registers the difficulty of believing in his death but also the conscious futility of this return to roots that go back before her own birth. Its bitter humour arises from the knowledge that this is all a compensatory activity, a need to do something in the face of a bewildered loss – to do something when nothing meaningful can be done.

Identity is firmly established in Wordsworth with the help of continuities which work as premises in his poems – the cyclical rhythms of Nature, the organic development of the child into the man, the immortality of the soul. Such continuities are inevitably in question to a poet like Adcock who has absorbed the lessons of modernism. In fact, she dwells on discontinuities so that her experience of "cultural displacement", with which I started, can be seen as a synecdoche for a series of displacements which preoccupy her work.

There is a constant movement in her poems between times and places and points of view which unsettles any reliable sense of ontological stability. Even if the poem concerns the poet herself in the present tense there is always the post-Freudian possibility that her self is split, that there is a stranger within. So, running counter to a powerful realist impulse in Adcock – a concern to render experience in all its detailed and vivid assymetry – there is an equally powerful insistence that there is another world with its own quite different laws running collaterally to the "real" one and inhabited by an entirely different person from the conscious self. "Mornings After" (35), for example, shows her deeply troubled by her own implication in that world:

> I flush and shudder: my God, was that me?
>
> Did I invent so ludicrously revolting
> a scene? And if so, how could I forget
> until this instant? And why now remember?
>                                        (35)

On the one hand, some of Adcock's most characteristic writing employs a robustly commonsense tone, a technically adroit (but often inventive) formalism, a wry irony and vigorous wit that suggests that her poetic amounts above all to a feminine response to the Movement. "Smokers for Celibacy" (*TZ*, 36–37) for example expresses in rhyming couplets (some containing comically much over-extended lines) a preference for cigarettes to penises:

> Above all, the residues they leave in your system are
>   thoroughly sterilized and clean
> which is more than can be said for the products of the human
>   machine.

> Altogether, we've come to the conclusion that sex is a drag.
>   Just give us a fag.

Such poems occupy a world of public consciousness and address themselves (albeit sceptically) to the values of that world.

On the other hand, however, she has written poems which suggest that those values are maintained by ignoring or suppressing irrational forces that run counter to them, by placing "a Hans Anderson cover/ on a volume of the writings of De Sade" (35) as she says in "Mornings After". Here, as elsewhere, she employs the Freudian metaphor of surface versus depth combined with subterranean imagery: "I dream one of my sons is lost or dead,/ or that I am trapped in a tunnel underground". This suggests that this world is a constant presence below the rational and the everyday, which it may undermine.

However, the underside of consciousness is not simply sinister – it can also be a source of creativity. So, in "The Water Below" (16–17) it is regarded in Jungian rather than Freudian terms, and its constant under-presence is linked, through the symbol of water, to the idea of the past and continuing origin of life. The hints of mysticism in this early poem are rare in Adcock, but taken together with the disturbing images in "The Mornings After" they indicate the way that the many dream references in her poems should be understood. "The Water Below" begins with a description whose plausibility is encouraged by its painstaking precision and its matter-of-fact tone, but which is eerie and dream-like:

> This house is floored with water,
> Wall to wall, a deep green pit,
> Still and gleaming, edged with stone.
> Over it are built stairways
> And railed living-areas
> In wrought iron.

Adcock has dismissed surrealism as "a tired old tradition by now, and surely never one which was as much fun for its readers as for its practitioners"[5] and she does scrupulously avoid it in its fully-blown form. However, her poems are repeatedly fascinated by the boundary between waking and dreaming experience and these lines are poised deliberately between the two. Moreover, they lead to a memory of a childhood belief that there was water under her grand-mother's house – a belief held in the face of knowledge that when she played under the house there was "only hard-packed earth,/ wooden piles, gardening tools". It may be, then, that "The Water Below" is structured like "In Focus" and moves from a dream to a childhood memory.

However, what is most important is that the poem indicates the presence of other actual and possible worlds existing alongside the familiar one. That the point is made here through a reference to water – whose symbolic associations are with femininity and crea-tivity – may be especially relevant to Adcock as a woman poet. For she has become increasingly concerned with the feminine as itself an alternative world and has drawn attention to the analogy be-tween this kind of alternativeness and that between nationalities:

> The question of my nationality has always seemed at least as significant as the question of my gender. I write a good deal about places; I have passionate relationships with them. Wher-ever I happen to live I have always some residual feeling of being an outsider: a fruitful position for a writer, perhaps, if it means one takes nothing for granted. But now I wonder: has being a woman contributed to this? Are women natural outsiders?
>
> (*CWP*, 202)

It is interesting here that Adcock refers to her gender as a "ques-tion" – especially when it is equated as such with her nationality, which is genuinely questionable. No questions arise over what her gender is – the speaker of Adcock's personal poems is unambigu-ously feminine and heterosexual. But they do arise in her poems over the issue as a whole, in the way she interrogates gender, and they cause displacements and disorienting shifts of perspective which are analogous to the cultural displacements I referred to at the start.

These displacements are at their least complex in those poems where Adcock explicitly satirises institutionalised masculine author-ity. In "The Soho Hospital for Women", the lines "I have admitted the gloved hands and the speculum/ and must part my ordinary legs to the surgeon's knife" (81) suggest that the masculinity of the surgeons makes the operation seem like a cruel parody of the sexual act. In "Witnesses"[6] it is central, and there is a stark opposition between the women referred to in the title and the aggressively masculine officialdom who run the court that will decide whether another woman will get custody of her child. Once again, however, suspicion takes a disturbingly sexual form as the court proceedings are described as "these ferretings under her sober/ dress, under our skirts and dresses/ to sniff out corruption".

More complex is the clash of registers in "Clarendon Whatmough" (21–22) which subverts the official discourse of psychiatry. The analysand refers to her desire to pray (even though she is an unbeliever) after a friend's death, and then the poem imagines the psychiatrist's response in satirical free indirect speech – while suggesting, with powerfully expressionist imagery, the bland inadequacy of this:

> A hypocritical thing to do,
> would you say, Clarendon Whatmough?
>
> Or a means of dispelling buried guilt,
> a conventional way to ease
> my fears? I tell you this: I felt
> the sky over the trees
> crack open like a nutshell. You
> don't believe me, Clarendon Whatmough:
>
> or rather, you would explain that I
> induced some kind of reaction
> to justify the reversal of my
> usual kind of conviction.

Two voices vie with each other here, and overlap. However, they do not mingle and there is certainly no synthesis. Masculine analyst and feminine analysand infringe on each other in this poem as they do in the processes of transference and counter-transference which contain their own sexual components. So their voices form what Adcock refers to, in the literally sexual context of "Tokens" as a "compound,/ not a mixture" (60). In that context it is the "joint essence" of a man and woman which is laundered from their sheets.

Other compounds, however, remain – his pipe, tobacco and books on her table, and his "voice speaking in her poems".

This indicates the way that Adcock has introduced a dialogue of genders into her work which produces something explicitly well short of "androgyny" – for it allows gender to continue being a "question" and refuses any easy synthesis. It produces instead an unstable "compound" of voices, not a "mixture".

This has involved an increasing concern in her work with what constitutes the "feminine". As she has said:

> In my early poems there were few women apart from fabulised or fictionalised versions of myself; the men and the children were real, because I knew about men and children, but I had to play most of the female roles myself. My more recent poems are full of women and girls, real or imaginary, seen from inside or outside.
>
> (CWP, 202)

So some of Adcock's latest work has set out to explore aspects of feminine experience and to determine in what senses it is accurate to define them in that way. "Blue Glass" (122–123) is like a feminine response to the Martian poetic of Raine and Reid: its "underworld of children" is characterised by an "innocent eye" and its "sandals/ that softly waffle-print the dusty floor" seem directly to refer to their characteristic metaphors. However, the poem adds to this an explicitly girlish fantasising in which a stolen necklace becomes "like a chain of hailstones melting in the dips/ above her collarbones". A daydream is allowed more associative room here than it ever would be by the Martians whose poems tend to employ wit and irony to call a halt to such extended flights: in contrast to their detachment, Adcock's poem follows the girl into a blur of subject and object, girl and necklace, so that she

> . . .slithers among
> its globular teeth, skidding on blue pellets.
> Ice-beads flare and blossom on her tongue,
>
> turn into flowers, populate the spaces
> around and below her. The attic has become
> her bluebell wood. Among their sappy grasses
> the light-fringed gas-flames of bluebells hum.

Where the most apt painterly analogy for Martian poetry is with cubism and its hard edges and plural perspectives, these lines seem close to impressionism in their concern with dissolving outlines, the mingling of water and light, and in their exploration of the tonal effects of varieties of blue.

To what extent all this represents an assertion of a "feminine" sensibility remains deliberately open to doubt, however. Here, as with the questions of place and identity, Adcock insists on the way the ground shifts. The two genders question each other in her poems so that she avoids essentialist assumptions and retains creative tension between masculine and feminine (something which has been lacking in the recent poems of Adrienne Rich whose lesbian separatism has made her work increasingly single-minded and abstract).

So discontinuities, displacements, shifting angles of vision characterise Adcock's treatment of gender as they do her treatment of place, and raise questions, in a similar way, about identity. "Double-Take" (*I.B.*, 44) for example, is premised upon the effects of a literal angle of vision: "your next-door neighbour from above/... reminds you/of your ex-lover, who is bald on top". In this way the two, in a sense, become doubles even though at "ground level/ there is no resemblance". It is the capriciousness of this that is important because it reveals how unexpectedly sexual feelings can intrude. And also with what perverse gratuitousness, for the poem insists that "you don't fancy" the neighbour and then (at the next meeting) "you don't fancy" the ex-lover. Somehow the unstable compound of the two, and perhaps an obscure mingling of memory and desire, arouses a dismaying yet exciting response:

> ...why that sudden
> something, once you get outside
> in the air? Why are your legs prancing
> so cheerfully along the pavement?
> And what exactly have you just remembered?

She is both repelled by and attracted to the two men who are simultaneously familiar to her, and strange. Furthermore, though, there is a split in herself – similar to that mentioned earlier between her conscious, waking self and her unconscious, dreaming self – so in her responses, too, there is something both familiar and strange, in accord and at variance with her conscious wishes.

What Adcock's dialogue of genders involves, then, is a questioning of the mutual perception of men and women and an exploration of their bafflement about what they want from each other. Identities on both sides are unstable and this is the cause both of endless precariousness in relationships, and of occasional moments of fraught oneness achieved through shared but transcended scepticism and confusion.

So "Kilpeck" (54–55) describes the hesitations towards, and falterings away from each other of a couple who have spent the previous night talking, "instead of going to bed". The poem moves between sharedness and separateness of consciousness and so between the pronouns "you" and "I" and "we", and this has its physical expression in the way the terrain affects their progress – at one point, "we clamber awkwardly, separate", at another, "Slithering down the track we hold hands/ to keep a necessary balance". The poem very subtly hints at the way the man and woman (clearly Adcock herself) are conducting their own separate and internal arguments for and against coupling, and reflects this in the church and landscape that they visit. The woman feels a wryly amused shock at the sexual and procreative excesses in the building the man has brought her to see – its "serpents writhing up the doorposts", "beasts and fishes", its "Whore of Kilpeck" who "leans out under the roof/ holding her pink stony cleft agape".

The couple are middle-aged and this is reflected in the late summer in which the poem is set, but again subtly – there is an implied question whether they should think of themselves as mature or simply old, think in terms of harvest or of autumn. Certainly they are "dried and brittle" and are contrasted with the vitality of the soil (which "is coloured like brick-dust" and whose fruitfulness they regard "uneasily") and with the youthful flush of the "red sandstone" which gives the gargoyles "the colour of newborn children".

However, that last detail, which makes the idea of procreation (and therefore sex) seem briefly monstrous is the product of the woman's vision and there are hints that the man feels differently. His words are reported twice. He counters the poet's sexually preoccupied description of the Whore of Kilpeck with the remark that "There was always witchcraft here". And the night before he is said to have asked "if poetry was the most important thing". Both remarks are disruptive. The first suggests that his own doubts about sex relate to the alienness of women. The second, even more radically, questions the genre in which it is placed. So the way that the experience has been mediated through a feminine vision and translated into poetic codes is subverted by this sense of another voice, masculine and unpoetic, speaking in the poem.

What is characteristic about this is the way it keeps the poem open and deliberately unsettles any easy stability of point of view. The way the remarks are given in free indirect speech suggests a joining together of the man's voice and that of the poet – for the device involves the poet paraphrasing what the man said. This is ambiguous in its effects in that it indicates both the poet's attempts to understand the man and the way that his voice gets subsumed, and thereby distorted, by the poet's. However, both effects contribute to keeping the dialogue open – the first by enacting the attempt to understand differences and the second by revealing how much remains to be understood. So when Adcock says that the product of their having avoided sex is that

> We are languourous now, heavy
> with whatever we were conserving,
> carrying each a delicate burden
> of choices made or about to be made

it is clear that *some* sense of what they are feeling is being conveyed but also that the references to lack of sex producing a kind of paradoxical pregnancy (in the words "heavy" and "carrying") are characteristic of the woman poet's voice, rather than that of the man. So to what extent, if at all, the reader is getting the man's point of view at this point is left deliberately open to question.

# 5

# Carol Ann Duffy:
# Monologue as Dialogue

At one level, Carol Ann Duffy's use of the dramatic monologue allows mostly marginalised social types a voice. Her experience as a dramatist (she has written two plays, for example, that were staged at the Liverpool Playhouse) has helped her in her mimicry of contemporary speech rhythms and idioms and she is clearly concerned to introduce shockingly "unpoetic" material into poetry. The juxtapositions, for example, in "Psychopath"[1] – sex, gratuitous cruelty, excrement – suggest that what is being evoked is well beyond the literary pale, the articulation of the inarticulate, a naturalistic exploration of a low life normally unheeded by those who read poetry, the authentic voice of the eponymous psychopath.

However, what pretends to be a single voice in the poem is at least two. The shock tactics are experienced very much as tactics, the juxtapositions as juxtapositions, and in particular the phrase "dull canal", with its echo of *The Waste Land*, draws attention to a poetic voice speaking alongside the psychopathic one. The speaker reveals himself in a way that owes more to convention – to the speeches of villains like Chaucer's Pardoner or Shakespeare's Richard III – than to "real life". Closer still are the characters invented by Browning, the most influential practitioner of dramatic monologue and himself obsessed with male violence against women, as in "My Last Duchess" and *The Ring and the Book* in which some of the most memorable passages are spoken by the psychopathic Guido. So, too, the language of Duffy's poem suggests the poet's voice as much as the psychopath's – "my shoes scud sparks against the night" is imagist in rhythm and in the way it juxtaposes light and dark, and sounds like something that would be more comfortable in the third person rather than the first.

"Psychopath" works, then, not through the simple verisimilitude of its mimicry but more through something closer to parody, in which, according to Bakhtin:

two languages are crossed with each other, as well as two styles,
two linguistic points of view, and in the final analysis two speaking subjects. . .every parody is an intentional dialogized hybrid.
Within it, languages and styles actively and mutually illuminate
one another.[2]

Parody inevitably calls into question the whole issue of representation and "Psychopath" does the same by the way it makes languages clash with each other, for this arouses suspicions about the
distortions involved in the representation of the speaker. The imagery of the poem literally reflects this suspicion in its recurrent
dwelling on the psychopath's "image" – "I run my metal comb
through the D.A. and pose/ my reflection between dummies in the
window at Burton's". A few lines later he declares "Let me make
myself crystal" where "clear" is understood but is actually significantly absent. For he is speaking in a poem and therefore in a
distortive medium rather than a clear one, and he is actually being
transformed into something, as it were, crystalline – into a twisted
image of himself. So the last stanza starts: "My reflection sucks a
sour Woodbine and buys me a drink. Here's/ looking at you. Deep
down I'm talented."

The shifts that are involved as the reader watches the psychopath
watching himself are important because they draw attention to the
question of how what is seen is interpreted. So when, in the middle
of the poem, there is an emphasis on lack of reflection there is an
increased sense of difficulty, of seeing through a glass hardly at all.
The dullness of the canal in which he drowns his victim, then, suggests the near impossibility of fathoming his motives. Moreover,
this middle section starts with an indication that the ability to reflect
(and therefore to represent) is defeated by the nature of the man
himself, and perhaps by his language – "My breath wipes me from
the looking-glass". In a sense this is the psychopath answering the
poet back – rebuking her for speaking through him like a ventrilo-
quist. The reference to "dummies" in the second line is not an
accident, then, because it draws attention to the extent to which the
psychopath is a mere simulacrum and also suggests a link between
this poem and "The Dummy":

> . . .Why do you
> keep me in that black box? I can ask questions, too,
> you know. I can see that worries you. Tough.

(36)

Playful though this is it is a political statement that reveals one of the most important motives of Duffy's work – the desire to give a voice to those who are habitually spoken *for*. So, even a psychopath has aesthetic rights and deserves, as it were, to be adequately represented. The presence, so strongly hinted at, of the poet's voice in "Psychopath" is a way of owning up to the extent to which he is being caricatured, especially because the reader's sense of the implied author as a didactic feminist arouses an acute feeling that the psychopathic voice speaks very much against the grain of her beliefs. It is this feeling of the dialogic in the poem that makes it such an uncomfortable experience; it is very much what Bakhtin calls "a hybrid construction":

> an utterance that belongs, by its grammatical (syntactic) and compositional markers, to a single speaker, but that actually contains mixed within it two utterances, two speech manners, two styles, two "languages", two semantic and axiological belief systems.
>
> (*D.I.*, 304)

What makes "Psychopath" such an unusual poem is the width of the gap between the belief systems it contains.

The questions raised by this gap are those which are also raised in the arbitrations between postmodernism and feminism which are associated with Patricia Waugh and, more recently, Linda Hutcheon:

> Feminisms will continue to resist incorporation into postmodernism, largely because of their revolutionary force as political movements working for real social change. They go beyond making ideology explicit and deconstructing it to argue a need to change that ideology, to effect a real transformation of art that can only come with a transformation of patriarchal social practices.[3]

"Psychopath" is postmodernist to the extent that it gives so much self-reflexive prominence to problems of representation and sets readers a problem of identification which worries them with the feeling that they and the poet are complicit with the poem's speaker. Part of the importance of this is that it foregrounds reader-response – the feeling of complicity will vary according to gender, especially when the poem represents women through the psychopath's eyes.

The question that is raised here is similar to that which Hutcheon raises in discussing what she calls "feminist postmodernist parody" (Hutcheon, 151–160):

If the mastering gaze which separates the subject from the object of the gaze, projecting desire onto that object, is inherently masculine, as many feminists argue, could there ever be such a thing as women's *visual* art?

(151)

Hutcheon sees the only possible answer to this in parody which can subvert consensual thinking. In this way, even though, (as Derrida has pointed out) "representation constrains us, imposing itself on our thought through a whole dense, enigmatic and heavily stratified history" (quoted by Hutcheon, 151) nonetheless that representation can be "challenged and subverted". "Psychopath", as I have said, does employ something very like parody in its use of a double voice and so works in a way analogous to that of the visual art of Silvia Kolbowski and Barbara Kruger which, as Hutcheon says

parodically inscribes the conventions of feminine representation, provokes our conditioned response and then subverts that response, making us aware of how it was induced in us. To work it must be complicitous with the values it challenges: we have to feel the seduction in order to question it and then to theorize the site of that contradiction. Such feminist uses of postmodern tactics politicize desire in the play with the revealed and the hidden, the offered and the deferred.

(Hutcheon, 154)

So, in the struggle between postmodernism and feminism that takes place in "Psychopath" it is clearly the latter that wins and modifies the former. In the end the poem has to be seen from the kind of "priveleged position" (Hutcheon, 153) which is rejected by postmodernism – largely because that position is clear from the evidence of other Duffy poems. Nonetheless, the postmodernist elements are important – especially because of the way they suggest complicity. This acquires an even more disturbing significance in a poem about male violence inflicted on women because it reflects the way that women are made to feel complicit with the violence inflicted on them – how they are blamed by men for having provoked it and how the victims of violence feel guilty and blame themselves. The ambiguity of the poem's voice reflects the complex psychological interactions that take place.

One of Duffy's central preoccupations, then, is with representation which, as Derrida says, "programs us and precedes us" (quoted by Hutcheon, 151). A nightmare version of this is in "Eley's Bullet" (79–81) where a man's fate seems to have been determined because he finds "a bullet/ with his name on it". The name Eley is there in fact because it is the tradename of a company that makes bullets – nonetheless it seems to represent him and to program him to a violent act (either murder or suicide). Less surreal in their treatment of this theme are those poems where Duffy explores how masculinist ways of seeing determine how women are regarded, even by themselves, and how language determines the experiences it is supposed merely to describe, how representation makes dummies of us all.

"Standing Female Nude" (20–21) is a dramatic monologue spoken by a painter's model and as such reveals the advantage that feminist writers have compared with feminist visual artists. It is possible for a writer like Duffy to answer a gaze with a voice rather than another gaze, so there are more resources open to her than parody. Where the possibility of a woman's *visual* art is open to question, then, a woman's *verbal* art is not. This means that while the artist's model is inevitably complicitous with the masculine values she questions, the poet who makes her speak is not. There is no question where Duffy's sympathies lie – she constructs a privileged feminist position in the poem which allows her to expose the economic circumstances which impose complicity on the model, and she does so by her juxtaposition of languages – "He is concerned with volume, space./ I with the next meal."

Once again, then, there is a powerful dialogic element in this monologue, most importantly because it is designed as a response to a monologically masculine aesthetic. Duffy's poem works in a similar way to Angela Carter's short story about Jeanne Duval: "the woman to whom history denied a voice is the *subject* of Carter's 'Black Venus' – as she was the *object* of Baudelaire's 'Black Venus' poems." (Hutcheon, 145). The intersection of different discourses in the poem reveals how the model's body is transformed; her own familiar way of thinking about it is quickly reoriented in painterly terms – "Belly nipple arse in the window light". The use of dramatic monologue is all the more significant here because it suggests the extent to which she is made to rethink herself from the point of view of a masculine aesthetic. That she will be "represented analytically" is especially appropriate, then, because it suggests that the aesthetic involved is cubism but hints, at the same time, that

cubism's multiplying of perspectives actually occurs in an insuffi-
ciently multiple way – that in fact its perspective is too simply
masculine.

The model speaks about this masculinity with a directness which
is characteristic of Duffy and which at the same time satirises the
sophistication of painterly thinking – "He possesses me on canvas
as he dips the brush/ repeatedly into the paint". The crudity of this
is a deliberate affront but it also works as a way of characterising
the model as vulgar and energetic and, in the context of the whole
poem, suggests how inextricable the elements of the analytic and
the erotic are in the masculine act of the painting. The model's
impatience is made attractive, because humorous, and sympathy
for her is aroused deliberately at the expense of the painter (especially because his words are reported in her translation of them into
free indirect speech: "Further to the right,/ Madame. And do try to
be still.") The poem as a whole, though, is more complex than this
makes it seem because the model starts to sympathise with the
painter in a way that suggests they are both at the mercy of larger
economic forces – "Both poor, we make our living as we can". In
this sense they are complicit with each other but the real guilt lies
elsewhere.

More complex, though, and amongst Duffy's most important
achievements, are those poems where the question of guilt inheres
more closely in the actual characters of the poem. Strangely, in one
of the most powerful of these the speakers are not in the usual
sense characters at all, being two dolphins; for this reason, in "The
Dolphins" (25–26) the question of language is all the more acute
and the speakers use it as such an alien form of expression that it
is defamiliarised: "After travelling such space for days we began/
to translate". This is ambivalent – it suggests both how the speakers
learned to speak and how they were transformed; it recalls the lines:

I squash a fly against the window with my thumb.
We did that at school. Shakespeare. It was in
another language and now the fly is in another language.

(11)

There, in "Education for Leisure" the alienness of the language in
*King Lear* is compared with the alienness of death. Like the fly the
dolphins are translated in the sense of being turned into something
alien to themselves, as the model in "Standing Female Nude" is

translated into a painting which, she says, "does not look like me".
What makes "The Dolphins" so powerful is the way this translation
works as an analogue for representation, and the way this is reflected in the dolphins' struggle with language which they know
translates them into the terms of their keeper:

> The other has my shape. The other's movement
> forms my thoughts. And also mine. There is a man
> and there are hoops. There is a constant flowing guilt.

Representation involves such a complex interaction between subject and object that they become complicit with each other, and
"guilt" appears to flow freely between them. That this is also an
analogue for erotic interactions between men and women and for
violence inflicted on women by men is clear from the repetition of
the phrase "There is a man" and the complication of the dolphins'
feelings which are mostly desperate but also attribute positive feelings to their keeper: "The other knows/ and out of love reflects me
for myself." The dolphins have grown dependent on their oppres-
sor and by the end of the poem their interaction is so intense it has
become a form of identification – the dolphins cannot distinguish
themselves from the keeper who before was "the other": "There is
a man and our mind knows we will die here".

In "Naming Parts"[4] the shifts in interaction in a sexual relationship are reflected in the shifts from one pronoun to another. The
way that guilt is made to flow freely between the partners when
violence is inflicted by one of them is indicated in an alternation
between generalised and specific kinds of expression:

> A body has been discussed between them.
> The woman wears a bruise
> upon her arm. Do not wear your heart
> upon your sleeve, he cautions, knowing
> which part of whom has caused the injury.

The difficulty of accurately representing domestic violence against
women is suggested here in the way that the treachery of language
is indicated – its tendency to evasion and slippage into clichés of
metaphor that disperse and diffuse the reality of individual acts.
The woman's body has become the object of violence but when the
violence is discussed, the woman is required to think of her body

as an object in a way that divides her from herself. This poses a severe problem for her if she wants to represent this violence to others outside their relationship – so when, later, she is shown attempting to do so, she is again shown severely self-divided: "I cannot bear alone and watch/ my hands reach sadly for the telephone".

These self-divisions are so acute because responses to violence by the partners in sexual relationships are bound up with the strong ties of mutual identification which the partners feel. Duffy's deliberately mystifying use of pronouns and free indirect speech reflects this as the reader struggles to identify who is saying and doing what, and the obsessive references to body parts suggest the difficulty the man and woman have in seeing themselves whole. The reference to "parts" also indicates the role playing that further confuses their identities: "I am/ the Jack of Diamonds and, for this trick only,/ you my Queen."

However, Duffy's feminism is most accurately seen as part of a wider political protest against how representation "programs and precedes us". This takes its most obvious form in those poems where she employs a simple direct style to attack simplification, as in "Poet for our Times" (70–71), a monologue by a headline writer for a tabloid newspaper which satirises the way that British culture obsessively caricatures itself in its concern not to take itself too seriously – the conventions of headline writing allow simplistic messages to be transmitted partly because they have licensed themselves to be half comic.

A subtler simplification is in evidence in "Model Village" (37–39) which contrasts a primary schoolroom vision with an adult one. The child's eye here is not so much innocent as simplistic in a caricatural way, incapable of seeing the adults except as stereotypes – Miss Maiden, the Farmer, the Vicar, the Librarian – which represent the people involved only by externals which are the equivalent of "Grass is green/ and the pillar-box is red". This merely outward cosiness is subverted, however, by what these characters themselves say about their lives and yet, even then, there is considerable doubt that they represent themselves any more accurately than cats do by saying *Miaow* or horses by saying *Neigh*. The frustrated spinster who kills the mother who oppresses her; the previously down-to-earth farmer haunted by an apparition; the vicar who dresses up as a choirboy; the librarian frightened of anything beyond the library – these all seem to caricature themselves. Behind the cosy clichés of childhood are the *louche* clichés of soap opera or pulp fiction.

What Duffy consistently opposes to these simplifications – what constitutes the most reliable source of positive value in her work – is an appreciation, respect and understanding for otherness especially of the spontaneous and vivid kind that occurs in love. This has the opposite effect to that attitude to otherness that oppresses, as in "The Dolphins" – the attitude that must colonise the other and make it resemble itself – and the attitude that simplifies and makes crude what does not resemble itself. So love and other places, and their different languages, are repeatedly conflated in Duffy's work. In "Strange Place"[5] the familiarity of the place shared by the lovers is invaded, as they head for "an early night" by "news from other countries" and "weather somewhere else" on the radio: but later this domestic "here and now" will become "this strange place" because of the love it contains and so, paradoxically, makes the speaker "homesick". Love is traditionally written of in paradoxes and the one that most fascinates Duffy is the way it simultaneously makes strange and makes familiar – "Love makes buildings home" (57).

A loving interplay of familiarity and strangeness also characterises "Warming her Pearls" (60) which is spoken by a maid whose mistress asks her to wear her pearls, to "warm them, until evening". There is an identification between the two women which is a stark contrast with that between the man and woman in "Naming Parts" where the postmodernist confusion and fragmentation of bodies suggest a baffled ontological doubt. In "Warming her Pearls" the identification is of the sympathetic kind which is analogous to that of writers entering the minds of characters – it allows the maid to understand the life of her mistress, whose routine is mediated for the reader through the maid, who speaks the poem. She thinks of her all day:

> resting in the Yellow Room, contemplating silk
> or taffeta, which gown tonight? She fans herself
> whilst I work willingly, my slow heat entering
> each pearl. Slack on my neck, her rope.

The bodies of the mistress and the maid mingle via the pearls – the "faint, persistent scent" of the maid is imagined by her puzzling the tall dancing partners of the mistress. In this way love is shown tentatively negotiating otherness, enjoying its difference, influencing it (as the maid does both by her scent and, at least for the reader, by her personal interpretation of how the mistress lives) but not attempting to annex it, not resenting its freedoms.

For Duffy, love is another country and speaks another language and her vision of fulfilment requires that it be inhabited imaginatively and non-violently – without, that is, violating its rich otherness. So "In Your Mind" (89) starts "The other country, is it anticipated or half-remembered?" and so gives her latest book its title. It also recalls "Homesick" which suggests that love is really a pining for first love which is the country that we came from – a half-remembered place, "elsewhere possible" – for which we are homesick. This other country is latent below the actual – "Its language is muffled by the rain which falls all afternoon/ one autumn in England". It is more palpable in "River" (87) where it is seen across a border and where language is even more of a concern. As the river crosses the border, it "translates itself" but here the idea is not used in the oppressive way it was in "The Dolphins" and "Education for Leisure" – it is not a question of one system of beliefs erasing another, but of their mutual illumination. It is a celebration of the imaginative possibilities of the dialogic, the ability of one mode of expression to enrich itself with another. So a woman is seen across the border who "feels she is somewhere else, intensely, simply because/ of words; sings loudly in nonsense, smiling, smiling."

In a way characteristic of mainstream contemporary British poetry, Carol Ann Duffy has accommodated postmodernism but only up to a certain point. She has deployed postmodernist tactics largely in order to depict how women are represented in contemporary culture. However, because she wishes to condemn that representation she has found it urgently necessary to insert or insinuate feminist perspectives in dialogue with postmodernist ones. Because she has urgent political motives she has felt it necessary to place a limit on postmodernist free play; in this her motives are analogous to those of James Fenton. The power of her work arises from the persuasiveness both of her depiction of the distortive ways in which women are represented (the subtle, apparently "natural" means of representation, the complex ramifications of the ends of representation) and of her condemnation of these distortions. Moreover, she manages to do both, to depict *and* to condemn, through the deployment of the dialogic tactics which are available to novelised poets. These tactics enable her to suggest both how overpoweringly right and reasonable sexist attitudes can appear to those who hold them, and how wrong and oppressive their consequences are for their victims.

These tactics involve the subtle intermingling of voices and overlaying of perspectives and their deployments links Duffy to the narrative writing which is such a force in contemporary British poetry, and which I deal with in my next chapter.

# 6

# "Grapevine, barge pole, whirlpool, chloride, concrete, bandage, station, story": some versions of narrative

Blake Morrison and Andrew Motion were accurate, in their "Introduction" to *The Penguin Book of Contemporary British Poetry*[1], when they identified narrative as a key element in the development of the new mainstream poetry which they anthologised and which was, as they wrote, still developing. Most conspicuously, Paul Muldoon and James Fenton had written longish poems that playfully combined diverse narrative genres. Poems that tell stories have acquired an even greater centrality since the Penguin anthology was published, some of them influenced by the narrative poems it contained. "Greenheart"[2], by Alan Jenkins, for example, is indebted to Paul Muldoon's parodies of thrillers and detective stories. (However, its mingling of these genres with references to *Sir Gawain and the Green Knight* – which produces a disorientation that evokes the shifting boundaries of innocence and guilt – is entirely Jenkins' own.)

This importance, recently, of narrative is best understood as part of a larger process that has pushed lyric writing increasingly into the background. The Bakhtinian concept of "novelisation" comes closest to describing this process, involving as it does the introduction – self-conscious or otherwise – of a plurality of voices which baffles the personal authority of the lyric poet. There are notable precedents for this, for example in the tension between the voices of the speaker and the implied author in Browning's dramatic monologues, in the shifts of centres of consciousness in Meredith's formidable sonnet sequence "Modern Love", and the juxtaposition of conflicting points of view in early T.S. Eliot. But "dialogic" effects like these have acquired a dominance greater than ever before.

108

A reading of a recent British poem begins warily because the extent to which the voice speaking the poem is sanctioned by the poet is typically (at first) left open to question. Moreover, this question is especially fraught because poetry readers have been taught the opposite by some of the most influential poetic theory and practice of the 50s, 60s and early 70s – been taught to assume that this voice should speak directly, existentially, from the poet's own experience. The legacy of the Movement in Britain encouraged poets and readers to assume that the language of the poem was that of a no-nonsense male speaking to others similarly inclined. This legacy combined with that of the confessional mode, which, despite its US provenance, exercised much sway in Britain and encouraged an autobiographical poetic. Even outside the mainstream, the emphasis of Black Mountain poetry was that the poet spoke organically from an authentic self, and Frank O'Hara's "Personism"[3] was essentially a more playful (and naïve) version of the same belief – the poem would be placed between the poet and the reader "Lucky Pierre" style (like the partner in the middle in an act of troilism) – it would be not just personal but *like* a person, and one alive and sexy as someone sharing your bed.

The changes that took place in the 70s and 80s occurred without the backing of a similarly influential theorising or even interpreting. As a result, readers of recent poetry, while they have noticed the changes, are wary in the face of a kind of writing quite different from that which was previously dominant. Poems with questionable speakers are not a new phenomenon – the question of who is speaking is crucial, for example, at the start of *The Waste Land* where the famous first line could be spoken either by the implied author or by Marie, the character who colours the initial narrative. However, the modernist perspectivism implied in that ambiguity has become an assumption in recent British poetry and has been playfully multiplied.

In the case of Andrew Motion the shadowiness of the speaker is an effect that contributes to the atmosphere of mystery which he likes to evoke and is linked to his interest in ghosts and doubles (or twins). While telling a story, Motion draws upon the ability of poetry to suggest and hint and while his imagery is in itself solid and hard-edged, his problematic angles of vision give it a quality of wavering insubstantiality. The conflict between these two effects, in which an apparent definitiveness is subverted, is connected to the paradoxical effect of Motion's interest in secrecy – "secret narratives"

being his collective name for the poems collected in *Dangerous Play,
Poems 1974–1984*[4]. Ross Chambers has suggested that the emphasis
on secrecy is a strategy that in effect lies behind all story-telling:

> The possession of a superior insight or of information urgently
> required can be implied by a refusal to divulge. . .followed per-
> haps. . .by a "divulgation" so calculated that it acts more as a
> smoke screen, behind which the essential fact – which itself, per-
> haps, is a void – may remain undivulged. In this connection,
> secrecy – the claim to be in possession of a secret, together with
> an implied willingness to divulge it – forms the paradigm of all
> such tactics of narrative authority.[5]

So secrecy is a paradoxical quality in a poem – it allows definitiveness and mystery to be combined. In "Open Secrets" (Motion,
11) what appears to be divulged is that the father of the narrator
"had taken/ five shots that day to finish his stag" – a fact which he
wanted kept quiet to the extent of giving McDermot (who had
acted as gillie) the stag as a bribe to keep it secret. That this is a
smoke screen, however, emerges in the third stanza where the
narrator's motives in telling the story are laid open to question in
a self-reflexive way that draws attention to the deceptions involved
in story-telling and the strategies employed by the story-teller to
"seduce" the listener or reader. This is reflected, also, in the ambiguity of the "you" to whom the narrator speaks, a "you" that may
be either the reader or a figure with whom he is personally (and
probably sexually) involved. The complexity of the relationship
between the story-teller, the story and the reader is indicated, once
again, by Ross Chambers:

> Seduction as a narrative tactic takes the form of recruiting the
> desire of the other in the interests of maintaining narrative au-
> thority, so it is a duplicitous act to the extent that it introduces
> into the concept of "point" a *cleavage*, a conflict of motives, since
> the story that conforms to the hearer's desire has also the func-
> tion of satisfying other desires (e.g. the desire to tell the story) in
> the storyteller.
>
> (215–216)

Seduction is self-reflexively both a theme and a narrative strategy
in "Open Secrets". So "Florrie I sat on a grass-grown crumbling

stack of peat/ with the boy by her side" refers primarily to the story-telling act of situating two characters in a scene of seduction: but, despite his denials, the narrator may well be "the boy" and in that case may well have sat her there literally. However, there is a further question about the sense in which the narrator wishes to seduce the narratee. In the case of readers of the poem the seduction is metaphorical, but in that of their representative in the poem there are suggestions that the narrator's motives are to reignite a burnt-out relationship ("prolonging my journey home to you, I killed/ an hour") by telling, (or inventing?) a story that excites both him and his listener. The excitement will be all the more intense because of the illicitness with which the story is associated:

> . . .as soon as she whispered
> *Come on. We've done it before,* I made him imagine
> his father garotting the stag, slitting the stomach
> and sliding his hands inside for warmth.

The opening up of the stomach is an analogue for the openness referred to in the paradoxical title, which itself hints at the poem's seductive combination of hiddenness and "divulgation". The element of cruelty it contains is also linked to the way the narrator "made" the boy imagine this which in turn links the power exercised by authors with that exercised by seducers. To what extent all this will, in Chambers's terms, recruit the desire of the other will differ according to the narratee: while it maintains the interest of the reader of the poem, what it does for the narrator's lover will vary according to how well her desires rhyme with those of "the boy".

Nonetheless, the recruiting of the desire of the other is a key theme in Motion's work. His narrators tell stories partly in order to understand themselves by turning themselves into characters (this is what the narrator does in "Open Secrets" by becoming "the boy") or by identifying with other characters in the story – so the actions of the father and the boy become each other's equivalents. The stories shift between the point of view of the narrator and another character but then the other, through the process of identification or displacement, becomes the same. So, at the end of "Open Secrets" the narrator says:

> . . .He was never
> myself, this boy, but I know if I tell you his story

you'll think we are one and the same: both of us hiding
in fictions which say what we cannot admit to ourselves.

Something analogous happens in "The Pleasure Steamers" (Motion,
42–44) where the narrator becomes, in a sense, his father's double
– taking his place in a process that reflects the poem's concern with
repetition and change and the relationship between them. And in
"Coming to Visit" (Motion, 58–60) the focus is explicitly on twins
"breathing each other's breath" so that the gap between personal
identity and difference from others is closed in a way that surreally
combines comfort and alarm.

In "Dangerous Play" the narrator and the narratee are lovers
whose narratives intermingle because the narrator is telling a story
told him, paradoxically, by the narratee, and one in which he was
himself involved. The reliability of the narration is called further
into doubt because it is told on the verge of sleep:

> Or so you imagine it now. Or so you say,
> when you're telling me late in bed,
> and sleepy enough to confuse what was
> with what you're beginning to dream.

In the end, the truth of the story is not the point so much as its
power to establish the identity of the lovers, and their mutual identification with each other. The story is told to ward off a threatening
otherness which makes the narrator identify alarmingly with a
murdered man ("his face had been changed into one that I know/
or into my own") and makes the narratee have dreams which he
cannot share.

In this way the narrative tactic of recruiting the desire of the
other is repeated in the narrative itself and so made explicit. Many
of Motion's poems work in the interplay between the narrator and
another figure with whom he or she has a problematic relationship
which colours the narrative. In "Open Secrets" this takes the form
of recruiting one experience in the name of another in order to
compare two kinds of guilt. The analogy between hunting and
seduction, however, is long-established: the association that is made
in "The Letter" (Motion, 12–13) is more eccentric, though once again
it involves conflating sex and death. Here the narrator is a young
woman whose story juxtaposes a love letter she receives with the
death of a German airman. What makes her link the two is left

deliberately implicit in a way that emphasises that it is partly the power of secretiveness that does so – she has learned about male desire from her first love letter and the lesson seems to be reinforced by the disposition of the airman's body – "His face pressed/ close to the sweet-smelling grass. His legs/ splayed wide in a candid unshamable V". There is an ironic symmetry between the two kinds of "letter" of the sort usually associated with the short story. Both are "candid" where discretion is normally expected, and the airman's "V" is another "open secret" – divulging what is normally hidden – and evokes ambiguous feelings of fear and desire, sex (or victory?) and death. The capriciousness of the link between the two, then, is part of its point and suggests the way that the implied desire of the airman is recruited for the sake of the story and of the narrator and her lover.

"The Letter" suggests that, for the female narrator, language itself is an alien instrument deployed by men for the expression of their desires – the shock of the airman's symbolic openness arises largely from the extent to which it is the too literal (as in "letter") equivalent of the written language of the love letter. The implication behind this is that she is made aware of the extent to which the symbolic system she entered in acquiring language is secretly premised upon masculine assumptions. It is this which has much preoccupied women poets in their concern to tell stories from feminine perspectives – a concern I will explore in my concluding chapter when I will emphasise the impact that feminism and women's writing has had on mainstream writing as a whole.

Because of this impact it is important to stress the extent to which masculine and feminine writing are currently learning from each other. So Jackie Kay is very much concerned with feminine experience but her "The Adoption Papers"[6] must be seen in a wider context that connects it with the narrative concerns of other contemporary poets, including male ones. For it is profoundly dialogic in the way it tells a story by allowing three distinct voices to overlap each other. It resembles George Szirtes' sequence "Metro"[7], for this reason, in constructing a novelised, rather than a confessional version of family history – in the place of the single voice of Robert Lowell or Sylvia Plath pondering their constitutive experiences, Kay and Szirtes allow members of their families to express their own points of view.

So it is instructive to see how the closing poems in Jo Shapcott's "Robert and Elizabeth Sequence"[8] insist that the feminine and the masculine are not discrete categories and that the thinking of men and women can mutually enrich each other. It is certainly this enrichment that George Szirtes is looking for in "Metro" when he introduces the voice of his mother – she provides access to family history and so to domestic experience. More than this, though, since family history in this case is linked to wider history because it takes place in the last years of the Second World War in Hungary when many Jews were sent to concentration camps by the fascist government. Moreover, by enlisting his mother as a "psychopomp" he calls upon a notion of the feminine as being connected with particular closeness to the subjective underside of history; she becomes his guide to the eponymous metro which symbolises "the hidden half,/ A subcutaneous universe" (Szirtes, 19).

What is available to the poet himself is personal memory, like that of creeping into his aunt's lap when she "was sitting in the dark, alone/ Half sleeping" (17); hearsay "data": "*At the hour/ When the Germans entered Budapest we were/ Sitting in the Astoria*" (28) or a more objective kind of archaeology, "Old coins, components, ordnance, bone and glass,/ Nails, muscle, hair, flesh, shrivelled bits of string" (20). These are valuable in a limited way as components in a story manipulated by a "narrator", as Szirtes refers to himself (23) – but one "of morbid interest", too preoccupied with death and definition, too close to the cult of Terminus, preoccupied with "the skeleton/ Of something – body, city, staircase, wall" (28). However objective this all seems it is too retrospective and terminal, a "fiction/ Of history which makes up Budapest/ And what one thinks of as oneself" (28).

It is important, then, that this kind of definitiveness is subverted by the dialogue between the poet "narrator" and his mother. Through her the poem can enter what the experiences felt like from inside – she puts flesh on the "bare bones of the story" (28). More than this, though, in her capacity as psychopomp she has access to the underworld which symbolises the unconscious of history, where the dead and the living meet, and where non-realist kinds of writing can more fully express the reality of what happened, for "The tunnels creep/ Under the skin, the trains with their crew/ Of passengers can glide through unopposed". These passengers are the Jews murdered by the Nazis and it is through the poet's mother that their experiences are interpreted – they are the ignored of history so their voices are surreally muted, so that it requires "Her poetry (unseen and without sound)" to translate them:

> Their voices are not heard but seen, are moving
> Lips and tongues. They're well-behaved and quiet.
> To give voice is to lip read, to construe
> The contortions of a mouth, to place the living
> Where the dead are,
>
> (22)

"Metro" and "The Adoption Papers" are similar to the extent that they are both concerned with family experiences that have been formative for their authors and which are explored in a dialogic rather than a confessional way. However, "Metro" is written in a much more formal style and draws upon more conventional poetic effects than Kay's poem which has more in common stylistically with the poems of Simon Armitage, Glyn Maxwell and Matthew Sweeney. Kay and these three all give a high priority to the mimicry of a colloquial and vividly contemporary voice, though Sweeney is the odd one out to the extent that his preference is much more for third, rather than first person narration, which helps to give his poems characteristically, a much less excitable surface than that of the others. His coolness of tone excites sympathy by seeming to withold it, suggesting a disinterested and appraising gaze which narrates with an apparently unfeeling clarity. But since what is narrated is often deeply painful or disturbing or bizarre a surreal distance opens up between the manner and the subject matter. Moreover, the apparent coolness is often subtly undermined by the way the narrator insistently questions what is going on in the minds of the characters, so that their states of mind are insinuated into the poem while it still looks as though they are being observed from the outside. This is achieved with deft economy. "The Shadow Home"[9], for example, begins "As his daughter watches from the doorway" and so simultaneously establishes a centre of consciousness, her relationship with the central figure, and a scene of parting, so that the more objective narrative that follows is almost invisibly framed. Both the framing and the near invisibility are important because, like many of Sweeney's poems, this one is *about* consciousness, about how much anyone knows about anyone else, about the alienness of other people's experience. Ironically, at the start, the daughter "can't realise how exactly/ she has got him right" – she

cannot know that her knowledge of his double life with another
wife and another daughter is accurate. But beyond this, and more
crucially, there is ignorance and of a kind which suggests the distortions of identification: in trying to imagine the other family she
projects her own onto it, can only imagine it from that point of view:

> And does her shadow-sister look like her?
> Is she blonde, is her mother blonde,
> do they speak English, has her father
> hidden a language for years?

As in some of Andrew Motion's poems this closes the gap between
the self and others in a disorienting way and at the same time self-
reflexively mimics what happens in narrative in the process of
imagining the experience of other people. What it also indicates is
that inadequate understanding of others reduces our capacity to
understand ourselves:

> Does her shadow-sister know about her,
> or does she begin to suspect?
> Which of the two is the shadow home?

"Whatever"[10] is also written in this interrogative mode, this time
asking about the state of mind of two characters, each dealt with
in nine short lines, starting "What does he think" then "And what
does she think". In this way the story is divided between the two
of them but whether they are thinking about their half of the story
or whether that thought is imposed on them by the implied author
is itself questionable. The poem works in the interaction between
three angles of vision which question each other about motives,
so it ends "and all/ because of sex, love or whatever?" where the
language may be either that of the woman or the implied author –
or possibly (a fourth angle of vision) that of "the whole/ town"
which "is talking about her". The matter-of-fact manner in which
the story is told, culminating in the dismissive way in which love
is referred to, and the cool frame of questioned interpretations,
conflict with the passion implied in the story – a man swallowing
weedkiller because he hears his woman is sleeping with a neighbour who then also swallows weedkiller, both men likely to die.
And it is once again this stylistic conflict which gives the poem its
power and draws attention to how issues to do with the dialogic in

narrative, while they are complex and sophisticated, are also issues that are intimately bound up with the way that experience is felt and thought about.

"Blue Shoes" (Shoes, 51–52) illustrates this in a different form in the interaction between, for Sweeney, an uncharacteristic first person narration and the implied version of the central character who has himself written about the day when he suffered a heart attack – "I have his notes here,/ the last of any consequence". This sense of an interaction is reinforced by the way the poem shifts tenses between the day in question (which is referred to in both the past and the present tense), and the present in which the poem is being written. This is combined with a shift between what appears to be hard fact and what is speculation on the part of the narrator, imagining what happened – "I see him/ hurrying towards the train". This speculative element is reinforced by the reported attempts of the man himself to interpret what was happening – an interpretation that takes a self-consciously literary form:

> He played with patterns, with omens
> he deciphered later. That particular day
> it was blue shoes
> for want of any better.

It is the arbitrariness of this supposedly key image which is its point. It amounts to a mere freak of observation, or a meaningless obsession ("pretty women/ wearing blue shoes") which has only a circumstantial connection to the key event which itself is referred to in a disorientingly oblique way. The narration is perversely eccentric – placing something trivial in the foreground and something highly significant in the background. Nonetheless, it is the overlaying of the first person narration's interpretation on top of that of the central character which draws attention to the gap between the image and the event; and this gap evokes those between events and how our consciousness deals with them, and events and how they are described.

There is something characteristically sinister about the way this gap is perceived by Matthew Sweeney – a disturbance about how off-centre human awareness is, how it gets obsessed with trivia. Simon Armitage and Glyn Maxwell are also preoccupied with this, but their attitude to trivia is much more ambiguous and they tend to celebrate it in a tongue-in-cheek way. This is evident in Armitage's poems from the extent to which their effects are achieved on their surfaces, which tend to be charged with colloquial energy. There is an important sense in which his poems are *about* the language of which they are composed, that they play with contemporary idioms to indicate how much experience is coloured, or even determined by them. But the self-consciousness of his deployment of these idioms is crucial – he does not use them simply to evoke an authentic voice. Instead that voice is treated with a detachment that arises from the sense of distance that arises between the colloquial idioms and the poetic form in which they are placed, Armitage's symmetrical stanzaic patterns. This introduces a poetic voice speaking alongside the colloquial one – a voice that seems simultaneously to be identified with and sceptical of the colloquial voice and which simultaneously mocks its often trivial posturing and enjoys it. The speaker in "Ivory"[11], for example, undercuts himself by using too many words to demand an end to mere chat: "No more blab,/ none of that ragtag/ and bobtail business,/ or ballyhoo/ or balderdash/ and no jackassery, or flannel,/ or galumphing."

What this kind of writing most resembles, in fact, is parody. One effect which is especially characteristic of Armitage, moreover, is the comic mingling of a North of England idiom with an American one, as in "The Stuff" (Zoom, 68–69), a story mimicking a thriller about drug dealing in which a comic homeliness ("'Oldham – Home of the tubular bandage'") is mingled with an exotic danger ("Others were bundled in the back of vans/ and were quizzed, thumped/ finished off and dumped/ or vanished completely like Weldon Kees"). This mingling – which culminates here in a reference to the mysterious death of an American poet juxtaposed with one to a rail bridge in Oldham – suggests that the speaker has got alarmingly out of his depth. But it does so, typically for Armitage, in a way that emphasises how this is registered at the level of the language he uses:

> In Court I ambled up and took the oath
> and spoke the addict's side of the story.
> I said grapevine, barge pole, whirlpool, chloride,
> concrete, bandage, station, story. Honest.

This is a résumé of some of the key words in the story which, juxtaposed with the last two words in the poem deliberately raises questions about what language does to the truth of narrative.

It is clear, however, that this is less a source of anxiety to Armitage than of enjoyment – that what might seem the trivially off-centre diversion into the terms and images of the story and away from the facts of death and drug addiction is actually a spectacle in which the poem indulges. This, too, is characteristic of his parodic manner which is, if anything, even more pronounced in his latest book *Kid*[12] in which the title poem is about Robin overcoming, as it were, his anxiety of influence about Batman:

> Holy robin-redbreast-nest-egg-shocker!
> Holy roll-me-over-in-the-clover,
> I'm not playing ball boy any longer
> Batman

It might be possible to read this as an analogue for Armitage's casting-off of his own influences, especially that of Weldon Kees – except that Armitage seems always to have been sceptical and his own man. His parodies in *Kid* of Kees' "Robinson" poems (Robin, son of Batman?) are hardly even affectionate, in fact they mercilessly ridicule Kees' narcissistic *angst* and suggest that the Robinson persona barely functions as a Kees disguise, is largely an excuse for a displaced egotism, as in "Mr. Robinson's Holiday" (24–25) where the name is used twelve times ("Robinson thinking this is ridiculous, Robinson.")

This kind of intertextuality is also a feature of Glyn Maxwell's "Tale of a Chocolate Egg"[13] which is a postmodernist version of "The Rape of the Lock" to the extent that it takes pleasure in the way its eponymous confectionery enters and influences the lives of four or five recurrent characters. Its point is in the self-consciousness with which consumerism is recognised as such but still enjoyed, the way that a "vast advertisement/ for chocolate eggs" (100) evokes both shock and reluctant admiration – "the sheer nerve, the worthless new idea" (100). For mixed feelings like these Maxwell invents a poetry of thoroughly mixed-up languages which reflects the complexity of the messages that contemporary culture transmits and the equal complexity of responses to those messages.

Key effects in this linguistic jumble are Maxwell's use of free indirect speech and parody – in both of these the language of the implied author is mingled with others to form a (usually comic) hybrid. So, after buying his "chocko egg", the skinhead sees "his ex":

"Oi, sweet'art!" he shouted in the sun.
Not nobody's sweetheart, she carried on.
(100)

This moves from direct speech to the reporting of the inner speech of the "ex" – which involves the implied author paraphrasing thoughts of one character reflecting the language of another. What seems straightforwardly colloquial, then, is actually very complex at the linguistic level and this helps to explain why a poem that may seem simply obsessed with trivia ends up saying something powerfully significant about the way that contemporary experience is mediated through a bewildering variety of linguistic systems. This effect is reinforced by Maxwell's characteristic habit of repetition – "sweetheart", at one level, is uncomfortably close to confectionery, and the skinhead is in the habit of using the word both meaningfully and trivially, as when he says to the shop assistant "An I'll 'ave that chocko egg an' all, sweet 'art!/ Me fuckin' sweet 'art's buggered off, sweet 'art!" (106). What is important above all, though, is that the poem is very funny – this prevents a simply moralistic attitude being struck towards consumerism or, here, the reification of women. For the poem's mingling of languages deliberately poses problems of reader response which suggest the difficulty of adopting simple moral or political attitudes towards postmodernist culture, which suggest that reader and author are inevitably in an ambiguous position which wishes to condemn what is merely materialistic but finds itself nonetheless implicated in and complicit with it.

So the poem's parody of advertising mocks its claims but simultaneously backs them – there is an extent to which "Tale of a Chocolate Egg" is itself a camp advertisement which hopes the reader will be "totally/ and utterly, completely, creamily,/ dreamily, cremefondant centrally/ satisfied, delighted, nay amazed,/ converted, charmed and spellbound by our product" (105). There is a similar partial endorsement of the trivia in "Out of the Rain"[14] though this is more anxious and less celebratory perhaps because of the apocalyptic elements in the story which is a postmodernist retelling of Noah's flood with some debt, also, to Bob Dylan's "hard rain". It is a kind of allegory of the Cold War – the closeness to apocalypse figured in torrential, apparently endless rain. However, there is no sense that sins are being punished in this way – what looks like God is "just a cloud" (52) and the rain slackens off as meaninglessly as it began. The emphasis is not on moral or political misdemeanours but upon a kind of inadvertence and shallowness, an inability to concentrate on things of genuine significance which is reflected in the silliness of the first person narrator:

> I swam and thought of the dead. I thought "They're dead."
> (I was known as a thinker at school. I'll have you know.)
> I thought of the things I'd seen, and thought "I didn't
> see those things." (I was known as a liar, too.)

$$(57)$$

Once again there is in this poem a self-conscious montage of diverse languages, a careful notation of the cherished phenomena of contemporary culture (sport, pop music, different brands of bottled beer), and a refusal to distinguish in a moralistic way between the trivial and the significant. However, the weightiness of this new subject-matter has the effect of spoiling the fun, of insinuating an unpostmodernist worry, of hinting at an authorial unease that goes against the grain of mere perspectivism.

The narrative poetry that has been written recently in Britain is very various, then. What is clear, though, is that narrative is being used by poets as an opportunity to combine the traditional resources and expectations of poetry – imagery, rhythms, concentrated power, economy etc. with those of the novel – effects of narrative voice which raise questions about the value systems associated with different perspectives. The result is a self-conscious hybrid whose point is in its clash of voices, its juxtaposition of differently coloured narratives. The way, as a consequence, that different value systems are brought into contact with each other is implicitly political, and the dialogic element in this narrative writing is connected with the increasing cultural diversity that has been in evidence in British poetry after the Movement whose assumptions were monolithically those of white middle-class English males. Poets have increasingly drawn attention to their class, gender, nationality, regional identity or race and explored the value systems connected with them and how they compare and contrast with centripetal and consensual norms.

This is not merely a question of pluralism, of the bland tolerance of difference, but of a profound sense that the self has no meaning except in interrelation with others, and that the lived experience of the self can only be expressed through determined efforts to evoke the otherness with which the self interacts. Narrative has been one of the idioms some poets have used to achieve this partly because the act of story-telling inevitably raises questions about identity and identification. For as soon as a story begins the listener or reader is obliged to question whose experience it expresses and from whose point of view the experience is being described. Moreover, the dialogical tactics which story-tellers employ ensure that these questions continue to be asked.

It is worth looking, finally, at the Irish poet Paul Durcan because his poems work at the intersection between lyric and narrative modes and so he exemplifies most acutely the introduction of dialogic elements into a kind of writing that traditionally was purely personal. This is complicated because the narrative modes he calls upon are of both a written and a vernacular kind – as he says, "May I belong always to the oral tradition/ Who is a woman keeping her man on his toes:/ She permits him to speak solely from memory"[15]. So his stories seem closer, most of the time, to oral forms like tall tales, scandalous gossip and jokes than they do to the decorum of high fiction and Ross Chambers' concept of secrecy seems wholly inappropriate to them – given, as they are, to divulge all too easily but, at the same time, to call into question their own narrative authority. At times the meeting of this fabulatory vernacular with an almost obsessive dwelling upon objects and places (whose names Durcan characteristically repeats and repeats like an improvised refrain) produces effects akin to those in magic realist novels. But his tendency to include a version of himself and to write variations on the elegy and the love poem means that lyric expectations are felt but bewildered by questionable narrative – especially since these elements, irreconcilable though they may be, are seamlessly joined. For poetry, he says, can perform the impossible:

> Poetry! To be able to look a bullet in the eye,
> With a whiff of the bat to return it spinning to drop
> Down scarcely over the lapped net; to stand still; to stop.
>
> (245)

Returning a bullet with a table-tennis bat – this is a mixed metaphor that could function as analogue for the sleight-of-hand magic that Durcan performs in pretending that his texts are oral performances and for the way, in general in his poems, one thing keeps dissolving into another.

This is largely achieved by the fluidity of his free verse which keeps one thing running into another and by his habit of carefully notating whatever follows from his often impossible premises. "Paul" (172–173) is interesting in this respect because it exemplifies how his poems keep introducing possible shadow selves of the poet and also his characteristic insinuation, in a matter-of-fact tone, of surreal images and occurrences. The poem begins with some very self-conscious scene-setting – rush-hour traffic, city-centre church, traffic lights – which then becomes deliberately *too* self-conscious. "A Raleigh bicycle with upright handlebars/ That I had purchased for two pounds fifty pence in The Pearl" is so detailed it comically raises the question of how stories select their material. But nothing really untoward happens before the entrance of a priest (probably the most common character type in Durcan's poems) who asks the poet to act as a mourner at a funeral Mass for someone called Paul who was the same age as Durcan. This simultaneously suggests the figure of the double, which is so recurrent in fantastic literature, and the idea of attending your own funeral which is the stuff of urban myth – but both fit well into Durcan's oral idiom.

Two more lines of realist notation follow, with the poet kneeling in the front pew and the coffin alongside him on trestles, but the third, "Its flat abdomen next to my skull" seems to turn the coffin into a body and the poet into a skeleton. When Durcan then compares himself to a mother with her newborn baby the implication seems to be that he has given birth to his own corpse which is metaphorically what this poem does by linking creativity with death. But the next link is more purely playful, and one of Durcan's more thoroughly postmodernist moments:

> A feeling that everything is going to be all right
> But that we are all aliens in the cupboard,
> All coat hangers in the universe.

The words "aliens" and "coat hangers" seem to have changed places in these lines so that what would have been fairly banal has become unsettling and problematic. But this, too, is symptomatic of what happens in Durcan's poetic as a whole. He is very much concerned to draw attention to the kitchen sink (cupboard, coat hangers) but keeps conflating it with "higher" subjects involving the religious and the sublime (aliens and the universe seem to come from a populist version of Heideggerian ontology). This certainly suggests the influence of postmodernism and yet it is underpinned by a thoroughly grounded sense of Irish historical and cultural experience which is felt in particular through Durcan's obsession with the Catholic Church. Questions about narrative and identity continue to be asked in Durcan's work but he never ends up writing in a way that suggests that things have gone so far that the validity of the question is itself in question. His writing is dialogic in combining oral and written idioms, the "real" and the fabulatory, but this helps to define how the dialogic – which has its roots in Marxism and always takes for granted the reality of social experience – differs from an essentially conservative poetic like John Ashbery's. In the thorough postmodernism of the New York school *after* Frank O'Hara, voices are multiplied so endlessly that each becomes as meaningless as the next, and gets lost in white noise. The force of the dialogic, by contrast, is in its insistence on the individual shape and meaning of all the voices and idioms it contains.

What most characterises contemporary poetry on this side of the Atlantic is its tendency to place postmodernism in dialogue with realism. So it is the solid and familiar presence of the priesthood in Ireland that allows Durcan to confound its image with satirical jokes and unstable levels of fabulatory irony. In "Paul" the priest is "a seven-foot-tall, silver-haired peasant in his eighties" who tells the poet to put his bicycle "in the hearse beside the coffin". Above all, it is identity which is in question in this poem – at the graveside Durcan gets the feeling that the coffin is empty, "That Paul, whoever he was/ Was somewhere else". But Durcan's poems provide maps to help track him down – and those maps are *both* questionable *and* real.

# Part II
## Estrangement

# 7
# Estrangement and the Retro-Modernists

The publication of the Bloodaxe anthology *The New Poetry*[1] and the recent promotion of "New Generation" poets are symptoms of the emphasis in the poetry world on youth and the desire for novelty. This reinforces a tendency which too readily canonises some poets at the expense of others and then passes on, so that these others, no matter how substantial their achievement, are marginalised. The main contention of the second part of this book is that a number of poets, more or less contemporary with Philip Larkin, have suffered from the way he – and the Movement poetic with which he was associated – dominated the British poetry world in the 50s and 60s and that it is time their achievement should be recognised.

I have devoted chapters in Part II to three poets who have been neglected in this way – Edwin Morgan, Christopher Middleton and Roy Fisher. They were born respectively in 1920, 1926 and 1930, which makes them roughly contemporary with both Philip Larkin (born 1922) and John Ashbery (born 1927). However, where Larkin is most accurately regarded as antimodernist, and John Ashbery as postmodernist, these poets can best be seen as retro-modernist. In inventing this term I am referring to the extent to which they owe their most important allegiance to the classic modernism of the 1920s, to the generation of Eliot, Pound, Williams and Joyce, born about forty years before them, – though they have also built upon the assumptions of that tradition in their own individual ways.

This makes them profoundly unlike Larkin – most symptomatically in their anti-realism. Unlike his, their poems do not characteristically construct a reliable sense of the poet's personality authoritatively describing and commenting on self-consciously familiar slices of life. However, their anti-realism does not involve, as Ashbery's does, a playful celebration of the impossibility of ever fully apprehending the real: instead, it contains a fraught nostalgia both for epistemological assurance and ontological authenticity. Larkin and Ashbery both make assumptions, though of an opposite kind; for these retro-modernists, by contrast, the nature of the real is always in question and the experimental forms of their writing are evolved in an attempt to grasp it while simultaneously acknowledging its elusiveness. It is here that estrangement becomes a key concept for them, as it is for understanding classic modernism and as it is not for either Larkin – who harps on the familiar – or for Ashbery who harps on the strange or for whom reality is such an all-embracing problem it ceases to be a problem. For their constant interrogation of the real means that their poems enact continual but creative failures to grasp it which, in the process of that failure, continually defamiliarise it.

It is because they share this preoccupation with Viktor Shklovsky – himself very much a writer of the classic modernist period – that, like him, these poets are so concerned with issues of perception. Their poems repeatedly dwell self-reflexively on mind/object relations, on the status and meaning of their own images, and Shklovsky himself stressed the defamiliarising effect this self-reflexiveness has when he said that

> This new attitude to objects in which, in the last analysis, the object becomes perceptible, is that artificiality which, in our opinion, creates art. A phenomenon, perceived many times, and no longer perceivable, or rather, the method of such dimmed perception, is what I call "recognition" as opposed to "seeing". The aim of imagery, the aim of creating new art is to return the object from "recognition" to "seeing".[2]

For these retro-modernists, as for Shklovsky, this preoccupation has led to the foregrounding of images. It is this characteristic, above all, that distinguishes them from the novelised poets of the next generation: where dialogic poets situate the poem between mind and mind, estrangement poets situate it between mind and object and draw upon the image-centred styles (imagism, expressionism, surrealism) of classic modernism. So although retro-modernist poems are occasionally dialogic, they tend to be much more purely "poetic" than those of novelised poets like Craig Raine and Paul Muldoon, and they tend self-consciously to raise issues connected with the philosophy of perception and the dialectic between the mind and what it perceives. So Edwin Morgan is preoccupied with the influence that technology has had on the way that human beings interact with the world; Roy Fisher repeatedly dwells on the shifting subjective ground between the city and the way it is remembered or seen; and Christopher Middleton's ontological questionings are carried out largely by drawing attention to the fragmentariness of the world as it is experienced by modern sensibilities.

It is instructive, in this context, to glance at three other poets who are also retro-modernist in their different ways – W.S. Graham (born 1918), Charles Tomlinson (born 1927) and Jon Silkin (born 1930). Of these, it is Tomlinson who has been most urgently preoccupied with perceptual issues, so that his work can be read to some extent as an extended meditation on William Carlos Williams' insistence on "No ideas but in things". So "Swimming Chenango Lake"[3] is at its most basic level a painterly evocation of water. As such it most readily recalls impressionism, but Tomlinson's links with imagism counter this and produce a deliberate equivocation of perceptual modes, combining an impressionist "tremor" with an imagist "steadiness". This amounts to a hesitation between different ways of seeing, or of reading (a word used in the second line) but it is followed by a hesitation between sight and sound, or between the solidity of imagism and the fluidity of music: he stresses that the lake is a "geometry" rather than a "fantasia of distorting forms", but it is also a "Liquid variation answerable to the theme/ It makes away from, plays before". These equivocations are echoed, though, throughout the poem which is set on a number of thresholds – most obviously between autumn and winter, most importantly between the body and the water – that is, between the self and the world:

> . . .alone, he is unnamed
>   By this baptism, where only Chenango bears a name
> In a lost language he begins to construe –
>   A speech of densities and derisions, of half-
> Replies to the questions his body must frame
>   Frogwise across the all but penetrable element.

Here, perceptual concerns have led, via a concern with language, into ontological ones and it is important to stress that for all these retro-modernists this is precisely what is important about perception. It has a representative significance – focusing upon the process of perception defamiliarises what it is to be human and consequently being human is revealed with a new and strange density. (As I shall show later this to some extent takes these poets closer to the position of the Futurists than that of Shklovsky.) So in Tomlinson's poem the body and the water interrogate each other until the swimmer becomes a stranger to himself and grows "unnamed".

It was above all the act of naming which obsessed the mature W.S. Graham. He was older than the other retro-modernists and his early career was dominated by the influence of Dylan Thomas. However, he produced his most important work when he shook this off and moved from a Romantic view of poetry as verbal magic to a modernist view of poetry as troubled game. The question "What is the language using us for?"[4] dominated his work so that perceptual concerns are linked with linguistic ones: "The Secret Name" (59–60) is preoccupied with the possibility of a more authentic naming which would lead both to better communication and more direct seeing. It imagines a split in the self between a familiar "you" and an alter ego that defamiliarises that "you": "You maybe/ Did not know you had another/ Sound and sign signifying you" and hypothesises that

> If I had met you earlier walking
> With the poetry light better
> We might we could have spoken and said
> Our names to each other.

But what "the poetry light" stresses is that the perceptual element is inseparable from larger questions – it is not merely a matter of how things are seen but how those things are structured by the act of seeing, how that structuring occurs imperceptibly. The importance of estrangement is that it draws attention to that structuring so that it reaches beyond perceptual issues into ontological and even ideological ones. As Tony Bennett has pointed out:

the "reality" which literary works are said to defamiliarise is not some presumed raw, conceptually unprocessed, "out-there" reality but "reality" as mediated through the categories of some other form of cognition. Literature characteristically works on and subverts those linguistic, perceptual and cognitive forms which conventionally condition our access to "reality" and which, in their taken-for-grantedness, present the particular "reality" they construct as *reality* itself. Literature thus effects a two-fold shift of perceptions. For what it makes appear strange is not merely the "reality" which has been distanced from habitual modes of representation but also those habitual modes of representation themselves. Literature offers not only a new insight into "reality" but also reveals the formal operations whereby what is commonly taken for "reality" is constructed.[5]

Perceptual issues shade here inevitably into ideological ones and it is the intersection between them that has most preoccupied Jon Silkin. In his "Introduction" to *Poetry of the Committed Individual*[6] he quotes a prose passage from the Italian poet Giuseppe Ungaretti and then analyses its visual qualities in great detail – they clearly appeal to him deeply – but then he worries that "it precludes any sociality" that it "shares, but what it shares is not social". And then he wonders "how might a hermetic or imagistic art be engaged with an art that wanted without compromising its essentiality to be socially orientated, involving, as this does, some move towards the discursive" (26). His own poetic practice is marked throughout by this question; and yet, paradoxically, the very marks of this anxiety in his poems are themselves part of the answer to it – their tendency to dwell upon images, but also at the same time to fret over their insufficiency, opens cracks in the language which, as a result, continually insinuates political meaning into those images. "Lilies of the Valley"[7], for example, keeps slipping out of imagism into a questioning that introduces registers uncomfortably inappropriate to the floral context. The lines "With broad leaves, immobile;/ Are sheath-like, and fat" could almost have been written by H.D. – but "sheath-like" announces a sexual undercurrent that half-surfaces three lines later ("A fingering odour, clutches the senses") which then, five lines after that, takes on political meaning ("Its predatory scent/ Betters you, forces you") which connects with the theme of colonising that obsesses the "Flower Poems" sequence as a whole. This is all the more effective because of the deliberate artificiality of Silkin's poetic project in this sequence, which defamiliarises flower poems as a species: a gap opens up between the flowers and the poet's treatment of them which makes the reader repeatedly aware that the vision of the flowers is that of a committed socialist and anti-Zionist Jew necessarily preoccupied with issues of justice and territory.

So the flowers and the poet's vision continually defamiliarise each other. These poems begin with perceptual preoccupations but their implications extend far beyond them, as they do in almost all retro-modernist poems whose authors are most accurately seen in the formalist tradition of Shklovsky as it was modified by the Futurists.

As Tony Bennett has argued, for Shklovsky "The category of defamiliarization was. . .invested with a purely aesthetic, and not with an
ideological significance."

This ran quite contrary to the position of the Futurists who viewed
the devices of defamiliarisation as a means for promoting political
awareness by undermining ideologically habituated modes of perception. As Osip Brik summarized the Futurists' position:

> Thus art was still "a device"; what had changed from the original
> Formalist interpretation was the application of the device. The
> emphasis was shifted from the aesthetic function of the device to
> its use in the service of a "social demand".
>
> (31–32)

Retro-modernist poets do not believe, as the Futurists did, that
defamiliarization can penetrate to the "real" – but their poems keep
restlessly wishing that it could, keep evolving new forms in an
attempt to outwit the obstacles in the way of the real, and are
always at least implicitly political in believing that stale ways of
perceiving are "ideologically habituated". So where, for dialogic
poets, perception is always inter-subjective, for estrangement poets
the possibility of finally answering the mind/object question always
looms – even if it also always recedes. Perspectivism and relativism
are the air that dialogic poets breathe, although they place them (as
Ashbery does not) in carefully rendered social contexts which to
some extent limit their free play. Retro-modernists, by contrast, keep
arguing with those elements in the modern condition which frac-
ture the self and the world and baffle the authenticity of human
experience. It is for this reason that, for them, the perceptual aspects of the estrangement aesthetic are only the surface symptoms
of a multi-layered activity: and the belief in depths as well as surfaces is another characteristic that distinguishes retro-modernists
from postmodernists.

# 8

# Edwin Morgan's Metamorphoses

Edwin Morgan is now in his seventies and his *oeuvre* is a substantial one. *Themes on a Variation*[1] recently followed his *Poems of Thirty Years*[2] and both subsequently appeared in his *Collected Poems*[3]; there is also a *Selected Poems*[4], which is a useful introduction, and there are books of translations[5] and essays[6]. What sets him apart is his apparent refusal to forge a settled poetic identity and this despite the fact that he has material at his disposal which could have been used in this way. In particular, he could easily have defined himself simply as a poet of place – he was born in Glasgow and has lived most of his life there. Many of his best poems do have Glasgow as their setting. Mostly they present realist slices of urban life, but even within these boundaries Morgan has found plenty of room for manoeuvre. In "The Starlings in George Square" (165–166) the birds are a source, in the first section, of fondness for one man and wide-eyed awe for his young son, in the second section, of comic confusion caused by their terrible din ("the clerks write Three Pounds Starling in the savings-books") and in the third section of anxiety at their possible disappearance, then relief at their continued presence ("They lift up the eyes, they lighten the heart"). "Glasgow Green" (168–169), by contrast, moves from a scene of homosexual rape among the "meths-men" to a meditation on sexual desire and loneliness. "Glasgow Sonnets" (289–292), in depicting dereliction, deploy imagism ("Under the darkness of a twisted pram/ a cat's eyes glitter") mingled with statement:

> . . .Hugh MacDiarmid forgot
> in "Glasgow 1960" that the feast
> of reason and the flow of soul has ceased
> to matter to the long unfinished plot
> of heating frozen hands.
>
> (290)

A more often repeated treatment of Glasgow, combined with a more explicit Scottish nationalism, could have produced a much more easily recognisable, yet still flexible, Morgan "voice". He has preferred a more centrifugal poetic, as the title of his second major volume *From Glasgow to Saturn*[7] playfully declares: he has set out to tackle an enormous range of subject-matter in an enormous range of forms – concrete and sound poetry, free verse, Persian *ghazals*, ottava rima and so on. Reading Edwin Morgan can seem less like reading and more like channel-hopping. Reviewers and critics usually admire his versatility, but they can also be a little suspicious. Michael Schmidt, for example, complains that

> there is a sense that many of Morgan's poems are *about* something, conscious attempts to accept a challenge of subject-matter or form and, willy-nilly, to forge a poem out of it. The challenge has replaced an inner poetic necessity; the very variety worries the reader. Morgan has an enviable facility, with all the implicit dangers of facility.[8]

When Morgan's work is considered as a whole, however, its variety no longer seems merely willed or whimsical – it starts to emerge as the necessary product of a consistent outlook. His poems relate to each other as much through their differences as their similarities: taken *en masse* they demonstrate a twentieth-century sense not only that experience may form itself into a bewildering number of patterns but also that each pattern is likely to dissolve into an entirely different pattern, or into chaos. Each poem within his canon, then, must be seen in the context of the others – in context, they reveal their momentariness, that they have issued into the brief shape of their constitutive subject.

This is most explicit in that group of concrete poems Morgan has termed "emergent poems", "where everything comes out of, but at the same time mounts towards, the last line".[9] Each of these poems seems to move through numerous attempts to arrive at the complete articulacy represented by this last line, but this eludes them because they have spaces where most of their letters should be. However, words assemble, before the last line, across the spaces. So "Message Clear", with its spaces removed, reads:

Am I?/ if/ I am he,/ Hero,/ Hurt/ There and/ Here and here/ And there,/ I am rife/ in/ Sion and/ I die:/ A mere sect/ A

mere section/ of/ The life/ of/ men./ Sure, / The die/ Is set
and/ I am the surd – / At rest/ O life! / I am here:/ I act,/ I
run,/ I meet,/ I tie,/ I stand;/ I am Thoth,/ I am Ra,/ I am the
Sun/ I am the Son – / I am the erect one: if/ I am rent,/ I am
safe/ I am sent,/ I heed,/ I test./ I read/ A thread,/ A stone,/
A tread,/ A throne./ I resurrect/ a life:/ I am in life;/ I am
resurrection;/ I am the resurrection and/ I am;/ I am the resurrection and the life.[10]

To remove the spaces from the poem like this, though, destroys it,
for the spaces are as important as the letters – they are cognate with
the silences that have preoccupied modernist literature. The letters
strive for stability because, when they emerge, they always do so in
the place they occupy in the last line. The spaces, however, undermine this stability – they keep shifting in the line, so that each line
has a different shape, and its sounds and its silences (and therefore
its meanings) vary each time.

"Message Clear" can be seen as an analogue for Morgan's work
as a whole. Each line within it is a brief variant shape, a unique
pattern discovered by dismantling a traditional message and working defamiliarising variations on it. The poem represents multiple
fissurings of a traditional assurance of transcendent coherence: "it
is supposed to be a monologue spoken by Christ on the Cross",[11]
and yet the Word finds it difficult to speak His words. The words
sit with their feet hanging over a void, but they are not anxious
about this emptiness – they use it as a background for their own
expressiveness so that where previously there was a single monolithic meaning the poem discovers numerous other possibilities. So,
within Morgan's canon, individual poems can be seen as variant
shapes and unique patterns which are the product of a defamiliarising vision that transforms conventional modes of perception
and expression.

Moreover, the loss of such traditional assurances is not a source
of anxiety to Morgan. In "Message Clear" the splinters from the
Christian message build tentative other messages ("I am the surd/
. . .I am Thoth,/ I am Ra,/ I am the Sun"). So everywhere in his
poetry he responds optimistically and playfully to the modern as
a fascinating challenge – another reason that his poetry is various
is because it responds to a sense of its period as quickly changing
with a quick-change art. Morgan's emphasis is on the human capacity to cope with change, and to create

new ways of overcoming even very great disasters. . .This is part
of our species and I don't think it's entirely irrational that one
can have a hopeful or even a *very* hopeful long-term view of the
possibilities of the human race. I think it's because we're so flexible.
The species that died out were very rigid. The great Saurians
were very impressive creatures but they hadn't the kind of flexibility to master changes in the environment that man has.

(*Interview*, 22)

There is a continual fascination in Morgan's work with human
flexibility and the endlessly inventive and diverse behaviour that
results from it. In responding to this his poetry has itself needed to
be extremely flexible, needed to evolve forms and techniques to
solve diverse poetic problems. In particular, Morgan has been consistently concerned to give poetic representation to technological
change, as he himself said in his essay, "A Glimpse of Petavius":

What I want to express is concern about the very incomplete way
in which poetry since the nineteenth century has reacted to
changes in society and in material surroundings. It is because
these changes have been so great that I am made conscious of
this strange communicative gap. . .between poetry and life. Our
poetry needs greater humanity; but it must be the humanity of
man within his whole environment: not just the drop of dew, the
rose, the lock of hair, but the orbiting rocket in Anselm Hollo,
the lobotomy in Allen Ginsberg, the lunar mountains in Hugh
MacDiarmid.

(*Essays*, 15)

So Morgan ranges himself against those poets (Eliot, Yeats, Stevens,
Muir) who, explicitly or implicitly, condemn technology and mostly
exclude it from their work, and alongside those (MacDiarmid,
Mayakovsky, Voznesensky) who, with some qualifications, accept it
and explore its human implications.[12] This concern is the starting-
point for most of Morgan's work and his variousness is best understood when viewed from this perspective. Having set out this
programme for himself Morgan necessarily evolved a poetic premised upon change in order to evoke a world which is "continually
changing and changing fast" (*Interview*, 4) and it is in this continuing exploration of change that his paradoxical consistency lies. Instead of staking out a carefully bounded poetic territory (like Eliot,

Yeats, Stevens and Muir) Morgan has set out to be inclusive and to reflect as much of twentieth-century change as he can manage, and his variousness arises largely from the changeableness of what he reflects.

In describing the poetry of Voznesensky, with whom he obviously feels affinities and whom he has translated, Morgan could be describing the consequences of this inclusiveness for his own work. Having suggested that a "poetry which wants meaningfully to interlock with this age must be prepared to be vulnerable, fluid, various, adventurous and searching" (*Essays*, 72) Morgan goes on to discuss the theme of "metamorphosis" in Voznesensky's work and to discern in it "three aspects":

> It reflects the quite real blurring, overlap, interchange, and evolution of forms which fast travel, cinema and television, modern art, and newspaper and advertising techniques have made a familiar part of experience; it has, in its Russian context, a quasi-Aesopian function in that without lifting the blunt instrument of allegory it helps to recommend disavowal of the monolithic; and perhaps most important, it tries to resurrect the creative imagination through a development of that linguistic *ostranenie* ("dislodgement", "alienation", "making strange") which the Russian formalist critics of the 1920s saw as central to poetic vigour.
>
> (*Essays*, 73)

Much can be revealed about Morgan's work if it is examined from the point of view of the three aspects of metamorphosis which he identifies in Voznesensky, and I shall do this later. However, if Morgan's range is to be fully represented it is important to start with a qualification, for he has written a number of love poems, in particular, which are designedly traditional, in the sense that they suggest that some experiences have only been superficially altered by taking place in the twentieth century. "When You Go" (184), "Strawberries" (184–185), "One Cigarette" (186), "The Picnic" (186–187) and "Stanzas" (507–511) draw their strength from directness and simplicity; stylistically they have the "daring baldness and starkness" that Morgan praises in the Wordsworth of *Lyrical Ballads* (*Essays*, 133). They suggest that love, even now, can sequester itself from circumambient experience – with Morgan's hectic canon in the offing all around them, these poems offer a surprising harbour, an almost quaint calm. Against the movement which Morgan insists on everywhere else – except, for quite different reasons, in "Instamatic Poems" (217–224) – these poems present a stasis which suggests the feeling of unreality that love can cause. "One Cigarette" is consciously atavistic, for though, as R.S. Edgecombe has pointed out, its "conventional Petrarchan statements about burning love are quietly, unforcedly modernised", nonetheless they retain their "paradoxicality and intensity"[13]. Moreover, the poem finally uses its imagery of burning, not to suggest that love consumes, but to suggest that the departed lover's presence lingers in a cigarette that is left behind:

> As the last spire
> trembles up, a sudden draught
> blows it winding into my face.
> Is it smell, is it taste?
> You are here again, and I am drunk on your tobacco lips.
> Out with the light.
> Let the smoke lie back in the dark.
> Till I hear the very ash
> sigh down among the flowers of brass
> I'll breathe, and long past midnight, your last kiss.

"The Unspoken" (182–183) is a more restless love poem than the others and appears to concern itself, like Morgan's non-lyric poetry, with change ("as you shifted in my arms/ it was the sea changing the shingle that changes it/ as if for ever"). However, it is personal, not social change, which is being described here, and this is emphasised by references earlier in the poem to personal memory, which are almost unique in Morgan's work.[14] By referring to the Second World War and to space exploration, this poem explicitly places love in a twentieth century context but it does this in order to emphasise continuity rather than change – to insist that the underlying experience is the same, to insist that it is telling "a story as old as war or man". Similarly, although "Floating Off to Timor" (233–234) and "In Glasgow" (234–235) employ a more tricksy style than the other love poems they do so to evoke the immemorial power of love to be both playful and transcendent.

These poems show that Morgan's statement "our poetry needs greater humanity" is not a tetchy concession that precedes his real point, but reflects a genuine belief that the work of twentieth-century poetry should be to explore the interaction between human sensibility and its changing environment – that the real point is in the interaction. So, the only reservation that Morgan expresses about MacDiarmid – who is otherwise an important model for him as a modernist concerned to write about both Scotland and science – is his lack of human warmth:

> Hardly ever, in any poem, do you get a sense of a man who is committed emotionally to something other than ideas, words or landscapes. The beautiful and terrible bonds that are not geological but between individual persons, bonds of love or friendship, of desire, misery, doubt, or forgiveness – these are strikingly absent. This is the greatest lack in MacDiarmid's poetry.
>
> (*Essays*, 220)

It is this interaction, therefore, that is in evidence even in Morgan's science fiction poems, which might have been his least human writings. As Robin Hamilton has pointed out, of "In Sobieski's Shield" (196–198):

> it is not finally the alienness of the planet to which the refugees from a destroyed earth have fled, or the physical changes which they undergo as a result of their journey. . .but the traces, inter- ferences, memories of earth, though of another earth than theirs, which "really" change them.[15]

This poem's hypothesis is of a kind of technology that treats human material in the most radical possible way – dismantling it atom by atom, despatching the atoms to a distant planet and reassembling them. In the end, however, this process emphasises the resilience of the human in surviving even this, it demonstrates how human beings can draw strength by transforming change itself into renewal. "In Sobieski's Shield" refers twice to a "second life", an idea that can be glossed by reference to the poem of that name:

> Is it true that we come alive
> not once, but many times?
> We are drawn back to the image
> of the seed in darkness, or the greying skin
> of the snake that hides a shining one
>
> (180)

"In Sobieski's Shield" shows how this can be achieved against terrible odds, and how even shock and pain can become ways of seeing ourselves from a new perspective and so defamiliarising and thereby reaffirming ourselves. So the speaker carries with him a race memory of the First World War and finds a tattoo from a dead soldier on his arm. There is human continuity in this but there is also change. The memory is altered by the radically different context in which it interferes; the tattoo, which is seen in Flanders as a symbol of tenuous hope – "a heart still held above the despair of the mud" – becomes a much more substantial symbol of hope in Sobieski's Shield – "my god the heart on my arm my second birth mark".


This, then, is the most accurate background against which to see Morgan's treatment of metamorphosis, of which the first aspect is "the quite real blurring, overlap, interchange, and evolution of forms which fast travel, cinema and television, modern art, and newspaper and advertising techniques have made a familiar part of experience" (*Essays*, 73). His interest is not in technological hardware *per se* but in its consequences for perception and in its social implications – so, while "From the Video Box" (480–500) takes delight in satellite TV and scratch video, and in some inventions by Morgan himself – "wristwatch television", "portable chameleon televisions" – it is more concerned to explore the way that TV is perceived and responded to. Here, "blurring, overlap, interchange and evolution" are very much in evidence as dramatic monologue, and the flights of subjectivity that are associated with it, encounters the astonishing variety and radical instability of television imagery. First of all Morgan manages, through the standard devices of dramatic monologue, to evoke a series of different personalities – a viewer who is unhappy, one who is colour-blind, one who has a fondness for italicised verbal preciosities and who has lost her cat, a flasher, a bigot, a hamster-owning, knife-toting psychopath, and so on. The range here insists that audience reception of television imagery is more important than the imagery itself. Having established this, however, "From the Video Box" does display the extent to which television and video have been forces for change, how they have shown that the human figure and its environment can be transformed into imagery and then dissolved, sliced up and spliced together, intercut, remixed and montaged.

It is with the points at which television and subjectivity meet that the sequence is most concerned – those points where the influence is mutual. One viewer, who is unhappy, thinks that in "that flurry of switched images" can be distinguished a sudden source of possible hope, a patch of "eggshell blue, a sky blue, blue/ of an innocent eye, not harsh or icy". Another speaks indignantly of waiting for an old film and finding instead that the screen had started bleeding, and protests "I want a clean dry screen from now on/ Let them bleed elsewhere, whoever they are". Another declares that, being colour-blind, he or she could identify a completely different message in a conventional film from the one available to normal eyes, an entirely different figure in the TV carpet. Another thinks that she saw her drowned son alive on television in a "split-second flash":

> It came in a blizzard of images,
> a speeded mosaic of change
> in the Americas, I watched
> half bored, irritated
> by the strident music, ready
> to switch channels – then!
> – not in his seaman's cloth
> but a camouflage jacket,
> looking straight at the camera,
> his fist in a revolutionary salute,
> a letter sticking from his pocket
> with writing I saw as mine. . .
>     oh images, images,
> corners of the world seen
> out of the corner of an eye –
> subversive, subliminal –
> where have you taken my son
> into your terrible machine
> and why have you peeled off
> my grief like a decal
> and left me a nobody,
> staring out to sea?

The second aspect of metamorphosis – its recommendation of the "disavowal of the monolithic" – is most evident in the way that Morgan's poems dismantle perception and representation, and so reveal that other perspectives exist alongside familiar ones. So

"Cinquevalli" (432–434) keeps shifting its angle of vision in order to insist that the conjuring up of historical figures is necessarily a restless activity and always a problematic one. Each stanza starts with the name Cinquevalli so that it appears to be a fresh beginning each time, and so that he is approached from several different perspectives – this produces an effect like the interpenetration of planes in a futurist painting. The famous juggler is repeatedly divided by these stanzas into different phases of his life, different activities and different poses, and within each stanza he is sometimes further divided – in the third he is described as "half faun, half military man" and as "half reluctant, half truculent,/ half handsome, half absurd"; in the second – through seesawing repetitions and diminishing line-lengths – the movements involved in his juggling are broken down into their constituent parts in a way reminiscent of Muybridge's photographs:

> . . .He throws it
> from hand to hand, always different,
> always the same, always
> different, always the
> same.

Repetition itself is analysed here and shown to contain variations:

> Despite the appearance of monotony we are shown that each single movement exists in its own right. The ball will never move through exactly the same trajectory twice, the speed at which it is thrown will always vary, and the position of the hands cannot be exactly repeated from one action to the next.[16]

Repetitions, variations, transformations, and the artistry in Cinquevalli that effects them, suggest the analogy between the juggler and the poet; the relationship between the technique of the poem and the techniques of its hero draws attention self-reflexively to the pyrotechnic artifice in both. This effect is especially marked in the third stanza where the poet introduces himself in the present looking at a photographic representation of the juggler – "Cinquevalli in sepia/ looks at me from an old postcard: bundle of enigmas." In this way the poem steps out of its historical frame to reveal its artificiality. Moreover, in "recreating" Cinquevalli, the poem shows him in the process of creating himself: it starts with the terrible fall from a trapeze which he miraculously survives and which leads to his second life as a conjurer; in this way it re-enacts a career that defies the monolithic by its ability to surprise and to perform the apparently impossible. Through this process Cinquevalli becomes a paradigm of human flexibility and aesthetic resourcefulness. One of his tricks – which involves juggling with three objects – becomes a wildly hyperbolic representation of the creation of a self-image:

> The last time round, the bowler
> flies to his head, the stick sticks in his hand,
> the cigar jumps into his mouth, the coin
> lands on his foot – ah, but
> is kicked into his eye
> and held there as the miraculous monocle
> without which the portrait would be incomplete.

Given such artistry both juggler and poet can transform their material and so radically alter the way their audiences see themselves and their experience; though saddened by what he hears about "the shells whining/ at Passchendaele"

> Cinquevalli tosses up a plate of soup
> and twirls it on his forefinger; not a drop spills.
> He laughs, and well may he laugh
> who can do that. The astonished table
> breathe again, laugh too, think the world
> a spinning thing that spills, for a moment, no drop.

By contrast with the use, in "Cinquevalli", of multiple perspectives, "Instamatic Poems" employ a photographic analogy that freezes their subject-matter (stories taken from newspapers) in a single action viewed from a single angle. In keeping with this deliberate reductiveness they employ, for the most part, a starkly flat and unfigurative language – a strategy which is thrown into even sharper relief if Morgan's linguistic richness elsewhere is considered – for example, the Hopkins-like verbal tumult of the early "The Cape of Good Hope" (61–75) and the exuberantly ludic porno-montages of "Soho" (250–251). Like all minimalist art, however, "Instamatic Poems" deploy simplicity to foreground representation; this is all the more important because they use one form of representation (poetry) to represent another (reportage) and they do this by employing an analogy to yet another medium (photography).

The effect is increased because poetry arouses expectations of aesthetic elaborateness and journalism of unaesthetic directness. The unsettling effect of "Instamatic Poems" comes from the way that the poetic structure jars against the journalistic, with a consequent "blurring, overlap, interchange" (*Essays*, 73). Its minimalism appears to affirm journalistic directness but ends up calling it into question – for the paradox of minimalist art is that its lack of expressive and illusory elements draws attention to expressiveness and illusion. So, in the first four lines of "Glasgow 5 March 1971" (217) – which describes a gang of robbers who have broken a shop window by pushing two people through it – the poetic and the journalistic have an unresolved dialogue with each other:

> With a ragged diamond
> of shattered plate-glass
> a young man and his girl
> are falling backwards into a shop-window.

The first line here is poetic – the isolation of the unusual collocation "ragged diamond" draws attention to the poem's lineation, because the phrase is inexplicable until the second line; this also serves to heighten suspense. This phrase is an oxymoron with at least three paradoxical associations: imprecise versus precise, poor versus rich, and soft versus hard. The line also serves a proleptic function through these associations – poverty and wealth are certainly relevant associations in the context of a robbery; diamonds may well be one of the objects in the shop-window; and softness versus hardness are associations that are taken up later in the poem, for instance in

> The young man's face
> is bristling with fragments of glass
> and the girl's leg has caught
> on the broken window

By contrast, there is nothing in lines 2 to 4 that might not be found in a newspaper report. However, the poetic context created by the first line, and the structure in which they are placed, surprises new meanings in them – they are shown, not simply to reflect the world, but to structure and thereby transform it. The monolithic singleness of meaning they apparently convey is fissured by their slow-motion dismantling by poetic lineation and rhythm.

Such effects are increased because "Instamatic Poems" everywhere convey a feeling of displacement through the way they have been removed from their familiar institutional context (shifted from a newspaper into a poetry book). In this way the sequence defamiliarises journalism and so can be said, as well as illustrating the second aspect of metamorphosis, to illustrate the third aspect which

> tries to resurrect the creative imagination through a development of that linguistic *ostranenie* ("dislodgement", "alienation", "making strange") which the Russian formalist critics of the 1920s saw as central to poetic vigour.
>
> (*Essays*, 73)

Moreover, it is not merely journalism which is defamiliarised in the sequence. By using the instamatic analogy to freeze significant moments and to reduce explicit comment to a minimum, the sequence defamiliarises human behaviour itself. Here, too, monolithic assumptions are undermined, especially since the sequence dwells upon the startlingly unexpected and the bizarre, to which the dead-pan minimalist style is particularly suited. Most conspicuously, there are a number of poems in the sequence which mimic photographs that Roland Barthes[17] would call "traumatic" – "fires, shipwrecks, catastrophes, violent deaths, all captured from 'life as lived'" (30–31) and which for this reason are the least connoted and the least institutional of photographs; such Barthes says:

> is the photograph about which there is nothing to say; the shock-photo is by structure insignificant: no value, no knowledge, at the limit no verbal categorization can have a hold on the process instituting the signification. One could imagine a kind of law: the more direct the trauma, the more difficult is connotation...Why? Doubtless because photographic connotation, like every well structured signification, is an institutional activity; in relation to society overall, its function is to integrate man, to reassure him.
>
> (31)

So while the sequence as a whole draws attention to poetry and journalism as institutions and as structures of significance, there are poems within it that suggest that there are experiences so shocking that they refuse to be structured, that remain anxious outsiders. It is appropriate that these are the most minimal poems of all, for their content is simultaneously irreducible and unchangeable; it offers extreme resistance to aesthetic transformation and therefore does as little as possible to "integrate man, to reassure him":

> A grey-haired man half-runs,
> carrying his white-haired mother on his back
> along a dusty road from East Pakistan.
> She is a hundred years old.
> What they own
> fills a knotted cloth at his hip.
> Even to them
> the hands of the dying are stretched out
> from both sides of the road.
>
> (224)

The instamatic presentation of these shocking moments provides a series of jolts to conventional ways of seeing and causes a disoriented revision of stereotypical thinking.

This concept of *ostranenie* is the most important key to Morgan's work. In pursuit of it he has consistently looked for the unexpected point of entry into his subject-matter; he has juxtaposed jarring voices and points of view on the same theme; he has destabilised the poetry of place – and undermined any possibility of his being defined as a "Glasgow poet" – by self-consciously introducing exotic places (notably the Middle and Far East) and other planets into his poetry; and he has drawn attention to poetic artifice by juggling self-reflexively with language and by employing such a vast range of forms that poetic form itself is called into question.

One device, in particular, has been recurrent – the use of unfamiliar perspectives, or, occasionally, the introduction of new perspectives that conflict with one already established. Dramatic monologue is a favourite form for Morgan and he has used it to suggest overlapping voices that half substantiate and half subvert each other, providing a picture that is fuller but at the same time more questionable. "Stobhill" (284–288) allows five speakers ("The Doctor", "The Boilerman", "The Mother", "The Father" and "The Porter") to tell their sides of a story surrounding an abortion. "The Whittrick" (79–116) is a series of eight dialogues that explore the idea of a

creative energy that is enormously stimulating and at the same
time terribly dangerous.

Most interesting, however, is Morgan's use of non-human points
of view (animals, aliens, mythical creatures, computers etc.) on
human experience. Of these the Loch Ness Monster's is the most
humorous – the human dismays him and his "song" is more like an
expletive dilated:

> Splgraw fok fok splgrafhatchgabrlgabrl fok splfok
> Zgra kra gka fok!
>
> (248)

"Interferences" (253–257) explores the idea of an alien's vision of
history, where the telling of each story is subtly wrong-footed by a
small linguistic slip, so that an otherness is hinted at both in the
story and in its narrator; this is a scene between Joseph and Mary:

> "it was a Roman soldier"
> he cried, his fist
>
> "it was our neighbour"
> pounded the table
>
> "it was a visitor"
> dropped wearily
>
> and she took his hand
> placed it on her womb
>
> "I am your virgian bride"
> with a smile worlds away
>
> (254)

"An Alphabet of Goddesses" (464–477) also retells familiar stories,
wittily modernising the Greek deities. This time, however, it is not
just the stories that are defamiliarised; the sequence dwells especially on sexuality in a number of its forms and shows how fantasy,
desire, jealousy, hatred and fear can transform those who experience it. Metamorphosis takes a traditional mythical form here but
is employed analogically so that the absurd ambitiousness of sexual
fantasy is celebrated by being given the hyperbolic expression it

seems to want. Rhea, for instance, describes what it was like when she and Zeus were snakes copulating – "the slow travelling ripple" that "catches every inch of you in its squeeze/ but in succession, severally, subtly" (473) – but even this is not enough for her awed interlocutor whose taste is for transcendence:

> . . .He must have coursed you
> like a spaceship, you are both such titans.
> You must have tangled like arms of nebulas,
> or two galaxies passing through each other,
> signals for some millenial dish.
>
> (473)

Characteristically for Morgan, though, the sequence has a vivid contemporary edge; some of its heroines resemble "screen goddesses" of the video age and as such are observed with sardonic enjoyment. Vixen is a sadist, a dream turned into a nightmare, who ties her victim to a tree and "loosens her skirt, draws his blood steadily" until he "stains the ground red and white together" (475). Circe is like a faded, slightly louche performer, who has lost most of her magic, but still relives her former glories:

> . . .pulls on her black stockings, right up,
> and screeches as she scrapes a nail
> along the nylon like a welder's spark,
> and pins on her old sphinx headdress from Cairo
> with its mortal colours, immortal desires.
>
> (465)

Edwin Morgan uses a bewildering variety of styles and techniques – however, this variousness is itself best understood by reference to the most crucial effect his poetry creates, that of "ostranenie" or estrangement. Terry Eagleton provides a useful definition of what this meant to formalist critics like Viktor Shklovsky:

Under the pressure of literary devices, ordinary language was intensified, condensed, twisted, telescoped, drawn out, turned on its head. It was language "made strange"; and because of this estrangement, the everyday world was also suddenly made unfamiliar. In the routines of everyday speech, our perceptions of and responses to reality become stale, blunted, or, as the Formalists would say, "automatized". Literature, by forcing us into a dramatic awareness of language, refreshes these habitual responses and renders objects more "perceptible". By having to grapple with language in a more strenuous, self-conscious way than usual, the world which that language contains is vividly renewed.[18]

However, what Eagleton goes on to say about this is even more interesting in its implications for Edwin Morgan:

The Formalists, then, saw literary languages as a set of deviations from a norm, a kind of linguistic violence: literature is a "special" kind of language, in contrast to the "ordinary" language we commonly use. But to spot a deviation implies being able to identify the norm from which it swerves. It is not that the Russian Formalists did not realize all this. They recognised that norms and deviations shifted around from one social or historical context to another – that "poetry" in this sense depends on where you happen to be standing at the time.

(4–5)

What is clear above all about Morgan's context is that the norm that had been established was above all poetic rather than social. Andrew Crozier describes, with succinctness and cogency, how this norm was established and sustained:

Since 1945 the major poetic controversies, through which current poetic concerns have received their most effective public exposure, occurred within the decade bracketed by the publication of the first *New Lines* anthology and the revised edition of *The New Poetry*. By and large our sense of the situation of poetry today is conditioned by the arguments of 1956–1966. The extent to which those arguments still determine our sense of poetic achievement since the war underscores the suggestion that, for all the differences and disagreements implied by those arguments, certain basic, undeclared – even unrecognised – agreements bound the controversialists together. Positions taken up on behalf of the Movement had the power and flexibility to absorb and merge with those of its successors; the non-partisan, individualist strategies of Movement poets enabled them, when the time came, to transcend their collective Movement in the mid-fifties.[19]

What Crozier is indicating here is the extent to which the Movement made itself appear the natural party of poetic government – so natural that it ceased even to seem "poetic". It achieved this, partly, by writing in a thoroughly anti-estrangement way: by employing language, for the most part, in as "ordinary" a style as possible, by avoiding the self-consciously poetic in which language is "intensified, condensed, twisted" etc. Behind its literary practices there lay an ideology of the familiar – a championing of Englishness, a mistrust of the exotic, a contempt for the theoretical and abstract. Much of its literary effort was expended in the construction of realistic slices of life which reassured rather than unsettled, which were designed to create such a sense of agreement between poet and reader that they hardly seemed constructions at all.

This was a dominant poetic, then, with all the appearance of "ordinary language" itself and which seemed a social as much as an aesthetic norm. It is as a deviation from this insidiously "natural" set of assumptions that Morgan's defamiliarising variety is most vividly understood. Morgan's emphasis on the metamorphic – on "blurring, overlap, interchange, and evolution of forms" (*Essays*, 73) – effectively calls into question the Movement's insistent attempts to impose stability. His restless experimentation with poetic form and incorporation of diverse generic elements everywhere interrogates the security of human knowledge in a way that contrasts starkly with the Movement's harping on the mundane and the thoroughly and collectively understood. And, perhaps most radically, his deconstruction of linguistic norms and his deployment of various kinds of non-realism – especially of science fiction – raise acute ontological questions which contrast with the Movement's tendency, as Andrew Crozier puts it, to dwell on an "authoritative self" (229). The most memorable example of this is how "In Sobieski's Shield" literally deconstructs the self – dismantling the body atom by atom, dispatching the atoms to a distant planet and reassembling them. But this collapsible view of the self is implicit throughout Morgan's work and, alongside his interest in estrangement, is perhaps the most crucial element he shares in common with the other poets in this section of the book.

# 9

# Christopher Middleton: Journeys Broken at the Threshold

Although he is English by birth and upbringing – born in Truro in 1926, educated at Felsted School in Essex, and at Oxford – Christopher Middleton has always been an outsider in contemporary British poetry. The fact that he has been, since 1966, a professor of Germanic Languages and Literature at the University of Texas is a symptom of this status rather than a cause – though it has also, of course, contributed to the effect by introducing Texan landscape and American idioms into his poetry. Even before this move his view of poetry was at odds with the English mainstream – in an interview in *The London Magazine* in 1964 he complained that "the experiences which most English poets seem to be writing about don't seem to be experiences which matter very much, even to them."[1]

On the other hand, Middleton is aware of his own Englishness, and seems to understand it all the more clearly through his detachment from it. So he suggests that his poem "The Child at the Piano"[2] is "a product of the educated English upper-middle class of today":

Notice the liberalism of "on both white and black notes", notice the "green air" which "lets us be", notice the introversions and mythological allusions, the gentility, the sense of music, too, – these could never have applied in a Jamaican shack, or in a Stepney amusement arcade, or in the plains around old Novapavlovka.[3]

This is astute, and suggests that Middleton was feeling some impatience in 1964/5 with the extent to which his experience had been culturally circumscribed. This is confirmed by the question he asks earlier on the same page: "Why should an English poem today about the terrible injustice and misery of the world be almost unthinkable?" At the time he gave this talk Middleton seems to have been feeling that his Englishness was a creative problem, one of the

151

sources of his creative difficulties: "My poems aren't what I'd like to be able to write. They are what I've been able to write so far, with much time spent in fumbling and confusion" (222). This statement draws attention to an important conflict in Middleton between aspiration and scepticism. Throughout his career he has formulated theories about how a poet should ideally write but has also been aware that what actually gets written is different. In this early remark he is largely expressing a sense of personal inadequacy – and it should be remembered that Middleton disowned his first two volumes *Poems* and *Nocturne in Eden*[4]. This conflict develops more complexity later in his career, moroever, when its influence can be discerned in an aspiration in his poems towards shamanic utterance constantly frustrated by modernist scepticism.

In this respect the best analogue for his career is in the journeys described in his volume of prose poems *Pataxanadu*[5] where he refers to "some kind of imaginary goal for broken, dislocated or frustrated journeys" (8). Middleton constantly gives the impression of setting off self-consciously with a pre-determined goal in mind, then finding this frustrated. However, this is not a source of failure, but of paradoxical success. Many of his poems enact this process and thereby are like "journeys. . .[that] penetrate alternative universes that are ingrained in this one" (8).

In 1964/5 Middleton's goal seems to have been to write political poems – hence the remark about "terrible injustice". At this period he made several remarks of this kind which have been siezed on and extrapolated by Stan Smith in his reading of Middleton[6]. However, when seen in the context of the priority he gave it in the mid-sixties, his political goal has to be seen as a broken journey – although a fruitful one because there is an important (if subsidiary) political element in his work.

When read together "The Child at the Piano" and his comments on it reveal the conflict between his aspirations and his scepticism. It is perhaps significant that Middleton chose this poem on which to focus his concern about being English and upper-middle class, for it can be read, on one level, as a reflection on his own expressive anxieties. The poem's questioning of the boundary between music and noise is a modernist questioning of form, of how raw material gets transformed into art:

> Handfuls of notes, all happening at once,
> her tunes do not occur; on their backs,

round they whizz like stunned wasps; contour
would crush that kind of mass.

This chaotic expression suggests possibilities which are frustrated:
if genuine art breaks new ground, opens up alternative landscapes,
the child at the piano can only hint at other places:

> Telescoping flukes and faults, their
> tenuous terrain dislocates
> no spheres I know of.

> (21)

"Telescoping" offers the hope that distances will be brought near,
but turns out to refer mainly to happy accidents sliding into mistakes;
the terrain is "tenuous", the listener is not so much "moved" as
baffled. The child's playing is too simply a form of self-expression to
be genuine art – it is too simply the equivalent of her other activities, like swinging from a tree: "Boughs of sound swoop through
the room,/ happily, for her to swing from." It is interesting, then,
that Middleton's comments on the poem draw attention to the
effects of his own sensibility in making it the kind of poem it is –
as though his own activity as poet had been too like that of the
child as pianist.

Of course this is too hard on Middleton and the poem because
"The Child at the Piano" incorporates the anxiety he expresses about
it – it reflects its own difficulties in transcending the accidents of
time and place. What makes it interesting is that it is English and
upper-middle class but also dissatisfied with being so circumscribed.
The poet thinks, as Middleton himself points out, of "Orpheus in
the underworld, making the stones dance" but the child's playing
"beckons no hell boulder up" (*Bolshevism*, 221). The poem contains
a Rilkean aspiration which the English subject-matter frustrates.

Middleton's status as an outsider, then, was a cause of his self-
exile, rather than a result of it. His sensibility rebelled against itself
as well as the mainstream of British poetry: in 1964 he was finding
both too genteel and it is clear that in leaving Britain he was simultaneously choosing a way of writing and a way of life, that the two
were inextricably linked for him. So, in a later essay, "For Marton,
Erwin, and Miklos"[7] he speaks of his lack of sympathy with the
English tradition as compared with what he calls the "archipelagic
structures" of poems by Apollinaire, Tzara, Eliot and Pound:

> a poetry balanced over gulfs of silence, a poetry of surprises, of enigmas, scrutiny followed by vertiginous distance, a poetry of broken uncertain surfaces, of foregrounded hinterlands.
>
> (48)

Middleton is tentative here, but he implies that his creative life has involved the discovery that, despite his English background, it was an unEnglish poetic which provided the most accurate structures for expressing his subject-matter:

> If I prefer the archipelagic zigzag to the sturdy continuous "prose tradition" of English, it is because the latter has been made, somehow, inaccessible to me by experiences of my own, which are not American experiences. I have battled, often tongue-tied, with my own ambivalences and uncertainties. The multiple "ego" can easily become a mass of variables which jam the line of perception.
>
> (48)

Middleton is characteristically unspecific about what these experiences are – he is a rigorously impersonal poet. However, his feelings of affinity with a poetic tradition quite different from that of his homeland have been crucial. For one thing it has helped to make him a brilliant translator of 19th and 20th century German literature, especially poetry. But most importantly for his own writing, the struggle that resulted was not simply a phase he passed through in acquiring a "voice" but something that has marked his whole poetic career – it is this that largely accounts for his stylistic restlessness, his endless experimenting, and it is not surprising that the work that has appeared has done so against a background of being "often tongue-tied". It also largely accounts for the sense in his writings of "ambivalences", "uncertainties" and the "multiple 'ego'".

In absorbing this unEnglish tradition and adapting it for his own ends, Middleton was remaking himself – he was involved in a process that was simultaneously poetic and psychological, which was similar to the one he describes Eliot and Pound submitting themselves to:

> I think the Eliot/Pound recognition of a technical problem was due partly to the fact that they were Americans colliding with a European culture which they wanted to assimilate; this was an

existential predicament for them. . .and there can be no technical problem unless it is very closely associated with the way one knows one's own mind to be working.

("Conversations", 79)

Middleton's predicament was that of an Englishman colliding with the radical modernist aesthetic of Germany, France and America. For him, as for Eliot and Pound, the choice of a poetic technique was an existential one for it also involved choosing one view of experience as opposed to another and this had implications for his way of life. The "archipelagic zigzag" and "the sturdy continuous 'prose tradition'" presuppose different views of the world. In rejecting English realism Middleton was rejecting a ready-made and firmly rooted system of coherence based upon an assumed consensus, and opting for fragmentariness, rootlessness and doubt.

The "existential predicament" faced by Eliot, Pound and Middleton is not merely a personal matter, but an important feature of the modernist sensibility. What it involves is not simply a series of encounters with alien cultures but a much more radical sense that it has become impossible ever to feel culturally "at home", a metaphysical sense that the self has become uprooted, that its origins have been lost, a sense most accurately characterised in the Heideggerian concept of "thrownness":

> This characteristic of Dasein's Being – this "that it is" – is veiled in its "whence" and "whither", yet disclosed in itself all the more unveiledly; we call it the "thrownness" of this entity into its "there". . .The expression "thrownness" is meant to suggest the *facticity of its being delivered over*[8].

This concept, then, defines the way that the self feels its presence in the world to have been torn out of context, that this presence is too simply an unexplained fact. One consequence of this which has been crucial for modernists is the feeling that the world is bafflingly foreign, so that we can have, in Eliot's words, "such a vision of the street/ As the street hardly understands"[9]. Heidegger is especially relevant to Middleton because he has been so deeply influenced by the tradition out of which Heidegger emerged, and he describes his own poetic in Heideggerian terms when he refers to his "compulsive themes of being and not-being, here and there, this and 'the other'" (*Kingfisher*, 46).

In "Moon Climbing", the moon is described in very much a "thrown" way;

> All night moon you are brought in
> To keep the empty space away
>
> A present image
> A present image washed clean by distance
> To keep the empty space away

The phrase "brought in" is similar to Heidegger's "delivered over" – in both the non-existence of the Agent that performs the action is part of the point. The moon appears vulnerable and "thrown" because it is "present" in the midst of so much absence. Even its presence is ambiguous because it is an "image" rather than an object, and as an image it carries with it symbolic associations of change-ableness. Moreover, through its roundness it is linked to the image of wrens that "Circle the house all day pecking for insects" and so envelop the house in the nothingness (the "nought") the poet fears ("Nine times circling the house I shelter in/ But saying *I* am seized by what I shelter from"). So what the wrens do on a small scale – by revealing that the house, as an inadequate shelter, cannot function as "home" – the moon reveals on a large scale, that we do not feel at home in the world, "This O is here for homeless homeliness".

In Middleton's prose poem "The Image" (262–263) "thrownness" is joined by "fallenness". These Heideggerian concepts are closely linked, but the metaphor of place that lies behind "thrownness" is exchanged in "fallenness" for the metaphor of time. Where "thrownness" evokes a shipwrecked "here", "fallenness" evokes an attenuated "now":

> Dasein has, in the first instance, fallen away [abgefallen] from itself as an authentic potentiality for Being its Self, and has fallen into the "world". "Fallenness" into the 'world' means an absorp-tion in Being-with-one-another, in so far as the latter is guided by idle talk, curiosity and ambiguity.
>
> (*Heidegger*, 220)

"The Image" describes a journey which takes its participants back to where they started – except that this starting-point is now unrec-ognisable. Life-as-journey associations are employed so that the baffled loss of purpose, and the disorientation experienced by the travellers, express an existential bewilderment – they are thrown into an environment that ought to be familiar to them but is shockingly foreign:

> they had arrived at the exact same spot, this was where they'd begun. There were no signs of the four rivers, no views of the mountain. As for the temperate climate some of the old hands had spoken of, now there came over them a blizzard, biting cold, now the withering oven heat of the desert.

Similarly, they have "fallen away" from their original potential:

> When they finally got around to where they had begun, it wasn't there any more. This was because they'd strung it out behind them. What had been a chariot of fire had become a rickety old wagon. Losing its parts as it bumped along. . .it had eventually, without anyone noticing when it happened, disconnected itself, then vanished into thin air.

In "The Image", as in many of his prose poems, Middleton calls upon the resources of myth in order to express an aspect of the human condition with primordial clarity. That it should be primordial is important to him – he is drawn to the aetiological element in myth because it claims to penetrate to the authentic origins of human experience. In "The Image" this is especially appropriate because, as myth, it attempts to commemorate how these origins were lost, how "being-in-the-world" or "Dasein" fell away from its potential.

The concern with lost origins is crucial in Middleton's work – it is an assumption underlying much of his poetry and is explored in some detail in his expository prose. This is something he shares with Heidegger, but its roots go further back in German philosophy:

> There is, . . .underlying Heidegger's analysis, an implicit historical account which his terminology of "fallenness", "thrownness" etc. indicated – namely of a historically primitive state of innocence, a golden age when relations between people, as of people to things, were genuine and whole. To what extent Heidegger is Hegelian, in believing that the primitive wholeness was characterized by lack of self-consciousness, is something I shall not speculate about.[10]

This is an assumption, generally, behind much modernist thinking – most obviously in Eliot's postulating of a period before "dissociation of sensibility" set in, but implicit recurrently. The use of a "palimpsestic" structure, for instance, – where one text is, as it were, written on top of others[11], as in *The Waste Land* and *Ulysses* – often suggests a hope in the continued presence, however "fallen", of the past, and that the surface of the present can be penetrated to unearth below it an original time of existential authenticity.

A hope of this kind is one of the basic motives of Middleton's writing:

> without being escapist, a writer can give his reader a taste of the life that is not politicized. . .The unmediated life, open and colourful, of the lost world we long to rediscover, a world such as is given to us in some music, our world as we dream it might have been long before our time.
>
> (*Bolshevism*, 156)

Middleton hopes that the role of the poet can be analagous to that of the shaman – that poetry can put its writers and readers magically in touch with spiritual origins that have been obscured or lost. In his "Introduction" to *Bolshevism in Art* he speaks of an "interanimation. . .between sound and meaning" (12) in poetry which he suggests

> marks a survival of a tradition of the sacred word, of the word which initiates being. This tradition empowered the poet (as shaman, in certain social contexts) to make utterances from that "centre" in which what we call soul and world are felt to be magically homogenous. . .A poem with this kind of magical centredness transmits, live, older or perennial forms of linguistic behaviour into a present in which people have become. . .dumbfounded by the blank obstruction of the world, by all the clichés, and by the arbitrary nature of the sign.
>
> (13)

In a later essay, "Reflections on a Viking Prow" (283–302) Middleton prefers to use the figure of the pre-industrial artisan as his analogue for the poet – but rather than take this as a shift from his belief in the poet as shaman it is more accurate to let it more fully explain that analogy. What Middleton stresses in both shaman and artisan is a social function which involves communication between people, between people and the material world, and between the material and spiritual worlds:

> Does what Heidegger called "the heavenly" talk to itself vicariously through us, or through our artifacts?. . .If things are mute to us, must our artifacts be mute to angels? Rilke did not think so, in the ninth Duino Elegy.
>
> (298)

Middleton is opposed to poetry as "self-expression" and poetry as a commodity produced by isolated individuals in a capitalist society, and wants instead a poetry that serves non-physical but still urgent community needs. He tries to remedy the "thrownness" of the contemporary poet by invoking a time when poetic activity had a significant social context, when a poem would function like the Viking prow his essay focuses on. It would be like an artifact – a product of great technical skill – which makes matter communicate a spiritual meaning.

This constellation of concerns reveals what is valid and what is distortive in Stan Smith's Marxist reading of Middleton[6], from which he emerges as above all a political poet. More of this later but it is worth saying here that while Middleton does regard all experience as social he also regards all experience as spiritual and that he is a passionate anti-materialist.

One consequence of Middleton's social vision, however, is that he is aware that his ideal poetic project is deeply problematic given modern experience. He envies the carver of the Viking prow his "natural" relationship with his medium. For that artisan, the message *was* the medium: the prow was carved into the shape of sea foam and this knew "how to deal with the sea. . .being made of the sea" but at the same time was "at home in the wood" and shared "the life of the wood" (286). This poses problems, however, if the carver is an analogue for the poet, whose "wood" is language. Here, too, Middleton's nostalgia for lost metaphysical origins is apparent: he longs for language to have the organic relationship with meaning he believes it once had. If this relationship could be restored a poem would be similar to a Zuni sculpture, it would be a "reinvention", "a restitution of the first creation, the dawn of being" (295). So, in "Ideas About Voice in Poetry" he expresses the hope that imagination can weave "tissues of linguistic sound, toward a restitution of the lost flesh of God...toward a re-membering of his forgotten flesh" (*Kingfisher*, 76).

It is the collision of this poetic project with the "fallen" circumstances that make him the poet that he is. The project turns out to be like the journeys in *Pataxanadu*: "broken", "dislocated", "frustrated". Middleton speaks of how "poetry's ground has shifted...The bridge...has been smashed. A poem is now...a contest with the opaque, conducted in silence" (*Kingfisher*, 48). He speaks, also, of a "profound grief which gnaws at the root of my consciousness" (*Kingfisher*, 67) and which he associates with the modernist sensibility of Eliot, Kafka, Mandelstam and Seferis. Whereas the carver's meaning felt at home in the wood of the Viking prow, the modern poet's meaning is subject to endless interrogation because "the image is an image, the sign a sign". This "wakens us to the world of difference, but also to the negations: not this, not that." (*Kingfisher*, 68)

The form of his poems enacts this collision. His "archipelagic zigzag" (*Kingfisher*, 48) is revealed as the product of lost coherence by the way that his "broken syntax, abrupted rhythms, free association"[12]struggle towards their own "gestalt". In the freest of his free verse the jagged isolation of fragmentary phrases is a kind of rhythmic "thrownness" – the sense of language as a mere presence, as merely "delivered over": but even here his characteristic use of repetition and assonance suggests a striving to heal the gaps between the phrases and to improvise a halting incantation.

"Rilke's Feet" (184–192) fears "It may be too late" (191) but hints that fragmentariness can be overcome. What seems here, at first, a merely fanciful conjoining of associations centred on physical and poetic feet leads into an exploration of how the body can express the spirit. The "pedestrian" is reflected upon, as feet are defamiliarised in a faintly comic way, but then it is transformed with references to dance and finally to flight. So the poem's twelve sections inch their way towards transcendence:

> Your invisible
> Feet can do nothing but insist
> Issue into a space all
> Rondure and volume void
>
> Of anything more dense
> Than the thrum of air you felt
> Around a seagull's wing
> (191–192)

What is characteristic in these lines is the way that transcendence is connected with loss – Rilke now is all afflatus and no body. The poem moves backwards in order to recapture what has been lost, but dwells on its being lost as much as on its being recaptured. There is a similar ambivalence in "Another Almost" (254–256) where Middleton evokes the way that memory mingles with fantasy to tease and frustrate the mind with missed possibilities – "zones of being I never knew", "Mysterious flesh", "lost hills/ tipped with frail churches":

> The time of a music
> almost now I hear the spell of it
> playing backwards

Middleton's own music often plays backwards – his poems often funnel back towards a point of origin. Sometimes this is self-reflexive, a concern to pursue the work of art back to its source. In "A Drive in the Country/ Henri Toulouse-Lautrec" (100–102) a series of starting-points is tried ("No, not that. . .Not even that. . .Not that . . .Not so, not so. . .") because the painting's motive force is elusive. As Middleton says in a later prose poem "Le Dejeuner", "A description of a painting. . .has to begin" (274) – a consecutive form inevitably distorts a static one. But one way of reducing the problem is to begin and stop and begin again. The final effect in "A Drive in the Country" is to imply that the painting is, as it were, *all* beginning, *all* origin. So Middleton dismisses all his attempts to anatomise the painting, to reveal its skeleton ("Drawn out of the bones of light") and declares the whole thing to be "an egg" ("Interior oval, its yolk,/ A yellow trap"). Then he presses even further back and insists that the oval is not an egg after all but "the eye of Henri Toulouse-Lautrec" itself. Finally he anatomises the eye and asserts that the figures in the painting:

> Healed, flawless, are the very nerve
> That sees, and they retreat from you
> Because of this,
> When all the time it happens to be there.

In other words, the painting is a "re-membering" of what the painter originally saw. The last line is ambiguous because it refers both to the painting and to the original perception. It indicates the apparent "thrownness" of the image in the painting – it seems to be a mere presence. But it indicates that the point of origin is also a constant presence, even though it constantly retreats from us.

Similarly, "The Prose of Walking Back to China" (120–123) follows itself, as it were, from its beginnings before the poet started to compose it, forward only slightly as it starts to be composed, and then back, before its beginnings to the origin of all poems. Its raw material is occasional – Middleton is walking in a French city in the early morning in summer. What interests him is the way that random and prosaic objects seen on this occasion ("a fish head in a heap/ Of trash in a pail, a flower, an egg shell") begin to be transformed. His interest is so much in the process that he stays with its beginnings, lets it remain as, in a sense "prose" on the threshold of poetry, by notating the circumstantial detail that surrounded the poetic event – some of which would be included and some excluded – and asking by what process of selection and transformation the prosaic becomes the poetic. He shows the selection process begin as he hears "Pure low Bach notes on a flute" and this provides an organising perspective from which the other material can be viewed, for it is at this point that the random material and the composing mind find an affinity with each other.

At the end of the poem, therefore, he is referring to an idea similar to that in the last line of Holderlin's "Andenken" ("Remembrance") "Was bleibet aber, stiften die Dichter", translated by Middleton himself as "But poets alone ordain what abides"[13]. In his commentary on this line (*Kingfisher*, 115) Middleton suggests that Holderlin is referring to a "poetic fiat":

> poets give speech to an energy in which spirit and nature are consubstantial functions of a signifying power invested in that energy. The poetic mode of gnosis, moreover, does not merely read the signs that phenomena deliver, for it consists, that gnosis, of originative acts of language.

So, at the end of "The Prose of Walking Back to China" Middleton is referring again to his ideal poetic project, in which the act of poetic composition – through its restructuring and defamiliarising strategies – can reconstitute experience by restoring its origins. The journey may be frustrated but is nonetheless fruitful because it discloses significance even through its dislocation:

> Nothing in the voice
> Guides the poem but a wave
> Continually broken,
> And restored in a time to be perceived,
> As the flute is perceived, at origin,
> Before creation.

However, this represents an unfulfilled aspiration – it imagines a poem that would penetrate to the origin of all poems but does not itself claim to do so; it remains, by comparison, mere "prose".

Moreover, China, the original country of shamanic song, and the metaphoric object of the "walk", is now, as "Anasphere: Le Torse Antique" (102–107) demonstrates, unreachable. In this poem, the concern with origin is more metaphysical than aesthetic. The "ancient Chinese shamanic motifs in sections III and IV", as Middleton calls them in his "Note" (107), do enforce a point about modern expressive difficulties, since they refer to "muscular forms of breath" which now "Never flow, leap/ Up the torrent and restore" (105). More importantly, however, they are part of a larger pattern of associations which suggests that the body of the world has been broken and severed from its spirit. So references in the poem to the beliefs of ancient Egypt and China are accompanied by imagery of fertility:

> Plant them giving shade in a field
> For five cows composing a sign for us
> The diagonals of a dice
> Or is it the pentagram –
> Hidden in a bed the conversation of bodies
>                                                    (103)

The pentagram "represents the 'earth spirit'. . .The sign represents all the creative forces in nature" and its "verticality signifies an aspiration toward the celestial" (*Kingfisher*, 125). Through these references Middleton declares that in the ancient world there was a direct correspondence between the body and the spirit and between earth and heaven. Shamanic song was one manifestation of this correspondence: the contrast between that and the modernist method of this poem is a manifestation of "fallenness". Correspondence has become a dead letter. Similarly, where before there was "Hathor", representing fecundity, now "Profit motive melts the poles" and "The time will not come again/ It will not come again" (107).

At one level the eponymous "Torse" is the body of the world which has become like the broken sculpture in "Archaischer Torso Apollos" by Rilke. It is headless – we can no longer understand the mind of the ancient world. It is not a real body but a representation – we can have no unmediated access to the ancient world. Nonetheless it is a link with the ancient world and challenges us, as Rilke says of the Apollo torso, to change our lives.

However, there is another meaning of the word – the one given by Middleton's "found" poem, "Definition":

> Torse 3
> [f.med.L *torsus*, -um,
> for L. *tortus* twisted.]
> *Geom.* A developable surface;
> a surface generated
> by a moving straight line
> which at every instant is turning,
> in some plane or other through it,
> about some point or other
> in its length.[14]

"Definition" defines much of Middleton's poetic practice. As such it can be regarded as his response to having been uprooted from both his native and his metaphysical origins: it simultaneously enacts rootlessness and hints at a solution to it, if only an unstable and merely aesthetic one. Taken in isolation, the "moving straight line/ which at every instant is turning" enacts a "thrown" consciousness: however, when the torse is viewed as a whole, the line develops a context for itself by generating a "developable surface" – which is the "constant from and about which the poem develops" (*Schmidt*, 354). Even then, however, the solution is viewed sceptically for the surface produced is only a torso – a piece of fragmentary and "fallen" representation.

The "torse" analogy, then, indicates the radical ambiguity that characterises Middleton's poems. He excels in creating rhythms and images that evoke instability on the threshold of stability, or an oscillation between stability and instability, or restlessness in search of rest. Most often the poem's "moving straight line" is a shifting perspective, what Middleton calls "a moving viewline" (*Bolshevism*, 217) which does connect it, as Middleton himself suspects, with "the optics of Cubism" (*Bolshevism*, 219). In this way the constant around which the poem develops is repeatedly interrogated by the multiple points from which it is viewed.

"In the Secret House" (108–109) brings the whole nature of perspective into question by reducing the role of the human observer to a minimum and allowing the objects in the scene to come into their own. The repetition of the interrogative "who" and the openness of the syntax (which makes subject-verb-object relations ambiguous) have the effect of keeping the nature of the poem's central consciousness in doubt. The isolation of the word "Being" in the second line ("who is this/ Being/ Vaguely human") allows it to be either a noun or a present participle. The first alternative connects it with Heideggerian explorations of being-in-the-world. The second implies that being human requires a conscious effort. This connects with the possibility hinted at throughout that the central consciousness is a "chameleon poet" who "becomes" the objects in the poem and whose ontological security is thus in doubt. However, the poem does not refer simply to the instability of human consciousness, it also renders unstable its component images, as though they too suffered from ontological insecurity:

> Various woods keep
> Recomposing themselves; nothing holds
> In the fire, the fire is always
> Less than it was

This is reinforced by the way that the fire, however negatively, takes over the poem's point of view – it "Does not hear. . .the little owl", it does not "give/ A thought to the petrified/ Print of a snail".

A "moving viewline" is connected in Middleton's work with his ruefully modernist view of language: "Knowledge that the image is an image, the sign a sign, wakens us to the world of difference, but also to the negations: not this, not that" (*Kingfisher*, 68). On the one hand, multiple perspective affirms the unique life of different states of mind and different natural objects: on the other it implies loss of an original coherence, "fallenness" into the mutual incomprehension of different kinds of consciousness. This accounts for the way that images in Middleton's poems seem like images, and signs like signs: objects waver on the edge of loss, presence on the edge of absence, being on the edge of non-being. The ending of "In the Secret House" is an affirmation almost strangled – but not quite – by negatives:

> Mud on my hands, little owl, it is
> No grief to share with you,
> Little owl,
> The one note, not lost, for nothing

A similar effect is achieved elsewhere by rendering sense of place problematic by making the setting of the poem ambiguous and unstable. So the title of "A Road that is One in Many" suggests that – although the poem seems to have a single setting – it is difficult to focus on the road in question because of remembered or imagined roads. The poem's repeated phrase "Hold tight" insists on the attempt to feel present in the scene, to live in the present moment in this place. The danger it hints at conjures up an existential anxiety which is necessary if being-in-the-world is to be properly experienced. However, the phrase is self-defeating since, being the wrong register for a quiet stroll, it introduces a surreal displacement – instead of enforcing single-mindedness it introduces another perspective. So the "constant" that lies behind the poem constantly retreats, partly because the poem draws attention to the tricksiness of language:

> . . .that is juniper, a cone, house
> Of a singing bird. The signs do not sing
>
> Being, but collisions, they take sometimes
> A life or two.

The "signs" here are primarily road signs, but they are also poetic signs which are unable to "sing/ Being" as birds do since they are inauthentic, because arbitrary. The collisions are primarily road accidents, but they are also poetic juxtapositions which suggest the mind's obsessive comparison of one place to another and its consequent inability to feel at home anywhere (unlike the bird that lives in the tree). And these "collisions" cause anxiety because the sense that each individual place is interrogated by the knowledge of other places is linked to the sense that being is interrogated by the knowledge of non-being, of death.

However, the special quality of Middleton's modernism arises from the context in which modernist techniques – multiple perspective, self-reflexive signification, "archipelagic structures" are placed. This context ensures that sceptical elements endlessly struggle with the constant lying behind all the poems – the aspiration towards an original unity. This means that most of his poems are structured around the attempted reconciliation of opposites, often with the sense that one pole is on the "threshold" of the other. The journey is broken on the very verge of its goal. The radical ambiguity of Middleton's poems comes from their being set on a threshold – between objective and subjective, "being and not-being, here and there, this and 'the other'" (*Kingfisher*, 46).

This crucial idea is most explicitly discussed in his essay "Holderlin's 'Andenken'" where he talks about elements of the poem having a liminal relationship to each other:

> images "flared up" (as Bachelard says) on this threshold between the land and the sea that this mind is beholding as presence: between the past and the present, here and there, action (the mariners) and contemplation (the poet)...the poem...marks a threshold between poiesis as a remembering, and reality – a threshold at which the remembering is found to be the initiator of the reality, its ground and shaper.
>
> (*Kingfisher*, 109)

This is the process he refers to at the end of "The Prose of Walking Back from China" when he hints at the possibility that "moving as you may, for luck" (123) might bring you to a single correct perspective, and so to the threshold of origin. The importance of Holderlin for Middleton is that he exemplifies the fulfilment of this ideal poetic project – remembering takes Holderlin to the threshold of original presence in a way that would be impossible for a sceptical modernist. Holderlin experienced what Middleton can merely struggle for, so the Romantic poet is useful as a model of what the struggle is about. In other words his importance for Middleton is similar to that which Paul de Man says he has for Heidegger:

> How are we to shore up our remembrance of authentic Being so that we can find our way back to it? This *Fund*, this find, it must

be somewhere; if it had never revealed itself, how could we speak of its presence? But here is someone – Holderlin – who tells us that he has seen it, and that, moreover, he can speak of it, name it, and describe it; he has visited Being, and Being has told him some things that he collected and that he is bringing back to mankind.[15]

The central preoccupation of Middleton's work, then, is existential. This is why Stan Smith's reading of him[6] accounts for only a small part of his work. Interesting as Smith is over this small range, his selectiveness is distortive, as, also, is his reading of "The Historian" in implying that Middleton shares Smith's Marxism. For Middleton longs for a pre-, rather than a post-capitalist society; philosophically he is an idealist rather than a materialist; and his most fervent wish as a writer is to "give his reader a taste of the life that is not politicized" (*Bolshevism*, 156).

Nonetheless, Middleton does believe that being-in-the-world, given the "fallen" circumstances, is inevitably political, and Smith's interpretation is useful in drawing attention to this element in his poetry. The political in Middleton is one aspect of his work that makes him a sceptical, rather than a mystical or nostalgic poet – though less important in this respect than his modernist knowledge of "difference" and "negations" (*Kingfisher*, 68). For it is always an oppositional stance that Middleton adopts when he deals with a political issue. Smith speaks powerfully of twentieth-century poets feeling a "crucial recognition. . .of *complicity*" in the history of their times, and this accurately reflects Middleton's own political concerns, which are essentially with the politics of being – with the way that such experiences as the death camps have altered both the subjective and the social life of twentieth-century people.

It is important, then, not to segregate Middleton's political concerns from his existential ones. There is, for instance, a political element in "Moon Climbing" (143) and "The Image" (262–263) which I discussed earlier in purely existential terms. "Moon Climbing" refers to the possibility of nuclear war and "The Image" to the way that the contemporary United States is a bewilderingly different place from the one its pioneers imagined it would be. However, these political points are made simultaneously with the existential ones and the emphasis is on the part they play in "thrownness" and "fallenness".

This view of Middleton's priorities is confirmed by "How to Listen to Birds" (128). The point this poem makes is, according to its last line, "not unpolitical" and this is because it calls everyday social existence into question by suggesting that birdsong, if properly attended to, will defamiliarise ordinary perception (as a poem might) and so hint that it can be transcended. More explicitly than elsewhere in his poems, Middleton is saying here that his main political desire is for the abolition of politics, and in saying this he uses the organic analogy so hated by Marxists. The importance of birdsong for him is that it is "at a variance" with "fallen" human language and provides a link with an original authenticity. If we "listen. . . bodily" we might "Inhale the first perfume on earth", for birdsong "modifies the whole/ Machine of being".

For Middleton, poetry should have the effect he ascribes here to birdsong. It, too, is political but strives to transcend politics – above all because, as he says in "Notes On Some Poems", it wants to safeguard pleasure and so "hatches quarrels with. . .ideologies that bury the spark under schemes and ashes, with the grossness of power, with all the defilers of human reality, who, for want of pleasure, spread greyness everywhere" (*Bolshevism*, 224).

So his greatest political concern ultimately is with civil liberty and, although he does express outrage as Smith demonstrates, perhaps his most characteristic political response is a kind of Dada subversiveness. This causes a satirical violence to erupt periodically into his work as a libertarian protest against ideological thinking of all kinds – it takes the form of sardonic wit, black humour, an anarchic impulse. He opposes the "fixed elements [in society], the clichés, which provide an illusion of coherence" (*Kingfisher*, 58) with "dangerous mischief. . .salutary chaos" (*Boshevism*, 8). He admires the armadillos that

> . . .climb to the tops of telephone poles
> and jam the exchanges of political assholes
> with the terrible sound of knitting
>
> (35)

# 10

# Music of the Generous Eye: The Poetry of Roy Fisher

Roy Fisher was born in Handsworth, Birmingham, in 1930. Until he took early retirement recently he had worked most of his life in higher education – in English and Drama at Bordesley College of Education and then in American Studies at the University of Keele. What fame he now has is of a paradoxical kind: he is famous for having been largely ignored. Until Oxford University Press published his *Poems 1955–1980*[1] when he was fifty, he had been published only by small presses, most of them now defunct – Migrant Press, Tarasque Press, Northern House, Fulcrum Press.

He continued to be ignored, moreover, despite the attempts of Donald Davie and Eric Mottram to promote him in the early seventies. Both wrote pioneering essays[2] that attempted to explain his work by placing it in context: what perhaps did not help was that they had radically opposed views of what that context actually was.

Davie's essay is the more eccentric of the two. He attributes Fisher's neglect to the fact that there are in literary England two distinct circles or systems of literary activity and literary reputation, and there is a sometimes rancorous rivalry between them. He takes Philip Larkin as an example of one "system" and Fisher as an example of the other and deplores the assumption that no-one can like equally Roy Fisher, who writes in free verse and in open forms, and Larkin, who characteristically uses closed forms and writes in meter. Davie's essay amounts to a plea on Fisher's behalf to what he calls the 'establishment' (the system that supports Larkin) and his strategy is to suggest that "Fisher and Larkin are very much alike" and that Fisher's "temperament is, like Larkin's, profoundly Hardyesque" (Davie, 154).

Opposing a paradox with a platitude is a risky business, but I want to explore what I take to be Fisher's uncompromising modernism and this seems to me to make him a very different poet

170

from either Larkin or Hardy. There may be some temperamental affinities between the three poets – they are all sceptics whose writings dwell repeatedly on an English landscape; in the case of Hardy and Fisher these revisitings become a kind of reality-testing, or a search for stability and certainty. Fisher's scepticism, however, extends to the literary medium itself and this results in his deployment of a wide range of techniques that suggest the distortiveness and complexity of the medium, its tendency to place reality at several removes; it results, also, in his avoidance of narrative and discursive writing. This is reflected, moreover, in his forms – in his characteristically tentative free verse rhythms and his open and fragmented structures. By contrast, Davie's contention that Fisher is "profoundly Hardyesque" implies that Fisher's forms are a kind of disguise that conceals the real nature of his subject-matter.

In this respect Fisher's affinities have always been with European and American modernism, and Mottram's essay was more accurate in pointing this out – although by mentioning so many names in locating Fisher he may have crowded him out of the picture altogether (Mayakovsky, Eliot, Lorca, Dos Passos, De Chirico, Paul Nash, Graham Sutherland, William Carlos Williams, Edward Burra, Wyndham Lewis, Whitman, Beckett, Robert Duncan, Zukofsky, Olson, Duchamp, Cage, Kafka, Robbe-Grillet, Borges, Oldenberg, Lichtenstein, Lundquist, Tzara, Creeley and Tony Hancock). These names do have a collective relevance, but the length of the list and its exotic appearance ultimately suggest the difficulty of the battle Mottram was fighting in the face of a poetry-reading public with mostly parochial and anti-modernist tastes.

Davie's essay contains much that is illuminating and its importance in drawing attention to Fisher was enormous. Its central thesis, however, cannot help a reader to understand Fisher's most characteristic work. In this way it represents a more sophisticated version of the kind of attention Fisher has received when he has not been neglected – a kind of attention that wants to turn him into a different poet. This was what Fisher was lamenting in an interview in 1973[3] when he referred to the disproportionate amount of attention given to his poem "The Entertainment of War":

I've written at least one simple narrative poem about some of my relatives getting killed in an air-raid. It's the thing most untypical of anything I believe about poetry that I ever wrote. But it's the poem which has been most reprinted, and which people remember

and like to hear at a reading. . .in a sense I don't too much regret
having some works like that in the book, although I'm usually
very aware of having them misused. I'm not meaning to sound
patronizing about people who like simpler poetry. . .I'm talking
about critics, quite skilled readers who will very characteristically go at my work from the representational end or the end
which appears to have morality in it, and might be what you
could call comforting in that the poetry might be left and the
concepts which it gives rise to can then be discussed away from
the poetry.

(25)

The misunderstanding of Fisher has been largely caused by this
tendency to approach poetry "from the representational end or the
end which appears to have morality in it", because a reader with
representational assumptions – a reader, that is, who assumes that
poetry is a clear medium for reflecting experience – is bound to
misunderstand Fisher's central concerns with the complexities of
perception and the *problematic* nature of representation. Fisher's
scepticism leads him to reflect upon perception to show how disconcertingly the ground between objective and subjective shifts and
to reflect upon representation to show how a further questionableness is introduced when perception is translated into language or
art. Fisher's poems are consequently indeterminate in their form
and meaning – they never present themselves as definitive or conclusive, but as provisional statements leading to other provisional
statements.

Fisher comes closest to making definitive statements at those
points in his work where he stresses the impossibility of being
definitive. The most explicit of these is in the prose passage beginning "I want to believe I live in a single world" in the early long
poem "City" (*Poems*, 14–39). Here, the vividness of individual experiences is acknowledged, but, at the same time, the difficulty of
defining their exact status and of connecting them meaningfully:

The imaginary comes to me with as much force as the real, the
remembered with as much force as the immediate. . .I cannot join
together the mild wind and the shallow ditches. . .Each thought
is at once translucent and icily capricious.

(29)

This passage provides a key to the fragmentariness of "City" just as the lines " 'On Margate Sands./ I can connect/ Nothing with nothing' " provide a key to the fragmentariness of "The Waste Land" – even if, like Eliot's lines, it effaces itself as a key. Moreover, the passage represents an important clue to Fisher's work as a whole, and when he later distanced himself from it in his 1973 interview (36) it was not because he no longer accepted its view of experience, but because he no longer saw such fragmentariness as a source of discomfort ("I would tend to enjoy it now"), because he objected to the posturing in the passage, and because, by 1973, he considered that the discontinuity of experience required an evolution of the self to attune itself to it, an evolution towards "the discontinuous self which I would claim to live according to now, and to have portrayed in later writing". In other words, where the passage in "City" implies a unitary self encountering an uncomfortably fragmented world, Fisher's development since "City" has been to suggest a fragmentariness in the self which corresponds to that in the world.

This is not to say that the relationship between the self and its environment is depicted as simple and stable even in "City". In fact, the passage "I want to believe. . ." – by presupposing a unitary self – tends to simplify the rest of the poem. Even in "City" there are elements that prefigure the later depiction of a discontinuous self because, even here, there are doubts about where the self ends and its environment begins. For the poem dramatises the conflict involved in its creation, the conflict between an approach which presents the city with documentary objectivity, and an approach which presents the city as transformed in advance by subjective meaning. The documentary approach is evident from the way, especially in the prose passages, "City" intermittently employs the register of urban history and/or geography:

> In the century that has passed since this city has become great, it has twice laid itself out in the shape of a wheel. The ghost of the older one still lies among the spokes of the new, those dozen highways that thread constricted ways through the inner suburbs, then thrust out, twice as wide, across the housing estates and into the countryside, dragging moraines of buildings with them.
>
> (17)

Such passages, which strive for objectivity, are juxtaposed with others which are so subjective that they can only be called expressionist, passages which suggest the way that the self has made the city a part of its emotional life, the way the city has been internalised through the distortions of memory and feeling. In the second section, "Lullaby and Exhortation for the Unwilling Hero", this is evoked, in the first twenty-six lines, through the rhythms of nursery rhyme:

> The pearl in the stocking,
> The coals left to die,
> The bell in the river,
> The loaf half eaten,
> The coat of the sky.
>
> (15)

Each image here has a vivid particularity, and the apparent lack of connection between the images is half overcome by the insistent cadence, which persists in trying to link them. The effect is to render the bewilderment of childhood, of the first attempts to make sense of experience – or of the bewilderment of adulthood in trying to remember or recreate such first attempts. The images represent those fragments of early experience – the product of fantasy, misunderstanding, or severance from an original context that would explain them – which return to haunt the adult mind. That this is an important clue to the long poem as a whole is confirmed by Fisher's own remarks about "City":

> I was. . .in a state of life when I could remember childhood – I was far enough away from childhood to have an intensity about some memories. And again I'd had a fairly inarticulate childhood, a childhood where I had a lot of sensations going in, but not a very – you know, I wasn't a child writer or anything of that sort, a child reader. There were still things left in my own perception which were unsorted.
>
> ("Interview", 19)

This, too, indicates a way in which the relationship between objective and subjective is complex and unstable in "City": much of what is presented comes with a history of feeling behind it, is "meant to be about a city which has already turned into a city of the mind" ("Interview", 12). This anticipates much that Fisher has written since – poems in which there is a deliberate ambiguity about whether what is presented is the product of direct observation or of one mental activity or another – remembering, imagining, or dreaming. However, "City" is unusual in the intensity of the state of mind that lies behind it. This is an intensity which takes a very indirect form, for Fisher, unlike confessional poets like Robert Lowell and Tony Harrison, very rarely mentions his personal life – there are very few direct references in his work to his parents, his wife or his children. But there is a sense in which "City" is a personal poem, that behind what Donald Davie calls its "animus against the new breed of city fathers, who are ingratiating and paternalistic" (Davie, 164) lies Fisher's sense of what the administrators are doing to the city he associates with his parents and his own earliest experiences and subsequent development:

> I was coming back to the city in my late twenties at a time when it was being rebuilt. . .And there was another thing which was again merely personal – my father was dying, and he was very closely associated with the city, with these areas over a period of forty years. Seeing this life ending, and the inevitable process of turning up old photographs, old apprenticeship papers, extended time that made you realise more than usually how much the place was dependent upon very evanescent, temporal, subjective renderings of it, which might never be rendered. And at this point my own lifetime was extended through his.
>
> ("Interview", 19)

Fisher's strong sense of the link between himself and his dying father, and his desire to find ways to give poetic articulacy to the unarticulated experience of the provincial working class, both suggest a similarity between Fisher's project in "City" and the more recent project of Tony Harrison. However, Fisher's concern with the unarticulated raises far more questions about the nature of representation than Harrison's concern, which is much more directly social and personal. Fisher is interested in "the phenomena [sic] of having a perceptual environment which was taken as read, which was taken as to be assumed and not a thing for which any vocabulary needed to exist". ("Interview", 19) This means that 'City' constantly deconstructs accepted readings of the perceptual environment by its repeated and self-reflexive shifts in style and register, and by how it reveals each successive reading to be unstable in containing a questionable level of subjectivity. So, the deadpan calm of the most objective passages is subverted by a dark expressionist violence that erupts into the poem:

> You can lie women in your bed
> With glass and mortar in their hair.
>                    (16)
> The foetus in the dustbin moves one claw.
>                    (16)
> The sun hacks at the slaughterhouse campanile.
>                    (21)

In an afternoon of dazzling sunlight in the thronged streets, I saw at first no individuals but a composite monster, its unfeeling surfaces matted with dust: a mass of necks, limbs without extremities, trunks without heads, unformed stirrings and shovings spilling across the streets it had managed to get itself provided with.

>                    (23)

Moreover, the whole of "City" should be seen in the context of the section entitled "Starting to Make a Tree" (25), which hints, in a playful and witty way, at the distortions involved in representation, at the nature of representation as a construct. The materials gathered to make the tree include "a great flock mattress; two carved chairs; cement; chicken-wire; tarpaulin; a smashed barrel; lead piping; leather of all kinds; and many small things". The artists are anxious to know "whose armpit and whose groin would help us most in the modelling of the bole, and the thrust of the boughs".

"Starting to Make a Tree" works self-reflexively to show what Fisher was attempting in composing "City" from the bits and pieces of experience which were available to him according to the passage "I want to believe. . .". Like each material gathered to make the tree, each bit of subject-matter that makes up "City" is a stubbornly diffuse and singular material derived originally from the local environment. Moreover, the language of the poem is analogous to the mattress, chairs, cement and so on available to the tree-makers in that, like all language, it is entirely different from what it is supposed to represent. So "Starting to Make a Tree" – especially when read in conjunction with "I want to believe I live in a single world" – deconstructs "City" by drawing attention to its nature as representation. So, "a perceptual environment which was taken as read"

("Interview", 19) is called into question by being subjected to a series of readings, each as provisional as the next.

Fisher's remark that the poet who wrote "I want to believe I live in a single world" lacks "the discontinuous self which I would claim to live according to now, and to have portrayed in later writing" ("Interview", 36) indicates the most important line in development that his work has taken since "City", involving a thorough calling into question of the way that landscapes and states of mind interpenetrate each other. As a result, Fisher's mature work presents an ambivalent context where objective and subjective are buoyantly mingled. In reaching this maturity, "City" was important as I have shown, but so, too, were other early poems which question the nature of consciousness and identity.

He talks, as I have said, about "City" originating when he returned in his late twenties when his father was dying and the city was undergoing urban renewal: the urge to write about it was similar to that urge to record which he describes at the end of "For Realism":

> . . .A realism
> tries to record, before they're gone,
> what silver filth these drains have run.
> (*Poems*, 55)

"For Realism" is cognate with "City" in its concern with how that urban renewal threatened to eradicate the experiences of the people who lived in the cleared houses; both poems respond to the threat by recording those experiences. As Fisher has said:

In many cases the cultural ideas, the economic ideas, had disappeared into the graveyards of the people who had the ideas. But the byproducts in things like street layouts, domestic architecture, where the schools were, how anything happened – all these things were left all over the place as a sort of script, an indecipherable script with no key. And the interesting thing for me was that the culture, particularly the metropolitan culture, the literary culture, had no alphabet to offer for simply talking about what I saw all the time. I mean, when I say in "City", "most of it's never been seen," it's a provocative phrase: it wasn't verbalised, it wasn't talked about. And there I wasn't interested really at all in the particular city, but in the phenomena [sic] of having a perceptual environment which was taken as read, which was taken as to be assumed and not a thing for which any vocabulary needed to exist. . .Seeing this life ending. . .made you realize more than usually how much the place was dependent upon very evanescent, temporal, subjective renderings of it, which might never BE rendered.

("Interview", 18–19)

What Fisher was hinting at here was his difficulty in finding a method of representation for these experiences which had never previously been represented. And what "For Realism" makes explicit is the distortion that intervenes between the realist impulse to record and the "real" object of that impulse: however "realistic" the aim of the recorder is, what he records is not reality.

Given such problems of representation, each successive passage in "City" approaches its urban subject-matter with a different strategy – the poem employs both poetry and prose, the poetry is by turns imagistic, expressionistic or surrealistic, the prose by turns documentary, historical, geographical or personal. Juxtaposing so many linguistic modes draws attention to the linguistic medium and indicates how each mode will take the poet only so far before it breaks down. This produces, in the end, fragmentariness and indeterminacy. "Each thought is at once translucent and icily capricious. A polytheism without gods." (*Poems*, 29). The realist impulse is treated with respect; the attempt to evoke reality is regarded as valid, even inevitable – but its success is only partial.

So Fisher has described his poems as "sceptical formulations of life" ("Interview", 17). What gives this scepticism added power, however, is that one of Fisher's greatest poetic strengths is his ability to write with minute and vivid precision about physical reality. This means that his scepticism does not result in an easy fictiveness but is made to do its work in the context of what are apparently thorough renderings of bits of the "real world"; the floors dissolve under verisimilitude with great subtlety. It takes repeated readings of "After Working" (*Poems*, 48–49) to identify at what point the poem slips into the surreal. This is partly because it happens gradually; first of all, for instance, there is an intermediate step which is probably an image seen on the threshold of sleep, a skewed memory:

> I squat there by the reeds
> in dusty grass near earth

> stamped to a zoo patch
> fed with dog dung,
> and where swifts
> flick sooty feathers along the water
> agape for flies.

But it is also because the thoroughly surreal scene at the end is rendered with such painstaking detail:

> signal to leave looking and
> shaded, to fall away
> lower than dulled water reaches,
> still breathing the dog odour
> of water, new flats, suburb trees,
> into the half-light of a night garage
> without a floor,
>
> then down its concrete stems,
> shaded as I go down
> past slack and soundless
> shores of what might be other
> scummed waters,
> to oil-marked asphalt
> and, in the darkness, to a sort of grass.

The impossibility of this is palliated by the way that "without a floor" is insinuated into the description by a rhythmic sleight of hand – a much shorter line than its predecessors, and lacking their spondaic weight – and by the way that the scene incorporates convincing fragments of reality, albeit magically rearranged.

With such techniques, Fisher's poems constantly expose the inadequacies of realism. They indicate that there are many realities, not one, since there are as many perspectives as there are states of mind, and they indicate that poets, like other language-users and other artists, have to filter these realities through a distortive medium. In early Fisher this was regarded as a source of frustration, while more recently it has become a cause for celebration.

The emphasis in these early poems is on the otherness of other people, and the most conspicuous poetic method defamiliarises them by the use of a technique that Donald Davie has related to Fisher's description of himself as "a 1920s Russian modernist", the use of a method of "making strange", "basically the slow-motion dismemberment of a ritual or routine action into its bizarre components" (Davie, 167). This is a concept associated with the Soviet formalist critic Victor Shklovsky and it is the method, for example, of "Toyland", involving the poet watching Sunday observance with a radically detached eye:

> Today the sunlight is the paint on lead soldiers
> Only they are people scattering out of the cool church. . .
> And we know what they will do when they have opened the
>     doors of their houses and walked in:
> Mostly they will make water, and wash their calm hands and
>     eat.
>
> (Poems, 3)

This is Fisher's most characteristic technique. "City" employs it to the extent that it contains, as Eric Mottram has pointed out, "nearly hallucinatory metamorphoses of the human, the transformation of the human towards the machine, or at least the reductive, simplified elements of body as operation barely covered by skin extensions called clothes". (Mottram, 10–11)

So, too, the figure in "As He Came Near Death" (*Poems*, 47) is shockingly defamiliarised; in the process of dying he becomes overwhelmed by objects until he, himself, turns into an object ("During this time somebody washed him in a soap called *Narcissus* and mounted him, frilled with satin, in a polished case.") By the end of the poem the interchange between objects and the human becomes so complete that, in an ironic and surreal reversal, an object acquires life: "After a time the grave got up and went away."

There are also two early poems – "Five Morning Poems From a Picture by Manet" and "Interiors with Various Figures" (respectively, *Poems*, 7–11 and 39–47) – which employ estrangement by raising questions about what happens to the human subject when it is represented in art. The earlier poem centres upon Manet's painting "The Boy with the Cherries", describing its nonchalant plenitude:

> Someone has given him cherries:
> untouched upon the wall

> they spill from yellow paper, crimson-heavy;
> glossy, their soft skins burst.
>
> (8)

But more importantly the poem explores the precariousness of this artificially stopped moment by placing it in the context of the boy's later suicide. There is no suggestion that this perspective is more "real" than Manet's. From this perspective, too, the reference may be to art rather than life, since Baudelaire wrote a short story called "La Corde"[4] based on the boy's suicide. Moreover, the style of Fisher's poem itself introduces an intertextual element: it frequently reads like a translation of a French symbolist poem:

> Trumpets of iron shake the sky;
> in chains of ceremony they spill
> out of the music of a
> generous eye.
>
> (10)

By multiplying perspectives Fisher's poem acts like a cubist rereading of Manet's painting: the boy's life and death are seen from several viewpoints, none of them more valid than the others. Or if one viewpoint is more privileged it is that of the dead who mutter about "legacies of wrong" – of which they consider the worst to be "the fiction of understanding" (10).

The "fiction of understanding" that is most important in this context is the kind imposed by Christianity, but Fisher's scepticism rejects *all* systematic generalisations. "No system describes the world" he says in "Metamorphoses" (*Poems*, 84). In his "Five Morning Poems" he replaces conventional assumptions with multiple viewpoints and so moves tentatively towards an explanation of the boy's experience without claiming to have the answer to it.

Similarly, in "Interiors with Various Figures" he exposes the inadequacy of familiar assumptions about character by presenting a series of scenes in which a relationship between a man and woman is viewed by one of them from a disconcertingly skewed angle. The scenes are made more questionable by being presented in a generically contradictory way – each section of the poem is spoken as a dramatic monologue by a participant in the scene, and yet the title suggests painting. So in this poem too there are multiple perspectives, here turning on a pun on "interiors" which refers, at its most obvious level, to a painterly representation of a domestic scene, but also refers, more deviously, to the human interior, to the idea that these figures are moving around as much in someone's mind as in a depicted room. And this poem too demonstrates how reality is never perceived directly – how, instead, it involves fictions of under-standing, elaborate and circuitous conventions whose results are endlessly partial. For this reason, each scene is a self-conscious fiction with much of its context bafflingly withheld.

Fisher's later poetic has developed from the questions about sub-jectivity which his early poems began to ask. It is likely that the experience of writing the prose piece "The Ship's Orchestra" (*Po-ems*, 165–191) was also important – having made that internal voy-age into the outlandishly surreal, Fisher seems disposed, afterwards, to imply that the poetic voice should never be entirely trusted, never be taken as read:

> With "The Ship's Orchestra". . .I wanted to be writing about some-thing I didn't know about, which was not entailed to any sort of reality and which was in fact made up of all kinds of fantastic impressions: you know it was a ship off a movie, a ship out of children's illustrations, a ship out of other people's poems, that sort of thing. And that is for me very important – to make it fairly clear that the thing that's being written is an artifact, is to do with the subjective.
>
> ("Interview", 12)

"The Ship's Orchestra" demonstrates how the self can create a world. With the experience of writing it behind him, Fisher has written poems which explore the boundaries between the self and the world and between the poem and experience. He speaks about this most directly in "If I Didn't":

> I could say
> the poem has always
> already started, the parapet
> snaking away, its grey line guarding
> the football field and the sea
> (*Poems*, 128)

Here the words "poem" and "parapet" are connected to each other through an ambiguity achieved by parataxis – a parataxis characteristic of later Fisher in the way it deliberately questions boundaries. In these lines there is a suggestion both that the poem is like the parapet (in marking a boundary) and that the poem can contain the parapet – "the poem has always/ already started" because the parapet is viewed poetically even before the poem is composed. This is similar to the point made at the end of "Glenthorne Poems" that "the trees. . .coming into leaf/. . .are already/ three-parts idea" (*Poems*, 77). At moments like these Fisher seems to be indicating – though with some reluctance – the impossibility of following William Carlos Williams' prescription "No ideas but in things". In "If I Didn't" what looks like a moment of perception in the present, "the parapet/ snaking away", is joined by a meditation on the way experience forms itself into patterns – this makes the moment of perception look, in retrospect, more abstract, more like a mere example of a moment of perception, or one of many remembered perceptions in a continuum. This feeling is reinforced by the way the meditation concerns itself with memory and leads to another remembered moment of perception which is also exemplary, which becomes in fact an analogue of the troubled inquiry into the nature of memory. For this moment brings with it a vivid imagery of uncertainty:

> and there I am,
> half my lifetime back,
> on Goodrington Sands
> one winter Saturday,
> troubled in mind: troubled
> only by Goodrington beach
> under the gloom, the look of it
> against its hinterland
> and to be walking
> acres of sandy wrack,
> sodden and unstable
> from one end to the other.

Given such a concern with instabilities it is not surprising that Fisher has evolved a difficult and rigorous poetic which moves fastidiously and sceptically through fine and serried distinctions. This may seem austere but in fact Fisher is always insisting on the pleasure to be derived from disciplined observation, from the rewards to be gained from avoidance of what is too easy. Here, it is

the eponymous hero of "The Thing About Joe Sullivan" (*Poems*, 52–
54) who provides Fisher with an occasion for displaying his own
artistic credo – Joe Sullivan is a jazz pianist praised for ignoring
"the chance of easing down/ walking it leisurely". Roy Fisher, too,
is a respected jazz pianist, and the ending of this poem surely reflects his activities as both pianist and poet, emulating a difficult
and subtle art, imagining fingers following Sullivan's "through
figures that sound obvious" but finding "corners everywhere",

> marks of invention, wakefulness;
> the rapid and perverse
> tracks that ordinary feelings
> make when they get driven
> hard enough against time.

This is why "Staffordshire Red" (*Poems*, 141–142) evokes the pleasure of discovery at the same time that it refers to the difficulty of
understanding; the effort to understand will produce surprises,
sudden insights like the one afforded by a "turn in the road, sheer
through/ the sandstone at Offley". The poem's imagery suggests
the unexpectedness and obliqueness of understanding, the hiddenness and oddness of meaning:

> . . .Some things
> are lying in wait in the world,
> walking about in the world,
> happening when touched, as they must.

The most important product of this artistic discipline in Fisher's
later work has been his composition of five sequences: "Glenthorne
Poems", "The Six Deliberate Acts", "Matrix", "Handsworth Liberties" and "Wonders of Obligation". Each of these is about seven
pages long and divided into brief numbered sections composed of
short, elliptical lines. In all these poems the boundary between the
self and the world is constantly in question so that the status of
their imagery is ambiguous, and the poetic voice seems always to
be asking what kind of statement it is making in the process of
making it. The analogy that first suggests itself for this is the creation, in modernist painting, of an ambiguous picture space; as in
"Interiors with Various Figures" these poems lay plural perspectives

on top of each other in a way that would be impossible in realist art.

However a more accurate anology for Fisher's sequences is with music. It is "The Thing About Joe Sullivan" that describes them most precisely:

> running among stock forms
> that could play themselves
> and moving there with such
> quickness of intellect
> that shapes flaw and fuse,
> altering without much sign,
> (53)

The sequences present "stock forms" as raw material for transformation, they dissolve into other, unexpected forms – all of this in a way that suggests improvisations that travel so far from their original theme that it seems almost lost, that it retains only a ghostly presence. So, the "Handsworth Liberties" (*Poems*, 117–124) are descriptions of places that "flaw and fuse,/ altering without much sign" under the influence of memory and patterns of assocation, for Fisher has written that "each of the poems. . .is a concentration" on images that had come to be arbitrarily associated for him with a piece of music:

> When I was fourteen or fifteen years old and heard new pieces of music, the hearing was often accompanied by a gratuitous visual impression, always of some actual but quite inconsequential location – a street corner or suburban-industrial vista – near my home. The impression would attach itself to the music and was revived every time I heard it again, or thought about it.
> (*Poems*, 193)

What this sequence represents, then, is a series of negotiations between the landscape and memory; it explores the way that landscape has entered the poet's mind and influenced it, and the way that the landscape has been altered in the process. For these locations have been altered by being perceived by a particular fifteen year old; by being absorbed into his mind; by being associated with music; and by being repeatedly recalled in different circumstances and in different moods. Necessarily, then, they carry a kind of psychological archaeology with them, alongside a tenuous objective residue.

For these reasons, the sequence deliberately keeps its options open stylistically: the literal continually dissolves into the metaphorical, visual impression into emotional expression, imagism into surrealism – and the point where such dissolves begin and end is impossible to locate exactly. In section 3, for example, there are a series of images which never quite mount up to a coherent scene though they are certainly definite enough in themselves ("unpointed brickwork/ lightly soiled" and so on). Instead they are made to suggest a place which is "thin" and which "will be dark, but never deep": the stylistic context is imagistic, which encourages a visual interpretation of the words "thin" and "deep", but they refuse to be disposed of entirely in that way. Instead, "thin" and "never deep" suggest either something insubstantial about the place, or how it was originally perceived, or how it was later recalled.

By carefully sustaining such ambiguities the sequence explores discontinuities in both the self and the world. In "Handsworth Liberties" references to place can easily be interpreted either literally as actual locations or metaphorically as states of mind. Sections 4 and 5, for instance, dwell repeatedly on interactions between "here" and "there" which can refer, at the most literal level, to two places in the present, but can also refer to mind and environment, or now and then. "Here" can become "there" as a result of movement, but also as a result of change, and it is when the interaction between them is attended to that their relationship begins to be perceived and understood:

> where here and there
> change places, the moment
> always a surprise:
> on an ordinary day a brief
> lightness, charm between realities;
> on a good day, a break
> life can flood in and fill.
>
> (118–119)

However, exclusive concentration on Fisher's scepticism – on his innumerable strategies for rendering the dubiousness of perception and the distortions of representation – cannot account for an important quality in his work, a quality which he himself indicated when he said, "I do like an AIR of reality about my writing." ("Interview", 32). He is not interested in fictiveness for its own sake; Philip Gardner is surely wrong in claiming that "the poet with whom Fisher has most in common is Wallace Stevens"[5]. For as Fisher himself has said: "I don't want ever to go over into an elaborated set of fictions like Wallace Stevens, I'd not find that congenial" ("Interview", 32). The nearest he comes to displaying such an interest are in his more playful poems, like "Paraphrases", and the poems collected in his book *Consolidated Comedies*[6], and these carry their fictiveness more lightly than Stevens ever does – in "Paraphrases", for instance, Fisher receives a letter from a man convinced that he has turned into Roy Fisher:

Dear Mr. Fisher I am now
so certain I am you that it is obvious to me
that the collection of poems I am currently working on must be
*your own next book*! Can you let me know –
who is to publish it and exactly when
it will be appearing? I shouldn't like there to
be any trouble over contracts, "plagiarism"
etcetera; besides which it would be a pity
to think one of us was wasting time and effort.
How far have *you* got? Please help me. I
*do* think this is urgent. . .

(*Poems*, 131)

Here the presence of Borges seems closer than that of Stevens.

Outside his comedies, Fisher is clearly interested in fictiveness, but this interest, and his scepticism, are accompanied by an almost obsessive concern *to approach* factuality and exactness, however much obliqueness and difficulty is involved. Much of the impulse behind this comes from Fisher's philosophical outlook; unlike idealists such as Stevens and Borges, who are obsessed with fictiveness, Fisher, like William Carlos Williams, is a materialist and "obsessed/ with cambered tarmacs, concretes,/ the washings of rain" (Poems, 162). That is, while Borges and Stevens believe that physical objects cannot exist separately from a mind that is aware of them, Williams and Fisher believe that reality is fundamentally material. Fisher's stylistic concerns certainly suggest a materialist outlook:

I am chiefly interested in hauling words towards concreteness –
I'm not so much bothered at this stage with the Pound precepts

about clarity of image and so forth, although those have gone in fairly deep for me. But with referring EVERYTHING to bodily existence, as simply as that, you know, referring language to it, the counters of language as a sort of sensory register.

("Interview", 20)

Perhaps the most characteristic element in Fisher's work is the precise naming of a great variety of objects, a relentless specifity that attempts to render the perceptual environment in its full sensory complexity. No British poet has described the appearance of a mid-twentieth century city with more memorable precision than Fisher; and surely no poet has described brick in its numerous conditions in more detail – Fisher knows brick the way an eskimo knows snow (although Fisher's landscapes are by no means all urban). Even in the thoroughly surreal "The Ship's Orchestra" the emphasis is upon the way that desire and fear take their forms from bodily interactions with physical objects (some of which are other bodies):

> Astringency, the prickling of the scalp, flexing of the feet, rotation of the wrists, passing the hands round the confining surfaces of the room where one is. That done, the thought of the scalloped alcove where the band might play. Combed plaster in swirls of rough relief, a deep pink rising from the floor to meet the powdering of gold that thickens and conquers at the zenith. Floor projection forwards, a curved apron, no higher than a tight skirt can step up from maple to black linoleum pitted with marks of casters, drum-spurs, bass-spikes.

(*Poems*, 171)

In fact, one of the most important surreal effects of this piece is the greatly enlarged importance given to sensations of touch, taste and smell, as though sensory priorities had been rearranged. Much of the environment is experienced through these senses in order to defamiliarise perception itself and bestow renewed attention on the physical nature of the world.

Fisher's preoccupation with physical factuality is linked also with his attempts to achieve a kind of impersonal observation. The passages in "City" which I mentioned earlier, where he employs the register of urban history and/or geography, are not present merely to be subverted – they represent a genuine desire to define the city as accurately as possible. And Fisher displays an effort towards unmediated perception in "The Memorial Fountain" (*Poems*, 60–61) where he describes himself as "by temper, realist," and "working/ to distinguish an event/ from an opinion". So the poem attempts to render the "real" fountain, not merely a view of it – its first twenty lines are a meticulous description of the fountain, using a method close to that of William Carlos Williams.

Similarly, in "City" and "For Realism" (*Poems*, 54–55) Fisher employs a kind of factual reporting against what he likes to refer to, ironically, as "conscience", defined by Donald Davie as the

> social conscience of the confident demographer and humanitar-
> ian administrator who has demolished acres of the inner city and
> rehoused their denizens in high-rise apartment-blocks on the ridge
> above their old dwellings, at whatever cost to the human associa-
> tions that those demolished dwellings had for them.
>
> (Davie, 163)

Fisher considers that such "conscience"

> involves a kind of abstract, generalised thinking which tries to
> impose a rigid pattern: the blocks of the flats were built on intel-
> lectual models of the people who were going to be moved into
> them, they were built graphed.
>
> ("Interview", 15)

In the face of such thinking, Fisher's impulse is to draw attention to the concrete particulars of people's lives and environment and to insist on their reality:

> For "realism":
> the sight of Lucas's
> lamp factory on a summer night;
> a shift coming off about nine,
> pale light, dispersing,
> runnels of people chased
> by pavements drying off
> quickly after them
>
> (54)

Although the word "realism" is placed in quotation marks, moments like this in Fisher's work represent his least sceptical writing;

in "For Realism" he invokes notions of observable social reality in order to oppose the monolothic thinking of city planners. In other words, he insists on a "reality" in order to oppose an oppressive fiction.

It is possible that there is some philosophical inconsistency between Fisher's materialism on the one hand and his scepticism on the other, since his materialism amounts, in the end, to a *belief* in the priority of matter. Poets, however, are not required to be philosophically consistent. Moreover, his materialism is largely a matter of temperament and is usually subordinated, in the end, to his scepticism. So, in "The Memorial Fountain" it is finally suggested that the idea that an event and an opinion can be distinguished is a "Romantic notion", ironically undercutting its pretensions to realism. And in "Of the Empirical Self and For Me" (*Poems*, 125) he shows how the self that observes must itself be subjected to empirical scrutiny, since the presence of the observer changes what is observed. So "there's seldom/ any *I* or *you*" in Fisher's poems because to say "I" or "you" takes them as read. The poem ends with an analogue of how we perceive reality:

> Thunder bursts across the mountain;
> the village goes dark with blown fuses,
> and lightning-strokes repeatedly
> bang out their own reality-prints
> of the same white houses
> staring an instant out of the dark.

The blown fuses and intermittent light here suggest the limitations of our senses; the transformation of reality into "prints" suggests the distortions of representation.

Fisher's materialism, however, does play an important role – it gives his scepticism something to brace itself against. Moreover, the sensory data in Fisher's work accumulates relentlessly like evidence in search of a truth that is never altogether proven; with a fastidious empiricism more and more vivid fragments of reality are assembled but will not fit together to define reality. In this way the accumulation finally contributes to doubt rather than certainty. But running into the stubborn resistance that Fisher's materialism provides, his scepticism becomes a much subtler and more complex instrument; encountering each other on ground favourable sometimes to one and sometimes to the other, they suggest the enjoyable variousness and odd particularity of experience. "The puzzle helps teach a fascinated resignation: any pavement, any dwarf wall, any old inside leg" (*Poems*, 149).

In the end what most reveals the wrongness of Donald Davie's attempt to suggest profound affinities between Larkin and Fisher is the contrast in their attitutides to realism. For Larkin, realism is an assumption and he deploys realist techniques with such bluff skill that they appear not to be techniques at all. For Fisher, realism is an impossible goal whose pretensions, nonetheless, annex experience even in the thick of perception and feeling and which therefore require painstaking vigilance and defamiliarisation. In particular, Fisher's desire to deconstruct the realist assumptions of a unitary self and its direct access to the phenomenal world have led him to slip from one modernist technique to another – imagism, expressionism, surrealism – in a way that draws attention to their differing arbitrations between subjective and objective. It is through these self-conscious slippages that the effect of estrangement is most consistently created in his work, for through them the nature and extent of the interpenetrations of self and world are interrogated from a series of adjusted angles.

What must also be said, however, is that Fisher's attitude to realism also starkly differentiates him from the tradition of self-reflexive fictiveness that leads from Wallace Stevens into the postmodernism of John Ashbery. For Fisher is as respectful of realism as he is sceptical of it, and insists on introducing realist inflections into even his most experimental poems. To this extent, at least, he is a retro-modernist rather than a postmodernist – his poems contain a nostalgia for the "real" and inscribe in their structures a significant sense of its bewildering loss, rather than a celebration of the freedoms attendant on that loss.

# 11

# A Various Art:
# Veronica Forrest-Thomson
# and Denise Riley

Even within the mainstream, contemporary British poetry is torn into factions, some of them comprising one person with an acrimonious internal debate. Outside it, though, there is one group which has achieved more cohesion than most, perhaps largely because of the way it has articulated its own outsider status. I am referring to the poets anthologised in *A Various Art*[1] and in the section of *the new british poetry*[2] headed "A Treacherous Assault On British Poetry" – most prominently J.H. Prynne, Andrew Crozier, Douglas Oliver, and Iain Sinclair. Their most important shared background is in what Crozier calls "an interest in a particular aspect of postwar American poetry, and the tradition that lay behind it – not that of Pound and Eliot but that of Pound and Williams" (*Various*, 12). It is clear that part of the impulse behind this is in an impatience with Englishness itself – to opt for Williams is to opt for a poet whose major concern was to cast off what he felt as the dead weight of English tradition and to invent for poetry a native American idiom, especially in matters of rhythm. To some extent it is unsurprising, then, that Eric Mottram raised hackles when he promoted this kind of poetry when he was editor of *Poetry Review* from 1971 to 1977.

However, – especially as a response to the way that a mere version of the English tradition had usurped for itself a reputation for being the whole thing – some of this impatience was justified. As Mottram has pointed out: "there are important traditions in British poetry other than those promoted by the Movement and their successors. For those who began writing in the sixties, the senior figures were Hugh Macdiarmid, Basil Bunting and David Jones – all poets deeply aware of and affected by the poetics of modernism" (*nbp* 131). I have discussed elsewhere the anti-modernism of the Movement and drawn a number of times in that context on Andrew

Crozier's essay in *Society and Literature 1945–1970* because it seems to me forceful and persuasive: "Traditional forms are invoked not so much for the freedom they can confer but for support. They define the space in which the self can act with poetic authority, while at the same time, in the absence of assurances provided by the conventionally felt poetic experience, they secure the status of the text."[3]

By contrast, Crozier, Prynne and the others have evolved a poetic in which mostly open forms are used to express both epistemological and ontological doubt. Crozier's "i.m. Rolf Dieter Brinkmann" (*Various*, 82) for example is composed of six free verse stanzas of five lines each unpunctuated except for a colon followed by the last three and a bit lines which serve as a summary of what precedes them:

> . . .all language is truth
> though a bed of dry leaves when evaporation
> ceases and our words turn and fall
> flickering with our life upon the earth

This poem is thoroughly informed with a Saussurian insistence on the arbitrary relationship between the signifier and the signified, and its scepticism about language is enacted by the syntactical ambiguities that arise through the way each clause runs into the next, as in the last lines in which "upon the earth" refers both to where the leaves/words fall and to a Heideggerian sense of being in the world. (A stark contrast to this view of language is expressed in the title poem of Simon Armitage's first book *Zoom*[4] where words are celebrated as "small" and "smooth" and yet at the same time with a "mass. . .greater than the ringed planet". As I point out in my concluding chapter, though, it is an indication of how much "estrangement" elements are now entering the mainstream that in *Book of Matches*[5], this most talked about of young mainstream poets has been influenced by linguistic scepticism.)

That word "flickering" in the poem's last line connects with the metaphor of light (or reflection) which it employs to suggest the shifting nature of language as a medium. By so conflating words and light it also implies that perception and linguistic expression are inseparable from and inform each other. And this in turn draws attention to a further implied theme of the poem – the relationship between the self and the world. This theme is much more explicit, though, in "The Life Class" (*Various*, 76–77) which insists that "no one/ can escape the ordeal of being with everything else/ in the world" and explodes realist assumptions about the unitariness and discreteness of the self through an emphasis on interpenetration first announced via imagery: "Overhead the sky merges through windows/ into neon". This merging is celebrated, moreover, because it encourages a kind of creativity – the world and the self act upon and transform each other. The poem's most crucial analogy for this – partially summed up in the pun in its title – is in painting, where in a "space eight by twelve" the miracle can occur of the world and the self transfigured by their being blurred one into the other.

It would be possible to discuss the ontological aspects of this poem in Heideggerian and, perhaps, in Lacanian terms. However, what is also clear is that it is connected with an English tradition that is preoccupied with a Nature/Mind dialectic – even though Crozier's stance on this is the opposite of Wordsworthian egotism. It is surprising, given their polemic, how often these Various Art poets turn out to be writing in an English tradition stretching back to the Romantic period. This is probably least true of J.H. Prynne, but even he, in a poem like "Thoughts on the Esterhazy Court Uniform" (*Various*, 246–248) turns out to be preoccupied with the theme of return which obsessed the Wordsworth of, for example, "Tintern Abbey" and the Yarrow poems. This is a source of strength and confirms Mottram's point about there being varieties of Englishness which the dominance of the Movement tended to obscure: what the Various Art poets claim is the right to discuss ideas in poetry – a right that seemed inalienable to Wordsworth and Coleridge, but which the Movement's deeply self-conscious insistence on unpretentiousness tried to suppress.

In referring to Esterhazy, Prynne is referring to a place and time which have become wholly absorbed in their association with music, which implies the way that the "real" can be almost wholly replaced by its representation. This idea is reinforced by a careful confusion of tenor and vehicle in the poem's metaphors, as in these lines where "home world" is both literal and an allusion to musical key and "pulse" is both bodily and an allusion to musical rhythm:

> . . .Each move
> into the home world is that same loss; we
> do mimic the return and the pulse very
> slightly quickens, as our motives flare in
> the warm hearth.

More importantly, though, these lines are part of a meditation on the existential meaning of theme and variation structures, the meaning, that is, of the relationship between repetition and change. The past informs the present so that what seems vigorous and fresh is nonetheless part of the pattern – "to advance in the now fresh &/ sprouting world must take on some musical/ sense". This is to some extent reassuring, as home always is, but there is also, as Freud insists, something deathly in repetition – what gets repeated is also "that same loss", something too much the opposite of the fresh and sprouting present. The importance of music is that its abstract patterns embody both repetition and loss and so express the elusive and shifting dialectic between them: in music "we most/ deeply recognise the home we may not/ have".

Alongside their sense of a shared interest in an American poetic tradition these Various Art poets share a knowledge of recent literary theory and the the philosophical and linguistic thinking that lies behind it – Saussure, Jakobson, Freud, Nietzsche, Heiddeger, Derrida, Lacan. Here, though, I think I have to own up to my own inability to read the work of most of them in any sustained way. I want to believe in a poetry that could absorb these influences and still be as exciting and moving as I find the poems of Wordsworth, Browning, Eliot – and also that of Pound and Williams. But in fact it is only the work of two women poets associated with this group – Veronica Forrest-Thomson and Denise Riley – that I respond to in this way because it is as intelligent as that of Crozier, Prynne *et al* but less concerned to keep reminding the reader of that intelligence.

Veronica Forrest-Thomson was born and grew up in Glasgow, but was a student and then a teacher in Liverpool, Leicester, Birmingham and most importantly Cambridge where she met and was influenced by J.H. Prynne and the group that surrounded him. She was only 27 when she died in 1975. Edwin Morgan has described her as a "spiky, difficult character of great intelligence and wit, engaging, vulnerable and lonely"[6]. Her output was inevitably small given the brevity of her life. It also contains some work that she had not acquired the expertise to make fully successful. However, this was also the product of her marked originality – she commanded a diversity of talents unique in British poetry. She knew about both linguistic philosophy (especially the later Wittgenstein) and deconstruction, and evolved ways of incorporating their strategies into her writing by combining them with lessons learned from modernist and postmodernist poetry (especially T.S. Eliot, William Empson, John Ashbery and J.H. Prynne). This is impressive enough in itself but what really distinguishes her work is the interaction it contains between these cerebral interests and a powerful lyrical impulse – she combined the talents of a linguistic analyst with those of a love poet.

"Ducks and Rabbits"[7] displays her cerebral side, combined with her characteristic playfulness. It refers to section IIxi of the *Philosophical Investigations*[8] where Wittgenstein distinguishes "Two uses of the word 'see'":

> The one: "What do you see there?" – "I see *this* (and then a description, a drawing, a copy). The other: "I see a likeness between these two faces" – let the man I tell this to be seeing faces as clearly as I do myself.
>     The importance of this is the difference of category between the two "objects" of sight.
>
> (193)

In other words he is concerned to distinguish between "seeing" and "seeing as" (197), between "seeing" and the organisation of what is seen into comprehensible information.

What is particularly relevant for poetry here is that Wittgenstein does philosophically in this passage something analogous to what is achieved aesthetically by the activity of "defamiliarising" – he reviews what is taken for granted from a new point of view. By severing the acts of seeing and of interpretation he opposes the way that habit conflates the two. So his philosophical method, which dismantles the act of perception, works as Victor Shklovsky describes art working, whose technique

> is to impart the sensation of things as they are perceived and not as they are known. The technique of art is to make objects "unfamiliar", to make forms difficult, to increase the difficulty and length of perception because the process of perception is an aesthetic end in itself and must be prolonged. *Art is a way of experiencing the artfulness of an object; the object is not important.*[9]

It is perhaps not an accident, then, that in illustrating his argument Wittgenstein uses an artifact of sorts. This is a drawing called a "duck-rabbit" which is used in Gestalt psychology and which "can be seen as a rabbit's head or a duck's" (*PI*, 194). He imagines himself seeing this "simply as a picture-rabbit from the first" (194) but then suddenly seeing that it could also be a duck:

> The change of aspect. "But surely you could say that the picture is altogether different now!"
> But what is different: my impression? my point of view? – Can I say? I *describe* the alteration like a perception; quite as if the object had altered before my eyes.
>
> (195)

"Ducks and Rabbits" refers to this idea of alteration in order to explore the relationship between perception and imagination. Duck-rabbits for Forrest-Thomson are to some extent like objects linked together through the activity of the Coleridgean fancy but which become more radically transformed through the imagination: "The Mill Race/ at Granta Place/ tosses them from form to form/ dissolving bodies in the spume." But the poem also mimics the idea of "change of aspect" through its use of footnotes, which effect a kind of double-take. So what is called "the stream" in the poem is declared to be the stream "Of consciousness" at the foot of the page – and this suggests, also, that the mill is the mind that imposes subjective transformation on objective fact.

The second and third stanzas discuss the effect of these mental activities on artistic creation. The footnotes here are quotations from the Wittgenstein passage I have been referring to. The crucial point is that these alter, but do not replace, our perception of what happens in the body of the poem, and they indicate this themselves: "The expression of a change of aspect is the expression of a new perception"; "And at the same time of the perception's being unchanged." This suggests the way that poems transform, and yet do not transform, their material – it suggests, that is, the effect of "defamiliarisation":

> Give B, see A and C.
> that's what metaphor
> is for.

This is what happens most conspicuously in the poetry Forrest-Thomson most approved of, the poetry of "rational obscurity". As she says in her critical book, *Poetic Artifice*:

If poetry is to justify itself it must. . .Assimilate the already-known and subject it to a reworking which suspends and questions its categories, provides alternative orderings. In the best rational obscurity external contexts are brought into the poem as a way of creating a new ordering which is nonetheless rational.[10]

There is a sense, then, in which a good poem for Forrest-Thomson is a kind of "duck-rabbit", a chimera that combines the familiar and the unfamiliar, the world and an interpretation of the world, meaning and form. "Rational obscurity" involves maintaining the double perspective and rejecting the simplistic view which sees only a duck or a rabbit.

A double perspective is also apparent in the way that Forrest-Thomson likes to mix cerebral elements in her poems with emotional ones. In particular she meditates hard-headedly about love, examining expressions of love as what Wittgenstein would call "language games", a term which "is meant to bring into prominence the fact that the *speaking* of language is part of an activity, or of a form of life" (*PI*, 12). To speak about love raises with especial acuteness the problem, which preoccupied Wittgenstein, of how private experiences are made public; to write a poem about love places the poet in a long tradition and so connects her with repeated attempts, throughout history, to place private experience in a public framework.

So "Zettel" juxtaposes quotations from Wittgenstein's *Zettel*[11] with a scene in which a pair of lovers lie together:

> With the configuration of chess-pieces
> limbs describe themselves in rooms
> under the angle-poise
>
> (23)

This reference to chess evokes the numerous passages in which Wittgenstein singles out that game to exemplify the rules which are deployed and the behaviour that arises in the use of language. This may suggest security at first because the rules of chess are reassuringly specific and precise. However, the fact that this is a poem suggests other references – in particular, because Forrest-Thomson quotes Eliot almost obsessively, "A Game of Chess" in *The Waste Land* with its own reference to sexual deception in Middleton's *Women Beware Women*. Moreover, the context of linguistic philosophy itself becomes a worrying one because it insists on calling into question what it means to say what we say. In this context, then, the references to language philosophy call into question what it means to say (as the poet does say, twice) "I love you":

> Love is not a feeling.
> Love is put to the test
> – the *grammatical* test.
>
> (24)

"Zettel" is riddled with doubt about what "love" is and the implied difficulty of knowing what a supposed "lover" is actually thinking. References to the play of light, to a mirror and to play-acting make the poem bristle with the possibility of deception. One of the basic problems of language as opposed to games, after all, is the difficulty of knowing what language game you are playing. You may have thought that love was, as it were, a game of chess but it may turn out to be more like the "variant of tennis" imagined by Wittgenstein, in which

> it is included in the rules. . .that the player has to form *such-and-such images* as he perform certain moves in the game. (Let the purpose of this rule be to make the game more difficult.) The first objection is: it is too easy to cheat in this game. But this is met by the assumption that the game is played only by honest and reliable people. So here we have a game with inner moves of the game.
>
> (Zettel, 113)

The trouble is that love is a game played by unreliable people, and, as Wittgenstein goes on to wonder about his subjective tennis: "What sort of move is the inner move of the game, what does it consist in?"

The acute linguistic questioning in Forrest-Thomson's first mature book *Language Games* is certainly anxious, then. However, the questions in fact become more sombre and painful in her later book *On the Periphery* and the "Further Poems" collected in her Allardyce Barnett volume. For example, in "Address to the Reader, from Pevensey Sluice" (65) language is envisaged as mined with pitfalls

– it is an object of wry apprehension rather than a problem to be solved or a game to be played. And this is the case even though these feelings are expressed through what James Keery calls a "joke at the expense of Chomskyan linguistics"[12]:

> If it were quicksand you could sink;
> something needing a light touch
> soon and so simply takes its revenge.
> Slightly west of Goodwin Sands
> the land hardens again with history,
> resists the symbol.
> Chalk requires an allegorical hand,
> or employee of Sussex Water Board
> who sets a notice here:
> DANGER SUBMERGED STRUCTURES
> and all at once Transformational Grammar
> "peoples" the "emotional landscape"
> with refutation.

The Chomskyan reference is witty but it is connected to a poetic tradition of "paysage moralisé" (and most obviously to W.H. Auden's "In Praise of Limestone") which also ensures its seriousness and suggests genuine anxiety. Forrest-Thomson was comparatively happy in "Zettel" that "Love" should be put to "the *grammatical test*" but "Transformational grammar" seems altogether more threatening. The reasons for this are not Chomskyan – the submerged structures to which the poem refers are as much geological and psychological as linguistic. In fact it is most accurate to say that the poem hesitates between its different perspectives, and works in the gaps between them, and that consequently any stability of meaning is deferred. It works, that is, through "différance" – the main influence behind the poem is not Chomsky but Derrida, who haunts her later poems, dwelling as they do on the loss of all certainties:

> You may hear its melancholy
> long withdrawing roar
> even on Dover beach watching
> the undertow of all those trips
> across to France.

It is "Transformational Grammar" here which is equated with "Faith" in Matthew Arnold's "Dover Beach". Religion had been under threat in the Victorian period: now even the certainties of grammar are being undermined by influences from across the Channel. And because Forrest-Thomson's intellectual and emotional concerns so thoroughly interpenetrate each other, the linguistic desperation she expresses is inextricably associated in her late poems with her grieving at the loss of love. "Address to the Reader" refers to the tradition of topographical poems only to negate it (to "people" it with "refutation") – the landscape it depicts is a non-place that expresses non-feelings. The relationship between writer and reader is conflated with that between lovers, but then both are deconstructed and dissolved, so that the human comfort which Arnold sought in the face of religious doubt is itself terminally doubted:

> Follow the reader and his writer
> those emblematic persons
> along their mythic route
> charting its uncertain curves and camber;
> for to be true to any other you must –
> and I shall never now – recover
> a popular manoeuvre known mostly as,
> turn over
> and go to sleep.

"Address to the Reader" is a complex and oblique poem, but what makes it more effective is the context of other poems which are direct and more or less transparent and which thereby help to define its emotional background. "Canzon" (102–103), for example, refers once again to love as a chess game and so evokes the Wittgensteinian context of her earlier poems. By now, though, the sense is more of an endgame: pieces (which represent selves or parts of the self) are being hazarded and lost, and that knowledge of the otherness of other minds and speakers (and lovers) which the chess analogy evokes is felt with despairing acuteness:

> You check my every move
> By being what you will do
> And not what I could say
> To you, my love, an other,
> Suffering more myself
> By overlove and desire.

The presence of Provencal love poetry, especially that of Arnaut Daniel, is felt as strongly in "Canzon" as Forrest-Thomson's more contemporary, and more rigorously cerebral influences. The last section of "The Garden of Proserpine" is even more direct:

> My dignity dictated
> A restrained farewell.
> But I love you so much
> Dignity can go to hell.
>
> I went to hell with dignity,
> For by then, we were three.
> And whatever I feel about you
> I certainly hate she.
>
> The god knows what will be the end
> And he will never tell.
> For I love you and you love me
> Although we are in hell.
>
> And what death has to do with it
> Is always simply this:
> If it isn't your arms I'm heading for
> It's the arms of gloomy Dis.

This eccentric syntax and the way these colloquial rythms slant their way across the quatrain form are more reminiscent of Stevie Smith than they are of Prynne's Cambridge school.

However, what makes Forrest-Thomson especially valuable is that as well as writing such unashamedly emotional quatrains she could write the surreal and difficult (but in the end equally powerful) free verse of "Richard II" (110–111). The poem is best understood by reference to Forrest-Thomson's theory of the "disconnected image complex" which produces a hesitation "between empirical reference to a scene and assimilation of another linguistic system" and "suspends our reading between empirical and discursive imagery and forces us to make connections which neither discourse itself nor the world already contains" (*Artifice*, respectively 73 and 74). "Richard II" hesitates between empirical references to a house which employ the register of a surveyor ("The wiring appears to be five years old/ and is in satisfactory condition") and the parodic use of a portentous poetic idiom resembling that of Dylan Thomas ("In the light of the quiet night and the dark of the quiet noon/ I awoke by a day side and walked in time's room"). "Différance", then, is again a powerful factor – the discontinuities in the poem draw attention to differences between poetic levels which mean that any stable meaning is endlessly deferred. The ghostly presence of Shakespeare's king increases this effect. His most important function is to introduce that sense of the terminal which I identified in "Address to the Reader" and "Canzon"; "Richard II" is, on one level, about the deconstruction of an ancient lineage, a royal "house" ("In the joinery timbers there is new infestation/ And a damp-proof course is urgently needed"). Connected with this, the poem conjures up an ontological insecurity more diffuse than Sylvia Plath's, but more disorienting and almost as profound. So these lines near the end combine a reference to Richard's smashing of the mirror that had contained his image – an action that suggests his self-destructiveness, expresses his loss of face and prefigures his loss of self-definition – with a reference, familiar from Forrest-Thomson's other poems, to her own emotional state:

And I turned back to my smashed self and the few looks pierced my own doll
    From the back-lash of the time brick and the last wall of an old love.

"Richard II" is a kind of elegy for coherent meaning, and it expresses what deconstruction means at a psychological level. For Forrest-Thomson, the idea that language is incapable of saying anything that is not subject to endless doubt and fracturing has deeply personal ramifications. It means that the self too (as lover, speaker and writer) can be deconstructed and is vulnerable to fragmentation and dissolution. The individual subject, like the author, is dead, and both become shadows of themselves:

The only coherence, finally, is on the level of technique. I think that "our metaphysics" is this new technique of disconnected imagery which is the doom of fate of the twentieth-century poet, who must simultaneously be detached and involved with language. This means that he has all the tricks of rhetoric and the skills of language but he must not make the mistake of thinking that they solve anything. . .Before he can appropriate the external

world he must deny it to himself, and this requires him to "learn",
as one of Empson's poems has it, "a style from a despair". He
must develop new techniques in order in the end to be able to
use the old; as Bradley said of the speculative philosopher, to
converse with shadows he must himself become a shade.

(*Artifice*, 86)

These ontological doubts seem to be the premise, too, of much of
Denise Riley's writing. They are reflected at a practical level, perhaps, by her deliberate cultivation of anonymity, which is very unusual at a time when most poets seem obsessed with self-promotion.
In "Dark Looks" [13] she expresses the reasoning behind this:

Who anyone is or I am is nothing to the work. The writer
properly should be the last person that the reader or the
    listener need think about
yet the poet with her signature stands up trembling, grateful,
    mortally embarrassed
and especially embarrassing to herself, patting her hair and
    twittering If, if only
I need not have a physical appearance! To be sheer air, and
    mousseline!

This poem is a typically wry treatment of the issue of the author's
presence in her work, taking in, as it goes, the opposite possibilities
open to that author – either to go for a kind of panorama that seems
collective ("anglo-catholic clouds of drifting *we's* high tones of feeling") or to opt for a close-up that is minutely personal ("micro-
scopic horror scans of tiny shiny surfaces rammed up against the
nose"). It is clear, though, that it is the latter temptation which is
most relevant to her concerns and this is the one she discusses at
greater length in "Cruelty Without Beauty" (50–51) which – as the
inverted reference to cosmetics in the title indicates – is a specifically feminine take on confessional poetry. It compares this kind of
writing to a form of narcissistic self-laceration ("Go on working
around my hairline with a blade") and is especially scathing about
its tendency towards self-dramatising ("Show your wound: Ah yes
mine's deeper"). But she is also wary of the opposite temptation,
towards total self-effacement – relevant here because they go hand-
in-hand in Sylvia Plath – referring to "the deadly/ wish to be white

eye stripped out of human motion/ as if sight crashed to clearness, clean of me".

In the end in "Dark Looks" she wants to be bravely indifferent to attention ("So take me or leave me") but then gets comically alarmed at her own insouciance: "No, wait, I didn't mean leave/ me, wait, just *don't* – or don't flick and skim to the foot of a page and then get up to go". And this ambivalence reflects a broader hesitation in Riley on the whole issue of the self: here, as throughout her work, the activity of writing is regarded as representative. In this respect, Riley's influences are similar to Forrest-Thomson's and it is valid to regard her as also pursuing the emotional and ontological implications, for poets, of deconstruction – though in Riley's case there are also felt influences, like Lacan and Kristeva, which have taken hold since Forrest-Thomson's death.

"Wherever You Are, Be Somewhere Else" (27–29) is characteristic of Riley, then, in declaring "I never have wanted/ 'a voice' anyway, nor got it" in the broader context of the question of personal identity. What Riley provides in this poem is a series of images to represent a Lacanian dispersal of the self, the sense that what Forrest-Thomson calls the "smashed self" (111) is actually the normal state of affairs: there is no separate, unified identity, instead there is something like "a tin sheet/ beaten out then peppered with thin holes" which is penetrated by light and voices. In particular, for individual feminine subjects like Riley identity is defined by the gaze of others – "all faces split to angled facets: whichever/ piece is glimpsed, that bit is what I am". But then this scattering is carried one step further; "what I am" is "held"

> in a look until dropped like an egg on the floor
> let slop, crashed to slide and run, yolk yellow
> for the live, the dead who worked through me.

This seems to be an explicit reference to the Lacanian notion of the "hommelette", a portmanteau word conflating the ideas of "broken egg" and "little man" except that the masculinist assumptions behind that notion are defused by the way this image is placed in the context of the feminist concern with the defining nature of the gaze.

All this seems to lead Riley to want to heal the Lacanian split between the I that speaks and the I that is spoken about – to the extent that she longs for a kind of comic union with her word-processor, longs "to be only transmission", or to be its Romantic equivalent, the flower that "breaks open to its bell of sound", a creature whose self and whose utterance are organically one. What happens instead is that the I gets translated into "a stream of specks/ a million surfaces without a tongue" for language makes being take on shapes profoundly alien to it. "Well All Right" (46–47) is a kind of allegory for this based on a fairy story by Grimm about a woman whose brothers have been changed into swans who tries to change them back into men: the woman's activity represents that of the poet and the incompleteness of the change she brings about represents the hybrid instabilities that arise when being and language collide. Yet paradoxically the poem also exemplifies Riley's language – couched in her characteristically breathless head-over-heels free verse – at its most turbulently evocative:

> . . .Leap to
> the crests of orange birds flickering along the long line
> of shoulders, hiss, warble in gaping whistles hoarse lyre
> chants of plumed and swollen throats whose glowing trills
> waver and zigzag the swayed neck heavy under the flare
> song of any body glittering with hard memory.

Two of Riley's longest poems, "A Shortened Set" (16–24) and "Stair Spirit" (65–71) are very determined efforts to track down the shaping influences of language and poetic form – in a sense – as they are in process. For she seems determined not to settle back into mere passivity in the face of what language does. What is noticeable about Riley's self-reflexivity here is its comparative urgency and lack of playfulness. "A Shortened Set" is deadly serious in comparing the constitutive brevity of poems – and the consequent insistence they make on the need for cuts – with abortion, and then deliberately mixing the metaphor so that the resultant lack of "fit" also enacts what is being said about unfittingness: "This cut/ my memory half-sealed but glued/ the edges together awry" (16). "Stair Spirit" starts from the idea of "esprit d'escalier" – "thinking if if/ only I'd thought to say that in good time" (65) and then steepens into textual vertigo, each line like a stair signifying a regret for what should have been said and implicitly mourning the loss of its appropriate occasion:

> sheen of waiting
> corridor lure

> gleam of black
> joy of can't feel
> sealant of self
> gloss leaper
> clown of sorrows
> (68)

Perhaps the most characteristic element in Riley's treatment of the question of identity is her restlessness in the face of the postmodern insistence on dispersal of the self – which she at one level accepts but at another resists, connecting it, in "Disintegrate Me" (62–63) to

> . . .an old self-magnifying wish
> to throw the self away so violently and widely that interrogation
> has to pause since its chief suspect's sloped off to be cloud, to be
> wavery colour bands
>
> (63)

This is one temptation. The other is its opposite – to believe in the self as "agent" and deny "a likely truth of helplessness". She regards this as especially difficult to bear – a compromise (and compromised) ontological position where the personal faces "impersonal hazard, the humiliating lack of much control". Riley's work is especially valuable because of her inventive persistence in tackling the issue of what the self has become – diminished, fragmented, infiltrated, but still an issue. It may be her feminist concerns which make this urgent for her to an extent it is not, for example, to Prynne and Crozier: the personal and the political are unquestionably intertwined for her. So "Laibach Lyrik" (7–10) is a poem about the disintegration of Yugoslavia but it treats this subject in the context of the ontological questions which preoccupy her other work. It deals with Bosnia as a real political problem. But it also treats it as a manifestation of how identity is problematically founded upon a constitutive splitting and exile which riddles the self with a longing for a coherence it cannot have expressed in a language which is also the source of the problem:

> The settling scar agrees to voice
> what seems to speak its earliest cut.
> A rage to be some wholeness gropes

past damage that it half recalls –
where it was, I will found my name.
A hesitant gap now stretches its

raw mouth: I will become this sex
and Istrian.

(9)

# 12

# John Ashbery and British Postmodernism

The complexity of postmodernism as a term has been compounded by its overuse. Critics and reviewers of contemporary British poetry have tended to employ it merely to gesticulate towards a number of various, and sometimes contradictory developments. The editor of *Bete Noire*, John Osborne, has been an exception to this but, as I indicate in my chapter on Craig Raine, even Osborne's use of the term is unconstructively broad in some respects[1]. Much more conspicuously, Blake Morrison and Andrew Motion suggested that the poets in their *Penguin Book of Contemporary British Poetry* "do represent a departure, one which may be said to exhibit something of the spirit of post-modernism"[2]. Some of the work of James Fenton and Paul Muldoon may be accurately referred to in this way but it is at best unhelpful and at worst simply wrong to apply it to the others – especially to the most copiously represented poets, Seamus Heaney, Tony Harrison and Douglas Dunn.

Motion and Morrison refer to Heaney as "characteristically more oblique" (13) than Robert Lowell and Ted Hughes and seem to regard this as a postmodernist characteristic. What they mean here may be better understood by reference to Morrison's book on Heaney[3], which suggests that it is wrong not to see his work "as part of a world that includes Ashbery, Ammons, Pynchon, Grass, Stoppard, Fowles, Barthes, Derrida and Foucault" (12) because it is "rather less comforting and comfortable than has been supposed":

Far from being "whole", it is tense, torn, divided against itself; far from being straightforward, it is layered with often obscure allusions; far from being archaic, it registers the tremors and turmoils of its age, forcing traditional forms to accept the challenge of harsh, intractable material.

(13)

All of this is true but it is also true of Tennyson and Browning and what it ignores are the atavistic elements in Heaney which, while they constitute some of his power as a poet, make him an entirely different writer from those in Morrison's postmodernist pantheon.

This is most evident in his view of language. It is true that Heaney's poems are self-reflexive – but in a similar way to Wordsworth's. He constantly compares writing to agriculture and language to land; he is always trying to insist that words have a "natural" relationship to their meanings and that poems have an "organic" relationship to their subject. His view of language is closest to that "mimetic theory" which Michael Schmidt attributes to Gerard Manley Hopkins: Heaney, too, "asks not only what language means but how it means to the senses, how it contains what it signifies"[4]. In "Digging", the poem with which Heaney chose to begin his *New Selected Poems 1966–1987*[5] spade and pen are equated; in "Anahorish" (*NSP*, 21) the eponymous name is treated as the immediate equivalent of the place it represents – "soft gradient/ of consonant, vowelmeadow"; "Glanmore Sonnets" treat language and land as interchangeable – "Vowels ploughed into other opened ground,/ each verse returning like the plough turned round" (*NSP*, 110). It is true that Heaney's organicism has become increasingly complex and self-conscious but it has not fundamentally altered and the mystical assumptions that lie behind the equation of an Irish place with its name in "Broagh" (*NSP*, 25) have actually become more prominent.

The title poem of his most recent volume *Seeing Things*[6] indicates, in its meditation on the Latin word "Claritas", an increased consciousness of the problem of representation. The word, he says, is "perfect for the carved stone of the water/ Where Jesus stands up to his unwet knees" – word and stone are distortive media. So far so postmodernist. But then the carving (and, by implication, the word) are said to transcend themselves and to evoke "life itself" through a mystical immediacy which ecstatically erases the gap between words and things, representation and thing represented. The sculpture and the Latin word "claritas" – which itself yearns for a language which will be a clear medium – combine in an epiphanic experience in which air and language become co-extensive with each other:

> . . .in that utter visibility
> The stone's alive with what's invisible:

Waterweed, stirred sand-grains hurrying off,
The shadowy, unshadowed stream itself.
All afternoon, heat wavered on the steps
And the air we stood up to our eyes in wavered
Like the zig-zag hieroglyph for life itself.

(17)

Much of this is powerful in its way but nothing could be further from the postmodernist view of representation and of language. Where Heaney wants the relationship between word and meaning to be mimetic, postmodernists insist it is arbitrary; where Heaney wants the relationship between language and the world to be organic, postmodernists insist it is constructed; where Heaney is mystical, postmodernists are sceptical. Whereas literary postmodernists largely adopt modernist forms and take them further, and accept modernist assumptions but are characteristically more playful and celebratory than their modernist predecessors, Heaney behaves more like other anti-modernists like Larkin who conduct a dialogue with modernist themes in order to argue, usually implicitly, against them, or allow them distortive room in a largely anti-modernist context and so defeat them by a kind of repressive tolerance.

So Heaney's "bog people" poems refer to the controlling metaphor of *The Waste Land* – the anthropological thesis, derived from Jessie Weston, that a sacrifice to the gods was required by primitive societies, a "scapegoat", in order for the dead land of Winter to be renewed by Spring. Eliot's poem treats this idea with a pervasive irony which insists on the difference between the modern condition (which is alienated, deracinated) and that of the much older societies who held these beliefs – societies which enjoyed an organic connectedness with their natural environments. However, where Eliot stresses severance from the past, Heaney insists on continuity. So he says that P.V. Glob (his equivalent of Jessie Weston) argues that a number of the "preserved bodies of men and women found in the bogs of Jutland, naked, strangled or with their throats cut, disposed under the peat since early Iron Age times",

were ritual sacrifices to the Mother Goddess, the goddess of the ground who needed new bridegrooms each winter to bed with her in her sacred place, in the bog, to ensure the renewal and fertility of the territory in the spring. Taken in relation to the tradition of Irish political martyrdom for that cause whose icon is Kathleen ni Houlihan, this is more than an archaic barbarous rite: it is an archetypal pattern. And the unforgettable photographs of these victims blended in my mind with photographs of atrocities, past and present, in the long rites of Irish political and religious struggles.[7]

So in "Punishment" (*NSP*, 71–72) Heaney declares that he has direct, unmediated access to the experience of one of these sacrificial victims:

> I can feel the tug
> of the halter at the nape
> of her neck, the wind
> on her naked front.

For Heaney there is unquestionably a community of mind between subject and object in this poem: he can "identify" with the sacrificed girl partly because he is a poet with ancient powers of divination or conjuration, but also because her social condition and his have profound affinities. What is no more than a black joke about resurrection in *The Waste Land* ("That corpse you planted last year in your garden,/ Has it begun to sprout?") is here taken seriously and death is transcended as it is in "Requiem for the Croppies", where "barley grew up out of the grave" (*NSP*, 12).

However, it is in this context – where Heaney's characteristic mysticism is mingled with politics – that it is at its most controversial. Edna Longley and Ciaran Carson both express anxieties about it:

> It is as if he is saying, suffering like this is natural; these things have always happened; they happened then, they happen now, and that is sufficient ground for understanding and absolution.[8]

What should be stressed, however, is that the "naturalness" that is evoked in these poems is a consistent resource in Heaney's poetic as a whole and reveals his links with a pre-modernist, Romantic theory of poetry and experience. In the "bog people" poems Heaney refers to one of the most famous modernist metaphors in a way that claims it for this older tradition. *The Waste Land* self-consciously deconstructs the metaphor; its formal effects of montage and self-reflexive fragmentariness work in a radically anti-organicist way.

Heaney, by contrast, heals the breach between past and present and magically restores the primitive mechanism to a renewed position of archetypal, "natural" power.

Heaney's struggle against modernism is conducted, not on behalf of realism, like Larkin's, but on behalf of a mysticism and organicism whose roots are in Romanticism. Nonetheless, his influence, like Larkin's, has worked powerfully against modernism and postmodernism in British poetry. For this reason it might be regarded as a mistake to have discussed him at all in this chapter. However, I think this discussion not only reveals what postmodernism most emphatically is not, but also suggests the difficulties facing genuine postmodernists. For in the 1980s Heaney rose to a position of enormous influence in British poetry which inevitably meant that he established an agenda from whose perspective other poets would to some extent inevitably be judged. Moreover, that important and youngish members of the establishment like Motion and Morrison could regard Heaney as, in his way, postmodernist suggests the extent of the difficulty genuine postmodernists would face in making themselves understood.

The contrast with America helps to define this more clearly – for there the poetic establishment in the 1970s and 80s was genuinely postmodernist and the most important figure was John Ashbery. Perhaps the most telling way to define this contrast is to compare the Motion/Morrison anthology with *The Best American Poetry, 1988*[9], edited by John Ashbery. These two anthologies say much about the two establishments. The series editor of the American book is David Lehman, who has edited a critical book on John Ashbery and whose own poems are influenced by Ashbery, so it was not surprising that he chose Ashbery to edit the first book in the series. Admittedly, there is a time-lag between the two anthologies but what lessens the importance of this is the extent to which Ashbery's selection reflects a superannuated view of the American poetry scene – reflecting the dominant poetic of the late 70s and early 80s rather than of 1988. By the late 80s in America, New Formalism, narrative poetry of various kinds, and women's poetry were all at least as important as the kind of thorough postmodernism Ashbery favours – that he failed to represent those kinds of poetry is even more glaringly shown up by the substantial way they *were* represented by Donald Hall in the following year's anthology, *The Best American Poetry 1989*[10]. At any rate, the starkness of the contrast shows how little there is, despite its "Introduction", that is genuinely postmodernist in the Motion/Morrison book: Ashbery/Lehman, on the other hand, contains little else.

For a start it is full of Ashbery's associates – his old friend Kenneth Koch; James Schuyler who co-authored a novel with him; David Shapiro who has written a book about him; John Ash, who is the British poet with most affinities with Ashbery. And so on. Martin Booth's comment on the Motion/Morrison anthology, that it contained "their immediate circle surrounded by a few others of like bent"[11] is actually far truer of Ashbery/Lehman. Even the poems by those not closely associated with Ashbery tend to occupy his poetic territory – there is much that is discursive and/or surreal and/or ludic, much that has a New York style or setting, quite a few touches of highbrow camp. There is little that concerns itself with society or history, little that is narrative or autobiographical or realist. An Ashbery perspective seems to affect even some of the established figures who are included, so that Gary Snyder and Charles Simic read like new recruits for Ashbery's postmodernist Village People. Admittedly, the only Ashbery element in the Snyder is that it is a poem about New York, but this is strange enough. The San Francisco Beat poet more recently retreated to the High Sierra seems, in this company, a kind of Zen Crocodile Dundee. Simic's poem is also about New York and its surrealism alternates between the dark elliptical kind he usually writes and the urbane playful kind more associated with Ashbery.

I was amongst those who found the Motion/Morrison Penguin too narrow but I find the quite different narrowness of the American anthology in many ways more disturbing because it is much more of a closed shop. Taken together the two anthologies rebuke each other by revealing the possibilities that each excludes. Moreover, the Penguin can to some extent be taken to reflect the way the British establishment has operated since in lowering the profile of most postmodernist poetry: though, as I shall argue, there are recent signs that this is changing.

What is valuable in *The Best American Poetry 1988* is the way it reveals how invigorating can be the influence of Ashbery's brilliant "Self-Portrait in a Convex Mirror"[12], and similar poems by him. The long poems by Clark Coolidge and John Koethe that display it draw upon its characteristic resources – the ease with which it moves between abstract discussion and vivid (often surreal) imagery – to interesting effect. This is a poetic that combines discursiveness with surrealism to enact the difficulties that discourse faces – difficulties that arise because our sense of reality is compromised by the way our minds and our language turn it into fiction. This is from John Koethe's "Mistral":

> ...What remains behind
> Is a kind of feeling of contingency, a gradual waning of the present
> Into a mere possibility, as though it were a dream of the extent of life
> In which there wasn't any tangible experience of finitude, only a dull,
> Unfocused anger as the words slide off the page and out of memory
> And the faces wash away like caricatures on a wall, and the sky fades
>
> (97)

There is relatively little of this kind of discursive poetry written by British postmodernists and I want to maintain that, while the influence of Ashbery has been important, its extent has been exaggerated. One reason for this is that the work of British modernists like those discussed in earlier chapters – Edwin Morgan, Roy Fisher and Christopher Middleton – has received too little attention, so that the extent of their input into younger poets like John Ash, Ian McMillan, Peter Didsbury and others has been underestimated. By contrast, Ashbery's high profile in his own country has caused him to be watched with some attention in Britain – though with that kind of apprehension (and, in some quarters, outright hostility) that characterises British responses to American reputations. As a result, critics and reviewers have tended to reach for the name of Ashbery when confronted by British postmodernists. This is distortive in a number of ways, not least because it tends to reinforce the idea that there is something unBritish about non-realist ways of writing.

However, because influence is such a complex phenomenon it is impossible to define where it begins and ends. Ashbery himself is most accurately seen as a late manifestation of a kind of profoundly sceptical modernism whose most important roots are in French post-symbolism. But it is undoubtedly the case that this provenance has powerful links with those of Morgan, Fisher and Middleton, and to try to disentangle all these interpenetrating roots would be a futile exercise. Consequently, the most efficient way to proceed is to describe those elements of Ashbery's practice that are also evident in British postmodernist poets and then to examine how accurately, or fully, these poets can be characterised by reference to those elements.

Although it takes John Ashbery's "It was raining in the capital" as its epigraph, John Ash's "October in the Capital"[13] has little connection with the subject-matter of Ashbery's quatrains. The real connection is in the method of Ash's poem, and the strategy involved in the epigraph – the allusion as red herring – is itself characteristic of Ashbery: the Marvellian hints in "The Picture of Little J.A. in a Prospect of Flowers" (Ashbery, 12–13) and "As One Put Drunk into the Packet-Boat" (Ashbery, 171–172) are similarly deployed. It is part of a larger poetic practice in which a hint is made momentarily and then overwhelmed by others that qualify or even erase it. As Ashbery said in an interview with Piotr Sommer, "understanding comes about. . .as a sort of Penelope's web that's constantly being taken apart when it's almost completed, and that's the way we grow in our knowledge, and experience"[14]. Without acknowledging it, Ashbery was here quoting from David Kalstone's essay on him: "Like Penelope's web, the doing and undoing of Ashbery's poems is often their subject: fresh starts, repeated collisions of plain talk with the tantalizing and frustrating promises of 'poetry'."[15]

This technique is employed as a way of rendering the enormous complexity of experience and the mind's bafflement in the face of it – its difficulty in finding significant connections between one experience and another. As Ashbery himself points out, in his essay on the painter R.B. Kitaj, this theme had been adumbrated by Eliot in *The Waste Land*, but Ashbery's poems have pursued its ramifications in subtly modulated detail, so that Ashbery's account of the passage beginning "The river sweats/Oil and tar. . ." reads more accurately as a depiction of his own work: "Such a passage is less a description than a miming of a way of seeing wherein objects will clear for a moment and then blur, adjacent phenomena are compressed into a puzzling homogeneity, and a clear outline abruptly turns illegible."[16] In the closing lines of "And *Ut Pictura Poesis* Is Her Name" this concern with "miming" is discussed together with the aesthetic difficulty encountered when it is attempted:

The extreme austerity of an almost empty mind
Colliding with the lush, Rousseau-like foliage of its desire
    to communicate

Something between breaths, if only for the sake
Of others and their desire to understand you and desert
   you
For other centers of communication, so that understanding
May begin, and in doing so be undone.

(243)

Understanding must begin, but it must never get too sure of itself – Ashbery has evolved a thoroughly sceptical poetic in order to render the sensation of living without any beliefs substantial or consistent enough to provide stable ground from which experience can be reliably viewed. The ground his reader is invited to stand upon may turn out to be dream, metaphor or artifact and so start to shift or even to open up vertiginously. Sometimes this may arouse anxiety but more often, in suggesting an infinite possible variousness, it arouses pleasure or even exhilaration. Sometimes, too – as in these lines from "Nymphéas" by Ash – it can disconcertingly suggest anxiety and pleasure at the same time:

> On the wall above the table a print,
> predominantly mauve, displays
> the victim of a recent bombing
> dissolved into luscious water-lights and lilies: it looks
> good enough to eat. . .[17]

The epigraph from Reverdy that Ash uses in 'Part Three' of *The Goodbyes* perfectly sums up this unexpected response – playfulness where you might expect angst:

> . . .La vie entière est en jeu
> Constamment
> Nous passons à côté du vide élegamment sans tomber
> Mais parfois quelque chose en nous fait tout trembler
> Et le monde n'existe plus[18]

In the face of meaninglessness, Reverdy's "vide", the poetic shared by Ashbery and Ash takes a determined pleasure – as Ashbery said in his *Quarto* interview: "There is a line in my poem 'The Skaters' that seems to be the sum of my hedonistic, my seriously hedonistic philosophy, which is 'nothing but movies and love and laughter, sex and fun'." (14)

Nonetheless, both Ashbery and Ash insist on the felt absence of centred meaning, and both employ effects to make "le vide" open under their poems. Ashbery's resources for achieving this are extremely various, though certain linguistic effects are most characteristic of him, especially quickfire shifts in register, involving, as Ash put it when interviewing Ashbery, "very shop-worn phrases, very slangy phrases, neologisms, and lyrical 'poetic' language and any kind of diction juxtaposed"[19]. Ash's resources are fewer, and most of them have previously been used by Ashbery, but he has added to their effectiveness in his own way – partly by simplifying them; most importantly they involve allusions to musical form and to the otherness of exotic places, and intertextual evocations of symbolism and surrealism.

It is Ash's preoccupation with music which provides the key to all these effects. For him its importance is that it momentarily suggests the possibility of astonishingly full understanding but then withdraws it. Similarly, symbolism is – as Ash in his essay "Reading Music" describes it – a method of "evocation, allusion and suggestion"[20], and offers a revelation which it never fully gives; it is a poetry of endlessly hesitant, and endlessly partial disclosure. Surrealism, by contrast, offers a paradoxical solidity, but though its images are specific, their status is always in doubt.

It is only when seen against this background that Ash's treatment of the exotic can be properly understood: for the solidity and specificity it appears to offer are illusory. Here, Ash has taken the example of Blaise Cendrars' "voyage" poems – which combine the apparently factual imagery of travel with a self-conscious fictiveness – and taken it further so that the importance of elsewhere is that is subverts the certainties of here, it insists that a poem's setting is provisional and can be altered at will.

So it is not surprising that the landscape in "October in the Capital", in *Disbelief* is impossible to locate. Like the American Type Founders Company, which is quoted in the epigraph to this volume, Ash has "modelled a world in miniature which exists only in these pages and is not to be found by the most enterprising geographer". It is a composite place of heat and political oppression, and the drought which it evokes so effectively carries echoes of the controlling metaphor in *The Waste Land*. It may also be that the sterile sexual encounters in Eliot's poem (which are linked, metaphorically, to drought) are being parodied in the third section of "October in the Capital" when a girl "returning from a party alone/

...having failed to speak to a man who had long fascinated her" gets aroused by a statue. However, this poem seems less concerned than its predecessors to display its scepticism, and its surreal imagery builds towards a political meaning. There is a repeated suggestion that life is being reduced: the place "dwindled/into formlessness", and "now it was drying out, –/a tray of tobacco leaves for an industrial tyrant's cigar"; the people "remained draped over balconies like laundry" or have been replaced by statues. And the closing image, "a statue made of very cold water" actually uses what Ash has learned from Ashbery – the way to open a perplexing vista in a poem, and keep it open – to suggest the complexity of political oppression, the complexity of its causes, its nature and its effects. For this surreal image of paradoxical fixedness evokes a society that appears stable because it is rigid with fear, but which is in fact constantly under threat of deep-seated change. It is as though Ash has taken Ashbery's largely aesthetic point from "Self-Portrait in a Convex Mirror", and made it political:

> ...The whole is stable within
> Instability, a globe like ours, resting
> On a pedestal of vacuum, a ping-pong ball
> Secure on its jet of water

*Disbelief* indicates an increase in Ash's interest in story-telling in both verse and prose. However, for Peter Ackroyd – whose *The Diversions of Purley*[21] collects three volumes previously published by small presses – the implications of story-telling have always been the central concern. His poems contain few of the references to music and painting that are so important to Ashbery and Ash, and Ashbery's concern with fictions (elaborating upon themes from Wallace Stevens) is adopted by Ackroyd and adapted as specifically a concern with fiction; his poems tend to be literary in their allusions, and the fact that he is also a novelist and literary biographer may largely explain why. For Ackroyd, as for Ashbery, understanding begins and in doing so is undone, but for him this undoing is effected through a sceptical unpeeling of layers of reality, in which reality looms but then recedes, in which activity in the world – through the distorting processes of being perceived and then translated into language – becomes a form of narrative, and men and women become "characters":

So winter is coming in, and the self fades
and flickers; we read novels late into the night,
watching helplessly as characters race toward each other.
So much has been written about this light, both for
and against, I don't know how to begin –
where the stars go? how the day starts?
Angel Clare bows his head against the wind,
thinking about the things he has to do today:
if I come out into the open will I be myself,
or will it be the beginning of another story?

(28)

Ackroyd's affinity is with the elliptical, fragmented Ashbery, not the expansive, Whitmanian Ashbery. He prefers short lines, he uses stanzaic patterns and his poems seem pared down – they give the impression of rigour, even of austerity. He is playful at times but this rarely seems gratuitous and his poems have few of the camp mannerisms which can be irritating in Ashbery and Ash. In these lines from "the novel" the discussion of the difficulty of describing the light is not merely self-reflexive, it also indicates that the light seems to vary according to how it is viewed, and by whom, and how difficult it is to see it as not pre-packaged by previous ways of seeing it, how difficult not to place it in a rigid structure ("landscapes, seascapes or family portraits/which seem most real when they are not so" as he says earlier in the poem). So "the novel" finally raises questions about the way even the self gets fictionalised; even an attempt to live more honestly, to "come out into the open" may only initiate a different set of conventions, may only "be the beginning of another story".

It may be that there are links between this concern with the elusiviness of self and Ackroyd's activities as literary biographer and novelist. Certainly, his *T.S. Eliot*[22] is a massively detailed attempt to locate the changing self of the poet behind his writings. As he says in his "Prelude", "the connection between the life and the work is here explicity made, and it will be the purpose of this book to attempt to elucidate the mystery of that connection". In this way Ackroyd has deliberately placed his enterprise in the complex and shifting ground between the poet's person and the poetry – all the more complex because the poet claimed the poems were impersonal. It is the difficulty of what the biography attempts that is its point; *T.S. Eliot* is about the difficulty of distinguishing the self from fictive versions of the self. And the word he chooses, "mystery", is significant – for this is surely his central preoccupation; it is mystery that is most conjured up in his own poems: "on the third stroke/it will be uncertain" (35). It is mystery, too, which prevails in his novel *Hawskmoor*[23] which is concerned, like Ashbery's "Litany", with the disorientation produced by the opposition of two voices. *Hawksmoor* alternates two first person narrations, one by an early 18th century architect, the other by a 1980s detective. "Litany"[24] is composed of two monologues arranged in parallel columns, which, as Ashbery said in this *Quarto* interview, "are supposed to be not read, but attended to simultaneously" (14). Both works compound the untrustworthiness of monologue with the jarring effect of vocal crossfire in order to suggest that meaning arises, if it does arise, not in one voice or another, or in a synthesis of the two, but in the unreconciled and mysterious distance between them. So Ashbery described, in the same interview, how

> I've taped "Litany" with. . .a woman poet; we both read simultaneously. . .Of course you lose enormous amounts of the text because of the clash of the voices, but what you hear seems to be very effective. . .it was my attempt at mimesis of the way experience and knowledge come to me, and I think to everybody. I think we're constantly in the middle of a conversation where we never finish our thoughts, or our sentences and that's the way we communicate.
>
> (14)

This feeling of incompletion is constantly suggested in Ackroyd's poems in juxtaposed, unpunctuated and broken pieces of speech, and in the subtle openness of his delicate cadences. But perhaps their most notable achievement is in their use of mysterious fragments of narrative to suggest a baffled and dreamlike inquiring:

> on the third stroke
> it will be uncertain
>
> my dreams meet me half-way
> stunned and incomplete
>
> you repeated something
> and then I walked forward

the lines meet in the distance
touching someone's life

there is a place I cannot reach
where the others are

(35)

Ashbery's influence is central to Ash and Ackroyd; it is much less so for Peter Didsbury. It has been important, nonetheless, and Didsbury's quite different use of the influence helps it to be more precisely understood in the case of the other two. What Disbury has learned from Ashbery is partly technical – his rhythmical flexibility and colloquial nonchalance – and partly an outlook on subject-matter, a belief in a self-conscious inclusiveness, an apparent open-ness to experience as the poem is being written that allows an improvisatory quality to be suggested. As David Lehman has written:

Virtually everything. . .can serve Ashbery as a source of material . . .Should the telephone ring during the hour or so a week that Ashbery reserves for the writing of poetry, he'll welcome the interruption – and allow it to modify the poem in progress. Noth-ing is excluded or suppressed. Ashbery can leap in an instant from Sidney Carton to a wrong number to an affirmation of love, and make it seem the most natural thing in the world. [25]

More weight is added to this method by the way – in evoking the moment of composition – it places itself *between* experience and language, interrogating the relationship between them. So, in "The Flowers of Finland"[26] the voice is tentative – ideas are proposed and then modified, or even erased ("Taken. Under-taken. Taken./ Words from a dream. . ./Stop. All wrong.") Other ideas are intro-duced whose status is in doubt – they may be bits of narrative, or they may be metaphors for what precedes or follows them ("After my head hit the windscreen/I thought of Auden's words. . ."). But the poem's discussion of language and poetry suggest that these ideas are being used as examples of what a poem can contain, and what language and poetic convention will do to them when the poem does contain them ("Anywhere will do to start/. . .Language is the propensity"; "telling the truth about the world/mightn't be the best way/of getting some things down").

In a similar way "The Smart Chair"[27] questions the way that poems connect distinct experiences. Its improvisational quality emerges from this because the experiences in question appear to enter randomly, so that the poem links a remark by an eleven year old girl ("Your chair looks smart") and a visit to a small island. One of the experiences is quite prosaic and the other is more conventionally poetic, and this adds a further Ashbery quality in the mingling of the two. These aspects are exaggerated, also, by the way the one experience is made more prosaic by being elaborated upon:

> My chair looked smart because it had a tie hanging over the
>    back.
> She's eleven years old, and although she knows that I don't
>    wear ties
> she didn't know I'd been to a funeral, wearing that tie
> which now improves my furniture.

And the other experience is made more "poetic" by having a fantasy appended to it:

> . . .a white farmhouse stood in the middle of the bay
> on a rock that was little larger than itself. *Not* a farmhouse,
> unless they farmed seaweeds, rats, and the voices of drowned
>    sailors –
> there wasn't enough room –

Juxtaposed in this way the prosaic and the poetic raise questions about each other; moreover, they remain unreconciled and they are not arranged hierarchically (as they are characteristically in Larkin's poems) so that the prosaic builds towards the poetic. Instead, there is a levelling of materials in an effect which is akin to (but not as extreme as) that inclusiveness in Ashbery which is indebted to Whitman's "democratic" aesthetic.

Where Didsbury differs from Ashbery is in his treatment of poetic meaning, and here the counter-influence of Christopher Middleton has been important. Both Ashbery and Middleton are experimental poets who have been concerned to face up to the problem of meaninglessness. However, whereas Ashbery's concern has most often been with mimesis, with evolving sophisticated techniques for the "miming of a way of seeing" meaninglessness, Middleton has striven for methods of assembling meaning, however dubious or fitful. For Middleton, poetry is an urgent activity (though one that allows a purposeful playfulness). In "Notes on Poems 1964/5" he describes the poems as "active structures of eccentric feeling, presenting truths of imagination"[28]. So, where Ashbery, Ash and Ackroyd walk elegantly by the side of the emptiness, Middleton urges "Fill the emptiness, facing it, raw grief/Now and really surrounds your face"[29].

Didsbury is never as urgent as this, but he has learned from Middleton's more oblique methods, his way of taking significance by surprise. Middleton provides the best analogue for this in his essay on Robert Walser when he refers to Walser's "discrimination of the symbolic pregnancy of commonplace evens by what astronomers call 'averted vision'" – vision by which faint stars can sometimes be seen "not by looking straight at them but by catching the light in the corner of the eye"(*Bolshevism*, 105). Middleton goes on to show how this method suggests that "the meaning is there, but always just out of reach" (106).

Examined more closely, "The Smart Chair" can be seen to work through this kind of indirectness, as the poem emerges as a deliberately circuitous investigation of the different ways that death can come to mind. Part of the point of the poem, however, is to demonstrate the inadequacy of putting it in this way, to demonstrate that it is necessary to avert the vision from death in order to see how it insinuates itself into experiences apparently unconnected with it, or each other. For this reason Didsbury will not refer to death as such, he forbids himself the use of "proper names", "for I will not have them do my work for me". Instead he wants his poem to speak through actions like that of the eleven year old girl when "Just to make it perfectly right she put a knot in my tie/so that it was really being worn by the chair". What Middleton calls "the symbolic pregnancy of commonplace events" is very much in evidence, therefore, when Didsbury returns from his visit to the island and finds the chair wearing a black tie: the more so because he felt, on the journey, a "fear when that truck moved over on the motorway", the island had a graveyard on it and the wind in its brown pines – "that freshened throughout the morning,/moving the flowering currants that grew among the graves" persists in his memory as a "voice".

So, from the randomness of "all the things that filled the last two days" – a randomness which Didsbury suggests by the use of techniques derived from Ashbery – a more unified meaning emerges because the poet is struck by a startling, even uncanny, connection between otherwise unconnected experiences. It is the arbitrariness of this which is stressed as much as its power. Nonetheless, "The Smart Chair" does demonstrate how, out of the fragmentariness of daily experience, pieces can unexpectedly fit together – especially when the vision is averted – to hint at a meaning. So, whereas Ashbery's work constantly explores ground broken by *The Waste Land*, a poetry of fragments whose only meaning he says are "their contiguity", "and it is implied that from now on meaning will take into account the randomness and discontinuity of modern experience, that indeed meaning cannot be truthfully defined as anything else" (*Kitaj*, 10), "The Smart Chair" takes randomness and discontinuity into account but then suggests that they can seem, briefly, to clear. It demonstrates how random and discontinuous experiences can accidentally coincide and form an associative pattern of momentary significance.

Even as I have tried to focus on Ashbery's influence on these British poets I have discovered other influences at work – Reverdy and Cendrars on Ash, the novel on Ackroyd, Middleton on Didsbury. Moreover, what is impossible to determine is the extent to which what looks like the influence of Ashbery is actually the direct influence of earlier poets who were also influential in making Ashbery the poet that he is. Certainly John Ash reveals, in both his poetry and his critical prose, a considerable knowledge of French symbolist and post-symbolist writing: this interest amounts largely to an affinity between the British and American poets. However, there is an important difference in their attitudes to its legacy. For Ashbery its influence is mostly stylistic; its profound non-realism, and its deployment of parody and irony, provide a springboard for him into his poetic of endless doubt, into his attitude of thorough detachment. There is something of this, too, in Ash's manner, but the very insistence with which he refers to things French and late nineteenth century or early twentieth, to the music of Debussy and Sati, the poetry of Baudelaire or Laforgue, suggests attachment rather than its opposite. This exerts a stabilising influence on Ash's work which counters the Ashbery-like instabilities which I described earlier. Moreover, it is joined in this respect by Ash's repeated references to his native city of Manchester, so that between them the

French *fin de siècle* and the English late twentieth century start to
define a more established sense of time and place.

As a result, there is a much greater sense of social rootedness in
Ash's work than there is in Ashbery's, and this is crucial because it
reflects a quite different outlook. Another way of accounting for
this would be to indicate how much smaller the impact of more
recent French thinking has been on Ash than it has on Ashbery.
Taken together, these two differences indicate that Ash is much less
thoroughly postmodernist than Ashbery and this is something he
shares – very significantly I think – with other British postmodernists.

This means that it is much more relevant to refer to the postmodernist theory of Jean-François Lyotard and Jean Baudrillard
when discussing Ashbery and his American followers than it is
when discussing British postmodernists. Lyotard's diagnosis of what
the postmodern involves also defines Ashbery's poetic very accurately – Lyotard sees that condition as premised upon "a shattering
of belief" and a "discovery of the 'lack of reality' of reality, together
with the invention of other realities".[30] And he continues:

> Moreover, the postmodern is that which puts forward the
> unpresentable in presentation itself; that which denies itself the
> solace of good forms, the consensus of a taste which would make
> it possible to share collectively the nostalgia for the unattainable;
> that which searches for new presentations, not in order to enjoy
> them but in order to impart a stronger sense of the unpresentable.
> A postmodern artist or writer is in the position of a philosopher:
> the text he writes, the work he produces are not in principle
> governed by preestablished rules, and they cannot be judged
> according to a determining judgement, by applying familiar cat-
> egories to the text or to the work.
>
> (81)

The extent to which assumptions like this lie behind Ashbery's
work is more evident than ever in his recent book *Flow Chart*[31],
which contains his most direct statements of belief (or disbelief). A
"flow chart" is "a schematic diagram. . .showing the progress of
materials through the various stages of a manufacturing process"
(*Webster's Dictionary*). It presents complex information in a structured, comprehensible and visible form. If Ashbery had written the
poetic equivalent he would have organised diffuse and difficult
material in a way that would have simplified and so clarified it.

So *Flow Chart* imagines, near the end, and as a hypothesis, a "regulatory system that organises us in some semblance of order" (199). This is evidently, in Lyotardian terms, the "unpresentable" – Ashbery is imagining a new presentation but he then reveals that it cannot perform the functions which are claimed for it. This glimpse of order is hedged around with such qualifications it nearly disappears. The "system" he refers to is something that might just possibly exist and which a "technically/ not unrealizable state of affairs" might "bring us closer, but only a little, to a vantage/ point" from which it might be approached. Then we are back to complete scepticism, from which perspective the pretensions of flow charts are present only to be undermined.

It is true that Ashbery is interested, up to a point, in the extent to which flows of various kinds make roughly accurate metaphors for human experience – especially the passage of time. He says, for instance, "Like a plangent river my life has unrolled this far" (59) and "I put my youth and middle age into it" (96). But he insists that the attempt to chart such flows is futile. A flow moves and a chart is still. Ashbery is in the line of Wallace Stevens here, as he was in "Self-Portrait in a Convex Mirror", in reflecting on the distortions of representation. Things as they are get changed by a flow chart as they do by a cubist guitar. A "plangent" river resembles music as much as water, "music that comes in sideways and afterwards you aren't sure/ if you heard it or not" (97).

However, a flow chart does not merely represent, it imposes order, and it is this above all which Ashbery opposes. He says that "One wants not to like, but to live in, the structure of things, and this is/ the first great mistake" (54). He imagines a researcher "at the library/ while it was still dark outside. . .all/ in the interests of some dumb theory [he] was trying to prove" who then goes outside to be "surprised. . ./ by every new dimpled vista" (94). In expressing a preference for the street to the library, the flow to the chart, Ashbery is opposing the epistemological project of the Enlightenment which took its most consummate form in the compilation of encyclopaedias and dictionaries – the desire to define, categorise and exhaustively explain the world. In this opposition he is at one with Lyotard, who refers to "that severe reexamination which post-modernity imposes on the thought of the Enlightenment, on the idea of a unitary end of history and of a subject" (Lyotard, 73).

Modernism also contained a critique of Englightenment values but postmodernism takes this much further – to the extent of questioning, altogether, the value of quests for meaning. This is what Lyotard is referring to when he describes the postmodern artist searching "for new presentations, not in order to enjoy them but in order to impart a stronger sense of the unpresentable" (81): instead of searching for or imposing significance postmodernist writers incorporate its unattainableness into their texts, and evolve forms that enact that unattainableness (this is linked to a postmodernist assimilation of the Kantian "sublime"). What *Flow Chart* does is to evoke such an enormous and complex "flow" that any attempt to "chart" it would inevitably be futile: but it also celebrates the postmodern condition and at the same time dwells on the virtues of a Lyotardian presentation of the unpresentable, advocating the conception of a "linear"

> space independent of laws in which blunted gestures toward
>     communication could advance or recede
> without actually moving from the spot to which they are rooted;
>     in other words, destiny could
> happen all the time, vanish or repeat itself ad infinitum, and no
>     one would be affected, one's
> real interests being points that define us, the line, which is
>     dimensionless and without desire.
> Thus, all things would happen simultaneously and on the same
>     plane and existence, freed
> from the chain of causality, could work on important projects
>     unconnected to itself and so
> conceive a new architecture that would be nowhere, a hunger for
>     nothing, desire desiring itself
>
> (200)

Ashbery is so embarrassed to be giving advice that he blows a raspberry at this passage straight after it ("Excuse me while I fart. There, that's better. I actually feel relieved.") But the fact he is embarrassed reinforces the feeling that this is genuine; we must accept randomness and lack of structure, stop looking for a "meaning", enjoy the incoherence.

Ashbery's way of putting it is, of course, more sophisticated – noone has a more intelligent style than him. Strangely, however, this very sophistication becomes a problem in *Flow Chart* because it seems out of proportion to the content: in this very long poem Ashbery has tried to speak directly about his outlook and this turns out to be almost exclusively aesthetic, and quite dull. In most of his earlier work, where he dramatises consciousness in the process of tackling incoherence, that process and the act of turning it into poetry inevitably involved a struggle which Ashbery's style was especially good at enacting. Here, the advocacy of acceptance means that consciousness and incoherence speak with one voice. The lack of resistance to the flow of experience results in monotony, paradoxical though this is in view of the number of voices and registers that the poem contains. All of these are too easily assimilated, as, too, are the (sometimes surreal) fragments of narrative – where in early Ashbery such fragmentariness produced vivid bafflement, here it has become formulaic and banal.

Perhaps this is caused by the pressure to conform exerted by the poem's prescriptiveness. The advocacy of passiveness in *Flow Chart* drains it of the puzzled, excited or worried energy of the earlier Ashbery and produces something near to complacency. The poem does represent very accurately some aspects of the postmodern condition – especially the way that consciousness is bombarded with second-hand imagery, half-baked opinion, inconsequential anecdote. But the poem celebrates that condition too undiscriminatingly. All of the voices in the poem seem to be more or less condoned and all of them seem fey and effetely self-absorbed – these are people who are "very particular about the trivia [they] associate with" [196] but find it hard to care about much else:

. . .As my cock hardens I can make out a group of primitive
    wattled structures
just below the horizon, and am allowed to wonder why, in such
    circumstances, anybody
would want to live from one day to the next, without
    assurances, no sketch
or dream of the morrow, and then it's gone. It disappears from
    view.

Both kinds of erection here may have "gone" and the difficulty of distinguishing between the two is characteristic and telling.


Where British postmodernists differ from Ashbery and his American followers is in the gravitational pull that is exercised in their work by a sense of time and place, or fact. This must be taken in the

mostly postmodernist context of radical instability that characterises their work, but it does make them less thoroughly postmodernist
than Ashbery by giving their poems more realist inflections. It is
also connected with the lack of interest which these British writers
have in the philosophical or mock-philosophical modes favoured
by Ashbery and the poets he anthologised in *The Best American
Poetry, 1988*: poems which employ such modes do not have physical settings and draw upon spatial or temporal imagery only ab-
stractly, as illustrations of their arguments. In some ways the absence
of such discursive writing in Britain represents a genuine lack –
poems that employ it can draw upon resources unavailable elsewhere, and are sometimes genuinely exciting. (The reluctance to
write discursively seems to me to be a general feature of contemporary British poetry and one that impoverishes it. In particular
when British poets try to write sequences based on poetic arguments, as for example an empiricist poet like Helen Dunmore does
in "The Raw Garden"[32], its consequences can be very damaging.)

However, in the context of the weaknesses to which Ashbery is
prone – as revealed in *Flow Chart* – the modified postmodernism of
British writers like John Ash, Peter Didsbury, Frank Kuppner and
Ian McMillan does seem to me to have its advantages. The way this
modification has arisen from a dialogue between postmodernism
and realism is hinted at in Ash's essay on Roy Fisher, "A Classic
Post-Modernist"[33] in which he says that Fisher's "exuberant virtu-
osity" in "107 Poems"[34] comes very close to Ashbery, but his realist
temper also pulls him in an opposite direction. "A highly elaborated
fictiveness (Stevens, Ashbery, Harwood) is uncongenial to him. It
remains crucially important to give at least "an air of reality" to the
poems. . .for Fisher the idea of a 'direct denotative language' remains 'a chimera' that is always with him – the idea that the real,
nameable objects floated into the self-contained fictive world of the
poem might be presented 'Without distancing them at all'" (47–48).

Ash is closer to Ashbery than Fisher in his enjoyment of a "highly
elaborated fictiveness", but he also displays an interest in denotation which is surprising given his reputation as a mere Ashbery
disciple. "Second Prose for Roy Fisher" (*BS*, 54) acknowledges the
older British poet as an influence in this respect, but also hints at
the presence of this kind of writing elsewhere in his work:

Flanged rails and flooded runnels. The wheels and circling currents
of the stopped wave. The pieces of the windowpane scattered

over the rough web of garden weeds by the missile thrown without anger: speculatively, *to see what would happen.*

These lines suggest that Ash has links, not only with Fisher's materialist philosophy, but also with the realist assumptions of imagism
– although this is prose, its rhythm closely resembles that of early
imagist poems (like those William Carlos Williams and H.D.) that
employ fricative spondees to arrest movement and focus upon the
material and stubborn fact of objects.

This is very foreign to Ashbery's relentless fictiveness and gives
the fictiveness of Ash's own work something to wrestle with in a
way that is analogous to what Ash calls the "tension between the
fictive and the real" in Fisher's work. That tension can be seen at
work even in these lines from "Second Prose for Roy Fisher" – for
the fact it *is* prose deliberately complicates its imagist provenance
(as it does also in Fisher's prose poems, which are Ash's model)
and transforms it with the addition of discursive and narrative
components. The presence of such denotative elements provides a
clue to a partially submerged realist impulse in Ash's poetic as a
whole. He has always been a poet of place in a sense that could
never apply to Ashbery, who has never been a "New York" poet in
the way that Frank O'Hara was. For Ashbery is much less interested in sketching specific (if apparently random) moments in New
York's ambient and ambulatory life than his predecessor. This,
however, is what Ash does in recent poems like "Following a Man"[35]
and before he moved to New York he did something similar for his
native city of Manchester. Moreover, the way he depicted it was
very close to the way Fisher depicted his own native city, described
by Ash himself as "unmistakeably the real city of Birmingham with
the usual complement of concrete towers, slum clearances and
derelict monuments from the Victorian era", but, as Ash goes on to
insist, "the total effect is fictive and dreamlike. A disused, Palladian
railway station is a 'gigantic ghost of stone': it is almost as if we
were looking at views of Birmingham painted by De Chirico or
Magritte" ("RF", 45).

This idea of the precarious stabilities of the local, and their transformation, is also important for Ian McMillan and Peter Didsbury.
In Didsbury's case, the city of Hull and its environs provide a
stable underpinning to his fabulatory flights into the exotic, and a

contemporary ground for his archaeological delvings into the ancient. By contrast, Ian MacMillan's poems are solidly grounded in the territory of social realism – set mostly in Yorkshire, they refer to mines and factories and to a landscape where the industrial and rural meet; their rhythms and assonances are vividly linked to the poet's own broad accent, and they occasionally employ dialect. This is connected to McMillan's concerns as a performer of his poems, and his ambition to be a stand-up comic. He takes for granted how much his realist subject-matter has become such a cliché that it has been parodied by Alan Bennett, Monty Python and, more recently, Harry Enfield – but his own comedy is much subtler (and funnier) than theirs. He does use parody but not, like them, crude exaggeration – partly because of a greater respect and sympathy for the realities behind the clichés.

Instead, McMillan mingles his evocation of social realities with a postmodernist fictiveness; his poems are self-reflexive and self-consciously intertextual, referring, in particular, to characters and incidents in novels. So "Propp's Last Case"[36] has an epigraph that claims to be from an unpublished critical work by McMillan himself, entitled *Trends in 't Yorkshire Novel*:

> Occasionally, during the late '50s and early '60s, the dominant position of the realist Yorkshire novel was challenged by a number of American-influenced works known as the *hardboiled* school of Yorkshire prose.

To say that what follows is a brief description of a sexual encounter that seems unsure whether it is being written by John Braine or Raymond Chandler, however, would be to underestimate its instability. "It was unthinkable midnight or Autumn/ in a blackish Barnsley of the mind" comically turns the reliable setting of a 50s novel into something questionable and subjective, or textual – a place out of a novel and therefore fictive (however realistic the novel). But the disagreement, as it were, between "unthinkable" and "mind" further suggests that this novelistic Barnsley is being defamiliarised by an unprecedented experience, or another text. The realist novel is in this way interrogated by conventions unfamiliar to it – first of all by those of the detective story which characteristically start with the central figure "in the dark"; this is partly why Barnsley is "blackish" and it is "unthinkable midnight". But then they are questioned much further by the conventions of postmodernist poems –

"midnight or Autumn" need not be alternatives, but presented as such playfully refer to the fictive activity of defining chronology, and this is made more explicit later: "it was coalblack midnight or Autumn:/ I guess the two are interchangeable." But not before a further generic doubt is introduced:

> She was kissing me
> like they kiss on radio plays:
> noisily.

Given the possibility that this is a narrative whose only medium is sound, the midnight or Autumn alternative acquires a new lease of witty irrelevance. But then this too is subverted when the joke about the arbitrariness of fictive settings turns into a joke about the arbitrariness of fictive naming, in a passage conspicuous for the brilliance of its comic timing:

> "Midnight or Autumn?" she asked,
> and I thought she meant her lingerie.
> She meant her dogs.
>
> As they chased me I tried to make a joke
> about not being able to run properly
> but my mouth was full of midnight
>
> or Autumn and she was laughing like they laugh
> on radio plays and I was gasping like they gasp
> just before they die
> on radio plays.

This kind of playfulness is McMillan's most conspicuous characteristic – and designedly so; in fact he advertises this characteristic in his titles: "The Crazy Horse Interview", "'Ilkley Moor Baht'at': Amplification", "The Harsh Stink of Mythical European Gypsy Violins", "The Texas Swing Boys' Dadaist Manifesto" and so on. But repeatedly his poems have a sombre undertow arising partly from a sense that the pervasiveness of the fictive may be connected with a sense of loss or of incapacity rather than increased potential. McMillan is postmodernist to the extent that, in Lyotard's words, he "searches for new presentations, not in order to enjoy them but in order to impart a stronger sense of the unpresentable" and

> the text he writes, the work he produces are not in principle
> governed by preestablished rules, and they cannot be judged ac-
> cording to a determining judgement, by applying familiar cat-
> egories to the text or to the work
>
> (Lyotard, 81)

This much he shares with Ashbery, but his attitude to the unpresentable is different. Lyotard's next point about the postmodernist artist
does not apply to McMillan – it is not true that his work "is looking
for" radically new "rules and categories" or that he works "without
rules in order to formulate the rules of what *will have been done*".
Instead, his poems work by referring themselves to (and ludically
conflating) defunct rules, and they are not at all sanguine that
"what will have been done" will have evolved innovatory rules in
that process. Moreover, they do to some extent express (as Lyotard
says postmodernist works do not) a "nostalgia" for the unattainable
(81) though "nostalgia" is too pejorative a word for this quality
in McMillan, which amounts to a kind of oblique elegy for the
unpresentable.

As I have said this takes the form of a sense of loss or incapacity.
This is expressed formally in the poems by a kind of open-endedness
which sometimes looks like a playful celebration of postmodern
possibility but can also look baffled, and more like a kind of modernist formal desperation. This is echoed in McMillan's imagery
which, surprisingly often, hints at a reification or mutilation of the
human. In "Just the Facts, Just the", "my daughter" is said to be
"jerking"

> about on the settee, bright red,
> making little cardboard cries.
>
> cardboard cries? Pull together yourself.
>
> Just the facts, just the
>
> (83)

The collocation of "cardboard" and "cries" is made even more disturbing here by the way it follows the syntactical ambiguity surrounding "bright red" which makes it able to apply both to the
child and the settee. This is all from the father's perspective and
registers his shock at finding his daughter's behaviour so alien that

she comes to resemble an object – a shock which is reflected in his recoil, in the next lines, from his own phrase, then in his jumbled word-order and finally in his lapse into silence.

Comedy is likely to erupt anywhere in McMillan's work, but in contexts like this it is as though comedy itself is being interrogated. McMillan's most important comic resource is incongruity, but "Just the Facts, Just the" presents facts in a way that implies a state of mind faltering in the face of them, trying to frame itself in an appropriate way but failing. There is, then, a lack of congruity between the facts and the feelings they arouse: consequently, comedy is present as a kind of threat, revealing a fear that the state of mind and the facts are inhumanly at odds with each other. This is presented in a postmodernist way in that the incongruity is enacted in the poem self-reflexively, as a breakdown in representation – but the poem registers this breakdown not as a source of new expression, but as a loss. Lyotard's "nostalgia" would be an inaccurate word for this because it is more complex than that, more sophisticatedly self-conscious – but there is here, certainly, an unpostmodern grieving.

"Grieving", however, would normally seem too specific a word to describe this effect in McMillan's poems. Mostly, it takes the form of a kind of bafflement, akin to that experienced in the face of the question of what is funny and why. The title of "Melville's 'Treasure Island'" (29–30), for example, reveals that its speaker has ontological problems about what text he is a character in; connected with this he has epistemological problems about the ship he is on: "we seem to be stuck/ to the harbour walls./ I don't think we're even floating." His inability to understand is echoed in the ship's apparent inability to move: "This is my first voyage/ but I thought that, on a ship/ there was at least the *sensation*/ of movement." But the most memorable image in the poem, as elsewhere in McMillan, is of disability:

> Blind Pugh stands on the bridge
> holding an ear-trumpet,
> listening for treasure.

These lines are haunted by the ghost of humour and so raise the same problem about the correct reader response as is raised by the generic instability in the poem's title (Melville or R.L. Stephenson: for adults or children?) More importantly, though, they connect powerfully with images elsewhere in McMillan that represent human incapacity to act with full appropriateness or fully to understand their experience.

In "The Meaning of Life (A Yorkshire Dialect Rhapsody)" (55) this theme takes on political implications with the suggestion, in this case, that the human damage has been caused by shiftwork in a coalmine. This damage is evoked at the linguistic level by references to deadening, merely phatic, speech: "I said 'Hey, you're looking poorly/ He said 'Them nights are drawing in'". But such language is then parodied with indignant surrealism ("up a ladder like a ferret up a ladder in a fog"; "like a lamplighter's daughter in a barrel full of milk"). The repeated references to eggs which seem not to have specific meaning at first are finally focused in the penultimate stanza where, compared to a head wearing a pitman's helmet (or "lit-up hat") they come to hint at human vulnerability.

However, it is in "The Tennis Ball Factory Poems" (51–55) where McMillan is at his most explicitly political. This short sequence works mostly through denotation – but the very objectivity with which images, conversational exchanges, and incidents are described is itself baffling because it raises the question of what this all amounts to, why it is being presented in this way, in this order, what the author's attitude to it is, what response is required from the reader. In other words the sequence has some of the effects of minimalism in questioning the boundaries of the aesthetic and the relationships between the author and the text, the text and the reader: as in Williams' "The Red Wheelbarrow", why does so much depend on all this? But the answer here is that, actually, not very much does; the question about meaning which is raised by minimalism is answered politically by this poem with the accumulating suggestion that these experiences are not meaningful *enough* – that they are trivia which loom too large because of the oppressiveness of this kind of work. A tennis ball factory is a perfect image for being oppressed by trivia, and the tension between the two is an appropriate way to guage the tension between postmodernism and realism in McMillan's work. In this poem as in the others I have discussed by British postmodernists, these two are a kind of quarrelling couple; so, in these lines, social realism is mingled with a slightly manic but inconsequential humour:

> Everywhere the lines. The balls
> falling in lines from the broken

> conveyor, landing on the greased
> head of a man in a white coat.
> Early in the evening at the bottom
> of the gently sloping ramp a boy
> tackles me about crossword puzzles.
> Everywhere the lines, the balls.
>
> (51)

The poem is in seven sections which may represent the days in the week – but anyway the poem gets increasingly desperate: "'Aye, Mac, we're just/ grovelling in the bastard dust, just/ crawling in the bastard muck'" (section 2); "Why are the wicked so strong?" (section 3); "'You calls this a life?'" (section 6). And the poem ends with another McMillan image of baffled incapacity:

> The telephone rings at five o' clock in the morning.
> No one in the canteen
> moves. We have lost our bastard hands.
>
> (54)

# 13

# The Estranging of the Mainstream

At the end of my "Introduction" I suggested that the distinction between the mainstream and the margins has become increasingly difficult to maintain. There are a number of forces at work here but the most crucial is in the influence that postmodernism has exerted – not because it has swept all before it but precisely because of the stubborn and varied resistance it has encountered in Britain. At the end of my last chapter I pointed out the extent to which poets like John Ash, Peter Didsbury, and Ian McMillan have transformed the postmodernist modes which, at a superficial level, seem most to characterise their work. Until recently the kind of poetry written by these poets would almost certainly have marked them out as outsiders. But it has become increasingly difficult to distinguish at times between their work and that of poets who are broadly mainstream but have been influenced by postmodernist techniques and pre-occupations. What I want to maintain in this concluding chapter is that the collision between postmodernism and realism in contemporary British poetry has produced instabilities so extensive that it is no longer possible to discern what the dominant mode of contemporary British poetry is – and that this has allowed various kinds of estrangement effect to enter by the back door.

The influence of women's writing has been crucial in this respect partly because British women poets seem to be mostly at their best when they adopt inquisitive or even baffled attitudes to gender, alongside their political ones. The effect of this is amply illustrated in a number of poems anthologised recently in *Sixty Women Poets*[1]. Hilary Davies' "The Opthalmologist" (96), for example, works in the ground between its female speaker and a man testing her eyesight. Gender oppositions between the two characters are hinted at as possibilities – the man associated with both science ("He has many categories of sight") and a desire to control ("He is completely in command down here") and the woman with a tendency towards myth-making ("All the kingdoms he shows me of letters/

From their different angles"). But the poem refuses to let these roles harden. Instead they start to interpenetrate because the central metaphor of sight insists on the transformative power of different angles of vision. What results is a dialogue of genders, with each character's point of view influencing the other's, and then a tentative synthesis: "the eye-doctor/ Offers the lure of many visions,/ The honey of his systems underground".

It is a similar open-mindedness that lies behind an especially exciting sort of poem that's been written by women over the past three or four years and whose emergence this anthology displays with great power. Influenced by feminism and by a growing tradition in women's poetry (fully illustrated in *Sixty Women Poets* by its selection of work by succeeding generations, from Elizabeth Jennings and E.J. Scovell on to Fleur Adcock, then to Carol Rumens and so on) a number of women at the moment are writing in a way that, by questioning gender, also calls desire and identity into question. The instabilities that arise from this result in a radically puzzled poetic mode that, in drawing on surrealism, is akin to the use of magic realism in women novelists like Angela Carter.

This kind of writing displays the boundaries of the self shifting, and is preoccupied with the themes of splits and transformations. So in a way similar to that in which Carter imagined hybrids of woman and bird, woman and machine etc, Jo Shapcott imagines a hybrid of woman and goat which suggests how that desire unsettles identity: "I wanted/ to eat everything. . .I tasted"

> that old sun and the few dark clouds
> and some tall buildings far away in the next town.
> I think I must have swallowed an office block
> because this grinding enormous digestion tells me
> it's stuck on an empty corridor which has,
> at the far end, I know, a tiny human figure.
>
> (259)

Bizarre though this is it works with its own precision as a metaphor for the way that desire causes the self to be invaded by a bewildering otherness which sometimes has, as it were, its physical expression in pregnancy.

Selima Hill is one of the most important writers of these fantastical poems and her "Desire's A Desire" (156–157) explores, more or less explicitly, why this drive is so subversive, so simultaneously desired and undesired:

> It taunts me
> like the muzzle of a gun;
> it sinks into my soul like chilled honey
> packed into the depths of treacherous wounds;
> it wraps me up in cold green sheets
> like Indian squaws
> who wrap their babies in the soft green sheathes of irises
> that smell of starch

Characteristically in those lines the exotic (Indian squaws) and the domestic (the smell of starch) are juxtaposed in a way that produces a disorientation sharpened by the extent to which the predominant womb/enclosure references are paradoxically linked to coldness. This is appropriate to the effects of sexual longing implied both by the images from traditional love poetry (honey, wounds, flowers) and by the Freudian genital symbolism (the gun, the sheathes).

It is perhaps a sign of the importance of this mode that a poet like Helen Dunmore, who normally writes quite differently, should have produced, in "Three Ways of Recovering a Body" (121–122), her own version of it, and a highly memorable one: "By chance I was alone in my bed the morning/ I woke to find my body had gone". What is questioned here is the extent to which women's identity is conjured out of their reflection in the masculine obsession with the female body: "Soon I recovered my lips/ by waiting behind the mirror while you shaved./ You pouted. I peeled away kisses like wax". Wittily she imagines the *reductio ad absurdam* of this, of becoming "the one woman in the world/ who was only present in the smile of her vagina" but then counters this with a closing pun: "Recovering/ I breathed to myself, 'Hold on! I'm coming'". This – in what looks like a reference to the emphasis on "jouissance" in recent French feminist theory – makes her re-establishment of her identity and her realisation of her own bodily pleasure coincide.

However, the importance of this kind of explicitly gendered writing is most fully felt when the larger structures that women poets have constructed are looked at. What was missing from my account of narrative poetry in Chapter 6 was the kind of stories that women poets have been telling – but this omission was partly caused by how those stories are often deliberately subverted as narratives by the way that questions of gender also become questions of language. This concern has also influenced male poets, sometimes explicitly. So Andrew Motion's "The Letter"[2] suggests that, for the female narrator, language itself is an alien instrument deployed by men for the expression of their desires – the shock of the airman's symbolic openness arises largely from the extent to which it is the too literal (as in "letter") equivalent of the written language of the love letter. The implication behind this is that she is made aware of the extent to which the symbolic system she entered in acquiring language is secretly premised upon masculine assumptions. It is this which has much preoccupied women poets in their concern to tell stories from feminine perspectives.

Selima Hill's *The Accumulation of Small Acts of Kindness*[3] enacts, in an acute form, feminine difficulty in the face of language. It depicts the stream of consciousness of a schizophrenic young woman and so dramatises her struggle with registers and voices (external, internalised or internal) as she tries to make sense of her experience. The poem's extreme fragmentariness and the disorienting lack of an organising principle in its movement from one idea to another bewilder the tenuous narrative line that nonetheless intermittently surfaces. What is finally evoked is a rebellion against narrative, a refusal to narrate in conventional ways that fulfill expectations which are alien to the mostly subjective events which constitute her story. What the poem does instead is attempt something similar to Luce Irigaray's project:

> What Irigaray is above all concerned to work out is the condition of women's subjectivity – how women can assume the "I" of discourse in their own right and not as a derivative male "I". This presupposes of course that what it is to be "male" and "female" is available to change, since they are possibilities provided by the symbolic order. Speaking (as) a woman is not only a psycholinguistic description, it is also the name for something which does not yet exist, the position of the female subject in the symbolic order.[4]

The way that *The Accumulation* ransacks language indicates the urgency of this need to assume a feminine "I" of discourse – but also how desperate it is. There is an extent to which the young woman in the poem is a paradoxical heroine as Freud's "Dora" is for Helène

Cixous in refusing to co-operate with a patriarchal psychoanalysis that travesties her psyche by imposing masculinist interpretations on it. But both women suffer terribly for their rebellions.

The examples in Jo Shapcott's "Robert and Elizabeth" poems[5] and Jackie Kay's "The Adoption Papers"[6] are more hopeful. Shapcott and Kay, like Hill, are concerned with feminine identity but their emphasis is on constructing, rather than deconstructing it. Nonetheless, they are sceptical and narrative "authority" is more questionable to them than it is to Andrew Motion. So Shapcott's sequence moves not only between genders but between historical periods. It is an argument of perspectives between Robert Lowell/Browning, on the one hand and Elizabeth Hardwick/Barrett Browning on the other and so explores the creative differences between men and women poets and, in that process, attempts to construct a feminine "I" of poetic discourse. It does this first by contrast with the masculine "I", which is obsessed with definition, hard clarity. So in "Elizabeth Looks at Robert" (55) the wife contrasts the husband's facility with "Terminology" and then equates it with "Terminus, rare god of boundaries" so giving due deference to this masculine precision while suggesting it is tainted with the deathly, the terminal – that this way of deploying language murders to dissect. This point of view is cunningly made to precede that in "The Goose and the Gander" (56) where Robert complains (with a disturbingly sexual ambiguity) that he "can't. . .pin her down" – in complaining that his wife is "nebulous" he seems to wish to turn her into a specimen.

This is partly a feminist reflection on the aggressively masculine aspects of Robert Lowell's work – its almost obsessive insistence on hard, physical images and precise historical fact. But it is cleverly linked with Robert Browning also in the way Shapcott associates the male poet's outlook with that of 19th century science, with a positivism that aggressively insists on understanding experience by classifying it. In "Robert and Elizabeth Visit the Norfolk Broads" (57) this sensibility is expressed through his preference for the hard, geological certainties of Dartmoor where "his footsteps/ clicked the granite" to the feminine softnesses of "acres of confusion between land and water" in the fens – "not an inch/ of sure footage on this raft of putrid stuff". This vividly combines an accurate picture of Browning's naturalism – his insistence aesthetically on hard physical fact, as in Fra Lippo Lippi's description of his formative experiences in childhood of near-starvation – with a wider fear of a chaotic otherness which masculine thinking associates with the feminine.

Unbounded softness and wetness is a nightmare for Robert: as he says in "Robert in the Kitchen in the Dark" (58), "Happiness,/...is only dry".

However, the last two poems in the sequence suggest the possibility of a truce between men and women poets, the hope that they can learn from each other and accommodate themselves creatively to the differences between them. In fact, "Robert Watches Elizabeth Knitting" dwells upon the expressive need for differences and suggests an analogy between those of a gender kind and those which constitute the symbolic system itself:

> I can't get my mind round knitting.
> It starts to have everything
> when you come down to it – rhythm,
> colour and slow but perceptible change.
> The meaning is all in the gaps:
> a pattern of holes marked out by woolly colour,
> a jumper made of space, division and relations.

In this play of differences, the possibility of a feminine discourse is envisaged, the possibility that poetry could be created out of "relations" between genders, wholeness out of "division". This would be "woolly" in a newly positive sense that opposes the masculine worship of "Terminus". It would be a gendered version of "différance" involving a creative evasion of closure in favour of a discourse in which the genders agree to differ and defer to each other. So "Robert and Elizabeth Sit Down Again" (62) ends the narrative with a prospective marriage of minds, with "minds in utter engagement,"/ mouths distorted in an ache of mutual beaming".

Shapcott is against the kind of feminine separatism advocated explicitly by Adrienne Rich and implicitly by Mebdh McGuckian. Jackie Kay is more concerned to concentrate on feminine experience but it is important to see her "The Adoption Papers" in a wider context that connects it with the narrative concerns of other contemporary poets, including male ones. For it is profoundly dialogic in the way it tells a story by allowing three distinct voices to overlap each other. It resembles George Szirtes' sequence "Metro"[7], for this reason, in constructing a novelised, rather than a confessional version of family history – in the place of the single voice of Robert Lowell or Sylvia Plath pondering their constitutive experiences, Kay and Szirtes allow members of their families to express their own

points of view. So "The Adoption Papers" mingles the speech of
three women as they try to understand what made them act and to
reflect on the motives, actions and desires of the others. In this way
the white woman who adopted a black child, the black woman who
abandoned that child, and the child herself, now 26, express themselves in turn in a free verse with minimal punctuation which suggests that the speech of each opens towards the others in a mutual
interrogation. All three are baffled in their different ways and these
bafflements multiply each other through juxtaposition and interpenetration: terminus, the masculine god of boundaries, is very
much opposed in this feminine polyphony where boundaries are
crossed and re-crossed, exploring the emotional bonds between the
voices. But it is through this radical openness that the poem acquires its power and speaks all the more meaningfully by avoiding
the too-easy definitiveness of obvious patterns of imagery and controlling metaphors. It is by fully measuring the extent of the otherness
it contains – the gaps between the women – that it finally evokes
sympathy for each of them, and a sense of genuine, if precarious,
identification, as when the adoptive mother says

> I always believed in the telling anyhow.
> You can't keep something like that secret
> I wanted her to think of her other mother
> out there, thinking that child I had will be
> seven today eight today all the way up to
> god knows when. I told my daughter –
> I bet your mother's never missed your birthday,
> how could she?
>
> (22)

As the epigraph to "Yesterday was Elizabeth's Turn to Cook"
(59) Jo Shapcott quotes Elizabeth Hardwick:

> It certainly hasn't the drama of: I saw the old, white-bearded frig-
> ate master on the dock and signed up for the journey. But after
> all, "I" am a woman.

This feeling is a premise of women's narrative poetry and leads
women poets, in the process of constructing a feminine "I" of discourse, to construct narratives whose focus is deliberately subjective, often playfully, even wildly so – Hill and Shapcott, for example,

are often wittily surreal. A similar impulse led Angela Carter towards her own European and feminist use of magic realism and she quotes the same passage from Hardwick in an interview[8] to explain her own motives.

There are dangers of essentialist thinking in this and Shapcott's closing poems in her sequence are meant to ward them off, suggesting as they do that the feminine and the masculine are not discrete categories and that the thinking of men and women can mutually enrich each other. So it must be stressed that the interest in surrealism which I have been pointing out in Shapcott and Hill is one that is shared with a number of male poets. Shapcott first drew attention with "The Surrealists' Summer Convention Came to our City"[9] which won the Poetry Society's National Poetry Competition in 1985. But this sounds very like John Ash at times:

> The Philharmonia played especially sweetly that summer;
> they made a recording of the Floral Dances
> which is still controversial because of the sound
> of chattering monkeys in the coda.

Moreover, "The Travelling Opera Plays Gluck's *Orfeo* for the Last Time" (18) shares much in common with Ash's "Incidental Music"[10] in that both poems centre on travelling musical ensembles with deeply troubled relationships to the music they perform and who suffer anxiety about the interpenetration of their lives and their art.

What is much more distinctively Shapcott's own is a mingling of surreal fantasy with a kind of naturalism – an emphasis on sometimes gross physicality, on the body and its functions, or its implication in animality. "With the Big Tray" (10) subtly suggests the effects of the purely physical by looking very closely at a woman's "long march/ up the staircase" – bringing the body into the foreground by dwelling on the difficult angles that must be negotiated. The short lines enact the great number of small manoeuvres involved, the great care, the precarious closeness to embarassment:

> . . .after wriggling and clinking
> round the door like a belly dancer
> she found herself inside,
> foolish on the Moroccan rug.

What is most characteristic here though is that Shapcott responds in both a straightforwardly physical and a fantastical way when

> Hilary surprised herself by breaking wind.
> Secretly, her large smell
> made her feel as real and salty
> as a merchant adventurer
> but she would take something for it
> from the bathroom cabinet anyway.

Much more recherché is the process of mummification which is the subject of "Electroplating the Baby" (48–51). This is described in a scientific register and with a relentless precision that are reminiscent of Marianne Moore but, given the grotesque context, this apparent objectivity itself suggests a surreal displacement – a dreamlike absence of emotion. Something similar is at work in "Twin Found in Man's Chest" (52) but there a reference to the register of sensational journalism is also present. The effect in both these poems of focusing on the body is to defamiliarise it disconcertingly – to suggest that what is most familiar to us actually contains a profoundly exotic landscape.

As I have pointed out this kind of writing is something Shapcott shares with other women writers, but it is important to stress that there is nothing inevitably feminine about it. It is instructive to compare Shapcott's "Love Song with a Flock of Sheep"[11] and Stephen Knight's "The Eyeball Works"[12] – both work by establishing a surreal hypothesis and proceeding matter-of-factly (but inevitably bizarrely) from there. Shapcott's poem is a response to an advertisement for malt whisky which boasted an entry form on every bottle for a competition in which the prize was a flock of sheep. The poet resolves to buy the whisky, enter the competition and win the sheep for her lover. When she then imagines the sheep grazing in his flat, the fantasy is more than merely fanciful because the physical detail gives it an earthily sexual quality, the flock "blowing in your ears" and "nuzzling across your hair":

> They will graze your legs, removing
> every hair with teeth
>
> so precise and shy you'll feel only
> a mist of breath and lips.

Knight's poem is premised upon the idea of a factory that supplies eyeballs with very precise specifications – *"Eyes for Librarians* and *Eyes of the Stars"* in colours from "Palimpsest Azure" to "Paul Newman Blue". Where Shapcott's "Love Song" is playful, Knight's poem is satirical and sinister: "the Eyeball Brochures.../whiff, unmistakeably, of Money and Success", recalling the titles of two novels by Martin Amis which dwell with appalled fascination on gross and grotesque materialism. But Knight's satire is more oblique and works largely through an uneasy ambiguity about the eponymous building. The word "works" has a designedly old-fashioned ring to it suggesting the kind of heavy industry which most characterised pre-postmodern capitalism. By contrast, the building itself seems more appropriate to commerce – it has "tinted windows" which "run cloud/ and passer-by at half their normal speed", "marble stairs", "an unlit foyer", "drapery and armchairs". These suggest an attempt at bland reassurance, but the building's function is a kind of institutionalised atrocity – the eyeball-slicing scene in Luis Bunuel's film *Le Chien Andalou* endlessly and routinely repeated: "to press/ drill, gouge and slice until it's dark". This gives the "works" some of the representative quality of the eponymous building in "The Dead Letter Office"[13] by Charles Simic ("They add my letter and your/ Telegram. They force them/ Through the rocks in the wall./ No one knows what goes on inside.") But the poem's concluding description of the building's human effects is more reminiscent of that use of disability (or maiming) as a political image which I pointed out in Ian McMillan in my last chapter:

> tapping the walls with his complimentary stick,
> the last of the donors to leave
> is "leaving" through the NO ADMITTANCE doors.
> He waves Goodbye. The doors go tick, tick, tick


What is clear is that there are forces currently operating in the culture that might collectively be described as postmodernist which have extensively impinged upon contemporary British poetry. One of the crucial points about feminism is that it is equally postmodernist and, as I indicated in my chapter on Carol Ann Duffy, anti-postmodernist: on the one hand it has worked to subvert previous assumptions and stabilities, on the other it has insisted on the need for a "privileged" voice that can make definitive statements of a moral, political and aesthetic kind. This internal hesitation in feminism is important for the poets under discussion because it is another force that operates to undermine any sense of a dominant mode, and more so because it is linked, complicatedly and subtly, to that hesitation between postmodernism and realism which I mentioned earlier. In drawing upon surrealism to express their gendered concerns about identity and desire, women poets are drawing on a standard postmodernist resource – surrealism was one of the most important influences on postmodernism. But in insisting at the same time on being able to make political points they are assuming that authentic statements can be made about the "real world".

It is therefore important – as I stressed earlier in comparing Shapcott and Knight – to be aware that male and female mainstream poets share much in common in the way that their work currently shows them both absorbing and, at the same time, resisting, postmodernism. The case of Sean O'Brien is interesting here because he might seem to occupy the opposite corner to a poetic with playfully aesthetic, self-consciously fictive and philosophically abstract concerns – his is a poetry with Leftist political preoccupations and a downright and aggressive social realist style. Even so there are clear signs in his poems that he has assimilated enough postmodernist lessons to immunise his realism against easy jibes from his political enemies that he is crude or naive. This is partly because, as John Mole has pointed out[14] he has absorbed the influence of Wallace Stevens, an important postmodernist precursor. But O'Brien's friendship with Peter Didsbury in their formative years as poets is also significant. In the 1970s they discussed each other's work, and poetry in general, and even co-authored some poems. This collaboration between Didsbury (whose basic impulse is postmodernist) and O'Brien (whose basic impulse is realist) can be taken, it seems to me, to epitomise the complexity of influences that is making recent British poetry what it is. It has meant that each has been aware of the poetic possibilities both of vivid directness *and* sophisticated obliqueness.

So O'Brien's poem "Before"[15] mingles a kind of lyric writing with an Audenesque montage that imagines society at a particular moment:

> This is before the first bus has been late
> Or the knickers sought under the bed
> Or the first cigarette undertaken,
> Before the first flush and cross word.

> Viaducts, tunnels and motorways: still.
> The mines and the Japanese sunrise: still.

Moreover, as well as being on the boundary of the lyric and the social, "Before" also stands on a post-symbolist threshold of absence and presence. This works self-reflexively by questioning the way that objects enter poems, and the poet's ability to recreate the world – so that the whole realist enterprise is called into question too, its claim to an accurate apprehension of objects. And "apprehension" is right – the attempt to imagine society evokes a sense of its vulnerability so that "Before" hesitates liminally between an apocalyptic anxiety and a realist assurance of the world's continuing presence:

> I declare this an hour of general safety
> When even the personal monster –
> Example, the Kraken – is dead to the world
> Like the deaf submarines with their crewmen
> Spark out at their fathomless consoles.
> No one has died. There need be no regret,
> For we do not exist, and I promise
> I shall not wake anyone yet.

I argued in my last chapter that the "spirit of postmodernism" that Andrew Motion and Blake Morrison discerned in the poets they anthologised[16] was confined – if the term is properly defined – to some elements in James Fenton and Paul Muldoon and, to a lesser extent, in Craig Raine and Christopher Reid. However, it does seem to me that a number of the poets who have emerged since the Penguin anthology, but are "mainstream" in the sense the word is used on the Penguin blurb, do have genuine postmodernist characteristics. They are *less* postmodernist than John Ash and the others I have discussed in my last chapter, and far less than John Ashbery and the discursive/surreal disciples he anthologised in *The Best American Poetry 1988*[17]. What marks them as "mainstream" is their greater adherence to metrical norms and sometimes to conventional forms and their habit of winning prizes or of publishing in magazines like *The London Magazine*, *The London Review of Books et al.* Nonetheless, their poems are sceptical about language, self-reflexive, playful, self-consciously fictive, and deconstruct themselves. Especially important here are Selima Hill, Jo Shapcott, Glyn Maxwell, Simon Armitage, Carol Ann Duffy, Stephen Knight and, not least, Alan Jenkins, who has been important, not only as a practitioner, but for how, as poetry editor there, he has published such poets in the *TLS*, the most "mainstream" publication of all.

The crucial point, though, is the way that postmodernist elements are combined with realist ones. This is especially conspicuous in some of the younger poets whose work is characterised by a particularly modish sort of realism which is associated with "the street". These poets tend to be influenced almost as much by rock music as they are by the poetic tradition and their poems draw on a kind of street knowledge which characterises the songs, for example, of the Fall and the Smiths. So, much of Glyn Maxwell's "Tale of the Chocolate Egg"[18], for example, is set literally in the streets of a new town, and makes continuous, witty and energetic references, in self-consciously current idioms, to bits of youth culture in ways that suggest rock journalism on an impossibly good day.

All this constitutes a very reliable underpinning of the "real": mingled with this, however, are obvious postmodernist elements. The poem dwells jokily on postmodern media like television (referring especially to soap opera and CEEFAX) and, above all, advertising, and does so in order to raise questions about "reality" and representation:

> You couldn't see its centre, it was whole
> and flawless, like a real egg. It *was*
> a real egg, or representation of
>
> a real egg, or a real chocolate egg.
>
> (98)

Moreover, the eponymous egg connects the poem to modernist metaphorical concerns with fertility but does so in a depthlessly postmodernist way by referring to two unrequited loves – that of a skinhead for his "ex" and that of an Indian shop assistant for the "Brown-Haired Bloke", the hero of the poem – and treating them in a detached and comic way.

Motion/Morrison's reference to a "spirit of postmodernism", then, can most accurately be seen, not so much as descriptive of the poems they anthologised, but as predictive of what would happen

– albeit in a limited way – to "mainstream" poetry in the decade after their book was published. However, British poetry does seem to have an astonishing ability to domesticate such influences and accept them only in an altered form, and it is the hesitations between radically contradictory modes which make contemporary poetry what it is. This can be seen even in the work of an important senior poet like Peter Porter whose realist sensibility used to make him write poems that solidified into statements constructed from his characteristically acute social observation placed, by his historical *nous*, in larger imaginative frameworks; however, over the past decade his work has been influenced by John Ashbery so that it now opens into questions – while still employing much the same raw material.

Because they are irreconcilable, what happens when postmodernism and realism interact is that they call each other into question and continually defamiliarise each other. As a result estrangement effects have started to acquire increasing importance, especially in the treatment of language and the self. The career of Simon Armitage shows the effects of this with especial clarity. The first poem of the title sequence of *Book of Matches*[19] describes a "party piece" which involves its speaker telling the story of his life in the length of time it takes a match to burn itself out. In the poems that follow it a series of speakers performs the same trick.

Much of this links with Armitage's previous work – in particular the idea of story-telling as a game. In "Snow Joke", which starts his first book *Zoom*[20], the bad pun in the title pretends to tick the poem off for its playful heartlessness, the way it seems to enjoy its own narrative panache even at the expense of its central character whose hubris leads to his being found "slumped against the steering wheel/ with VOLVO printed backwards in his frozen brow". The aspect of this which perhaps most helped Armitage's rapid rise to fame was the synergy – sometimes alarming – between the late 80s content and his style: the way that the dead man's driving ("he had a good car so he snubbed/ the police warning-light and tried to finesse/ the last six miles of moorland blizzard") can seem an analogue for the poet's look-no-hands story-telling, his witty and self-conscious facility.

However, an increasing sobriety is evident in Armitage's more recent work, accompanied by less concern with jaunty, polished surfaces. One of his match strikers is expert at ducks and drakes, but his poem contrasts such "skimming" with how he "drops down" afterwards "into a wider world". This depth versus surface concern is new but connects with a consistent preoccupation with the self which started to take on a more perplexed and inquisitive aspect in *Kid*[21], especially in that book's parodies of Weldon Kees' "Robinson" poems. These explore the relationship between authors and their characters in a manner which suggests that relationship as an analogue for the elusiveness of the "real" self. In "Looking for Weldon Kees" the futile search for the American poet, the way he gets confused with his persona, the mysteriousness of his disappearance, all serve to question the extent to which the self, and especially other selves, are knowable.

For all its apparent slightness, Armitage's "Matches" sequence has this weighty and complex issue as its central preoccupation and marks a development from *Kid* in the anxious note it strikes, in seeming (to use one of his favourite words) "bothered" by what makes people tick. What these poems most resemble are those modernist short stories which employ "epiphanies" which illuminate characters' lives, but do so with self-conscious artificiality and without authorial comment. The prototype for this in Armitage's own work is in "Poem" which seems to be in search of a moral but ends instead with a shrug of the shoulders: "Here's how they rated him when they looked back:/ sometimes he did this, sometimes he did that."

Matches are much briefer than candles. This, and the fragility of matchlight hint at a newly abashed scepticism about what happens to people when they get translated into literature; but also – since this is a party game – they suggest that such translations happen anyway, outside literature, in the ways that people talk about themselves and others. This is quite different from the attitude to language implied previously in Armitage's linguistic exuberance, and made explicit in "Zoom", the title poem of his first book, in which words are celebrated as "small" and "smooth" and yet at the same time with a "mass. . .greater than the ringed planet".

So "Book of Matches" is a sonnet sequence but it is not about love, and this is part of its linguistic point, which is to do with mismatches. "There are those who manage their private affairs/ and those who have to make a hash of theirs": the poem that starts like this is about a parachutist who is at odds even with himself:

> Things he should want: safety first,
> a perfect match, a straight indivisible two –
> he wouldn't dream of leaping.
> But he don't. So he do.

A safety match is a paradox that might appeal to a contemporary Petrarch, or it might represent an impossible ideal of domestic passion to a more modern Meredith, but the problem with this character is that what he should want and what he does want (which is gratuitous danger) cannot cohabit. It is appropriate that it is not the parachutist himself who speaks the poem, but a "friend of a friend" of his – we are at several unsympathetic removes from his state of mind and the speaker suggests that it is lack of imagination, inability to dream of leaping, that makes him leap.

Traditionally, poems should also want experience and its expression to be "a straight indivisible two", but Armitage's sonneteering suggests formal desperation rather than form – his sonnets are broken, buckled and ruinously lived in. And there is a sadness in the controlling metaphor that tends to make all the speakers seem burnt-out cases, and to hint at a deathliness in the very process of structuring experience in language. The mauling that Armitage gives the sonnet form suggests profound mistrust of its suave symmetry, the way that through its complex and insistent rhyming words and meanings, stories and lives get persuasively matched.

However, the case of Carol Ann Duffy is even more telling because her work has always shown such clear signs of being linked to mainstream realism in its calling upon of the reader to make acts of recognition which are also acts of agreement. Increasingly, though, other kinds of writing have entered her poems alongside these realist ones and insisted on forms of grotesque and sometimes violent strangeness existing inside the familiar. Much of this has its origins in the influence that feminism has exerted on Duffy's sensibility, making her think about the subtly political impact that language has on identity. So her latest book *Mean Time*[22] refers to language repeatedly, the extent to which it makes the self in its own distortive image: "These days/ we are adjectives, nouns. In moments of grace/ we were verbs, the secrets of poems, talented." (26) In the context of this self-reflexiveness, Shklovsky's point about the estranging effect of self-conscious artificiality is again relevant:

> This new attitude to objects in which, in the last analysis, the object becomes perceptible, is that artificiality which, in our opinion, creates art. A phenomenon, perceived many times, and no longer perceivable, or rather, the method of such dimmed perception, is what I call "recognition" as opposed to "seeing". The aim of imagery, the aim of creating new art is to return the object from "recognition" to "seeing".[23]

Modes of consensual recognition are increasingly being confronted in Duffy's work by modes of defamiliarisation. These express political alarm about what happens inside the familiar by dwelling on moments when identity is overwhelmed by a sense of otherness, when the "thin skin" which she punningly says "lies on the language" (26) is peeled away and the world is seen as though for the first time.

However, these new poems are preoccupied with deception and desire. In this context the self and the world are endlessly both travestied and defamiliarised through their shifting relationship with each other and as a result Duffy can sound at times like an expressionist:

> . . .Years stand outside on the street
> looking up to an open window, black as our mouth
> which utters its tuneless song. The ghosts of ourselves,
> behind and before us, throng in a mirror, blind,
> laughing and weeping. They know who we are.

Lines like this are not designed to evoke a nod of recognition – they insist on their unusualness and issue a challenge designed to make the reader see how unfamiliar the world can seem under the pressure of highly charged states of mind. They do this largely by the self-conscious way they focus on their own imagery and implicitly draw attention to the different status which the different images have – the street and the window are amongst the most common of real objects but they are placed problematically in relation to the metaphorical years and singing mouth. Before this problem can be resolved, the next sentence introduces the "ghosts of ourselves" which are probably summoned up by the personified years and which, being "behind and before us" are both retrospective and prospective. All this is so far by now from a realist idiom that it cannot matter whether the mirror is literal or metaphorical. And "blind,/ laughing and weeping" suggests that the ghosts are projections of emotions, which continues the theme which is present throughout *Mean Time* of ontological fragmentation and doubt. Given the extent to which self and world are confused by this point in the poem the last sentence, "They know who we are" is blackly humorous. Duffy is famous for her short sentences and mostly they signal a laconic matter-of-factness which suggests tough realism – this one, however, is a summary of what refuses to be summarised.

Only these ghosts can know who we are and their authority is in question to a grimly laughable extent.

That sentence exemplifies my main point – it is a composite of realism (in its style) and of the kind of epistemological and ontological doubt usually associated with postmodernism. More broadly, then, it exemplifies the confrontation between these two traditions and value systems. For Duffy identity has been continually defamiliarised through her tendency to explore gender issues through the medium of dramatic monologue, where there is pressure to mimic a "real" voice but simultaneously a dialogic sense of artificiality, of "ventriloquial" performance. Repeatedly used it suggests an interpenetration of identities and Duffy seems partly to be reflecting on this in "Small Female Skull" (25) where the self, surreally, is both split and doubled, as the poet looks at and handles her own skull as though it were an alternative personality assumed in a monologue: "I kiss it on the brow, my warm lips to its papery bone,/ and take it to the mirror to ask for a gottle of geer".

This is pushed one step further in "Steam", which imagines desire actually erasing identity. But there is also here, crucially, a sense of this whole process of questioning the self and the world coming full circle under the estranging pressure of the confrontation between realism and postmodernism that I have been stressing. For the poem's last lines powerfully evoke a conviction of a defamiliarised reality that might come *after* postmodernism:

> Quite recently, if one of us sat up,
> or stood, or stretched, naked,
>
> a nude pose in soft pencil
> behind tissue paper
>
> appeared, rubbed itself out, slow,
> with a smoky cloth.
>
> Say a matter of months. This hand reaching
> through the steam
>
> to touch the real thing, shockingly there,
> not a ghost at all.

(36)

# Notes

## Notes for Introduction

1.  Victor Shklovsky, "Art as Technique" in *Russian Formalist Criticism: Four Essays* trans. and ed. Lee T. Lemon and Marion J. Reis (Lincoln: University of Nebraska Press, 1965) 3–24.
2.  Donald Davie, "Roy Fisher: An Appreciation" in *Thomas Hardy and British Poetry* (London: Routledge, 1973) 167.
3.  Stan Smith, "Middleton, (John) Christopher" in James Vinson and D.L. Kirkpatrick eds. *Contemporary Poets* (London: St. James' Press, 1985) 576.
4.  Douglas Dunn, *Terry Street* (London: Faber, 1969).
5.  Caryl Emerson, "The Outer Word and Inner Speech: Bakhtin, Vygotsky, and the Internalisation of Language" in Gary Saul Morson ed., *Bakhtin: Essays and Dialogues on his Work* (Chicago: University of Chicago Press, 1986) 24.
6.  M.M. Bakhtin, *The Dialogic Imagination* ed. Michael Holquist, trans. Caryl Emerson and Michael Holquist (Austin: University of Texas Press, 1981) 271. Henceforth D.I.
7.  See my "'There are many worlds': The Dialogic in *Terry Street* and after" in *Reading Douglas Dunn* ed. Robert Crawford and David Kinloch (Edinburgh: Edinburgh University Press, 1992) 17–31.
8.  Sylvia Plath, *Johnny Panic and the Bible of Dreams and Other Prose Writings* (London: Faber, 1977) 63.
9.  Sylvia Plath, *Crossing the Water* (London: Faber, 1971) 19–20.
10. M.M. Bakhtin, *Problems of Dostoevsky's Poetics* (Manchester: Manchester University Press, 1984) 123.

## Notes for Chapter 1

1.  John Osborne, "The Incredulous Eye: Craig Raine and Post-Modernist Aesthetics," *Stone Ferry Review* 2 (1978) 51–65. Henceforth Osborne.
2.  Craig Raine, *The Onion Memory* (Oxford: Oxford UP, 1978). Henceforth *Onion*).
3.  Blake Morrison and Andrew Motion, "Introduction" to *The Penguin Book of Contemporary British Poetry* (Harmondsworth: Penguin Books, 1982) 11–20.
4.  Alan Robinson, "Theatre of Trope: Craig Raine and Christopher Reid" in *Instabilities in Contemporary British Poetry* (London: Macmillan, 1988) 16–48.
5.  Craig Raine, *Haydn and the Valve Trumpet* (London: Faber and Faber, 1990) 224. This volume henceforth *Haydn*.
6.  John Haffenden, "Craig Raine," *Viewpoints: Poets in Conversation* (London: Faber and Faber, 1981) 179. This interview henceforth *Viewpoints*.
7.  Craig Raine, *A Martian Sends a Postcard Home* (Oxford: Oxford UP, 1979) 13–14. This volume henceforth *Martian*.

8.  Craig Raine, *The Electrification of the Soviet Union* (London: Faber and Faber, 1986).
9.  Craig Raine, *"1953"* (London: Faber and Faber, 1990) 31. This volume henceforth *"1953"*.
10. M.M. Bakhtin, *The Dialogic Imagination, Four Essays by M.M. Bakhtin*, trans. Caryl Emerson and Michael Holquist (Austin: University of Texas Press, 1981) 7. This volume henceforth *D.I.*
11. Brian McHale, *Postmodernist Fiction* (London: Methuen, 1987) 166.
12. V.N. Volosinov, *Marxism and the Philosophy of Language*, trans. Ladislav Matejka and I.R. Titunik (New York and London: Seminar Press, 1973) 133. Bakhtin is now generally thought to have been the actual author of this book, which is henceforth referred to as *Marxism*.
13. Peter Forbes, "A Martian at Glyndebourne," *Poetry Review* 76 (1986) 7–11. This interview with Raine henceforth Forbes.
14. Bakhtin quoted in Tzvetan Todorov, *Mikhail Bakhtin: The Dialogical Principle* (Minneapolis: University of Minnesota Press, 1984) 95. This volume henceforth Todorov.
15. M.M. Bakhtin, *Problems of Dostoevsky's Poetics*, translated and edited by Caryl Emerson (Manchester: Manchester UP, 1984) 30. This volume henceforth *Dostoevsky*.
16. Ezra Pound, "Vorticism," *Fortnightly Review* 1 September 1914, 467.
17. Craig Raine, *Rich* (London: Faber and Faber, 1984) 18–20. This volume henceforth *Rich*.
18. Charles Forceville, "Craig Raine's Poetry of Perception: Imagery in *A Martian Sends a Postcard Home*," *Dutch Quarterly Review of Anglo-American Letters* 15 (1985) 105.
19. Raine describes his father's faith-healing at some length in "A Silver Plate" (*Rich*, 43–64).
20. Michael Hulse, "Alms for Every Beggared Sense: Craig Raine's Aesthetic in Context," *Critical Quarterly* 23.4 (1981) 15.
21. Edward Larrissy, *Reading Twentieth Century Poetry: The Language of Gender and Objects* (Oxford: Basil Blackwell, 1990) 159.
22. Katerina Clark and Michael Holquist, *Mikhail Bakhtin* (Cambridge, Mass. and London: Harvard UP, 1984) 70.
23. Dante Alighieri, *The Divine Comedy*, Italian text with translation and comment by John D. Sinclair, 3 vols. (Oxford UP, 1971) I, 186.
24. Craig Raine, *History: The Home Movie* (London: Penguin, 1994).
25. Andrew Crozier, "Thrills and Frills: poetry as figures of empirical lyricism" in *Society and Literature 1945–1970* ed. Alan Sinfield (London: Methuen, 1983) 22.
26. Philip Larkin, *The Collected Poems* edited, with an introduction, by Anthony Thwaite (London: The Marvell Press and Faber and Faber, 1988) 114–116.

## Notes for Chapter 2

1.  Paul Muldoon, *Selected Poems 1968–1983* (London: Faber and Faber, 1986) 34. Unless otherwise stated, all page numbers in the text refer to this volume.

2.  Paul Muldoon, *Madoc* (London: Faber and Faber, 1990) 10–11. This book henceforth *Madoc*.
3.  E. Cobham Brewer, *The Dictionary of Phrase and Fable* (New York: Crown Publishers, 1978) 69.
4.  Susan Stewart, "Bakhtin's Anti-Linguistics" in Gary Saul Morson ed., *Bakhtin: Essays and Dialogues on his Work* (Chicago: University of Chicago Press, 1986) 48.
5.  M.M. Bakhtin, *The Dialogic Imagination: Four Essays* ed. Michael Holquist, trans. Caryl Emerson and Michael Holquist (Austin: University of Texas Press, 1981) 76. This book henceforth *Four Essays*.
6.  Seamus Heaney, *New Selected Poems* (London: Faber and Faber, 1990) 74–75. Henceforth *NSP*.
7.  Michael Donaghy, "A Conversation with Paul Muldoon", *Chicago Review* Vol. 35 (1985) 85.
8.  Paul Muldoon, *Why Brownlee Left* (London: Faber and Faber, 1980) 7–8.
9.  See Ciaron Carson on this point quoted in Edna Longley's "*North*: 'Inner Emigré' or 'Artful Voyeur'?" in *The Art of Seamus Heaney* ed. Tony Curtis (Bridgend: Poetry Wales Press, 1982) 78.
10. John Haffenden, *Viewpoints, Poets in Conversation* (London: Faber and Faber, 1981) 133. This volume henceforth *Viewpoints*.
11. Paul Muldoon, *The Faber Book of Contemporary Irish Poetry* (London: Faber and Faber, 1986) 373–392.
12. Paul Muldoon, *Meeting the British* (London: Faber and Faber, 1987) 16. This volume henceforth *MB*.
13. Katerina Clark and Michael Holquist, *Mikhail Bakhtin* (Cambridge, Massachusetts: Harvard University Press, 1984) 287–288.
14. Edna Longley, *Poetry in the Wars* (Newcastle Upon Tyne: Bloodaxe, 1986) 238.
15. Clair Wills, "The Lie of the Land: Language, Imperialism and Trade in Paul Muldoon's *Meeting the British*", in *The Chosen Ground: Essays on the Contemporary Poetry of Northern Ireland* ed. Neil Corcoran (Bridgend: Seren Books, 1992) 135.
16. Linda Hutcheon, "'The Pastime of Past Time': Fiction, History, Historiographic Metafiction", in *Postmodern Genres* ed. Marjorie Perloff (Norman; University of Oklahoma Press, 1988) 54–55.
17. William Sherman, "1837: The Mandan Indians", *Anglo-Welsh Review* Number 69, 1981, 53.
18. Ibid., 59.
19. Jean-François Lyotard, *The Postmodern Condition: A Report on Knowledge* (Manchester: Manchester University Press, 1984) 81. See also my discussion of this passage in my chapter "John Ashbery and British Postmodernism".

### Notes for Chapter 3

1.  Nancy Glazener, "Dialogic subversion: Bakhtin, the novel and Gertrude Stein", in *Bakhtin and Cultural Theory* ed. by Ken Hirschkop and David Shepherd (Manchester: Manchester University Press, 1989), 109. Henceforth Glazener.

2. James Fenton, "Ars Poetica: 12: Extrinsic Interest", *The Independent on Sunday Review*, 15th April 1990, 19. This series of fifty "masterclasses" appeared between 28th January 1990 and 13th January 1991: they are referred to henceforth as "Ars Poetica" followed by their date and page number.

3. James Fenton, *The Memory of War and Children in Exile: Poems 1968– 1983* (London: Penguin, 1994). Unless otherwise stated all page numbers in the text refer to this volume.

4. John Fuller, *Selected Poems 1954–1982* (London: Secker and Warburg, 1985) 27. Henceforth Fuller.

5. James Fenton, "The Manifesto Against Manifestoes", *Poetry Review*, 1983, 73 (3), 15.

6. Quoted in the "Preface" of *The Order of Things*" by Michel Foucault (London: Tavistock, 1974) xv. This book henceforth Foucault.

7. James Fenton and John Fuller, *Partingtime Hall* (London: Penguin, 1989). Henceforth *Partingtime*.

8. James Fenton, "Introduction: A Western Observer", in *All the Wrong Places* (Harmonsworth: Penguin, 1990) xiv. This book henceforth *Wrong Places*.

9. James Fenton, *Out of Danger* (London: Penguin, 1993).

10. Alan Robinson, *Instabilities in Contemporary British Poetry* (London: Macmillan, 1988) 14.

## Notes for Chapter 4

1. Fleur Adcock, "Rural Blitz: Fleur Adcock's English Childhood", *Poetry Review*, 1984, 74 (2), June, 4. (This autobiographical piece henceforth RB). In a letter to me dated 8th March 1992, Fleur Adcock writes: "the title 'Rural Blitz' was given to my autobiographical piece by the then editors of *Poetry Review*, Mick Imlah and Tracey Warr. I was rather annoyed; it seemed too glib and clever-clever. My own title for the piece was "My English Childhood", with the stress on *English*; I wanted to make it clear that my childhood did *not* take place in New Zealand, as people in both countries still seem to assume."

2. Fleur Adcock's introduction to her work in *The Bloodaxe Book of Contemporary Women Poets* ed. Jeni Couzyn (Bloodaxe Books, Newcastle Upon Tyne, 1985) 202. This book henceforth *CWP*.

3. Fleur Adcock, *Selected Poems* (Oxford University Press, Oxford, 1983) 93–94. Unless otherwise stated, all page numbers in the text refer to this volume.

4. Fleur Adcock, *Time Zones* (Oxford University Press, Oxford, 1991) 4– 5. This volume henceforth *TZ*.

5. Fleur Adcock, "Introduction" to *The Faber Book of Twentieth Century Women's Poetry* (Faber and Faber, 1987) 14.

6. Fleur Adcock, *The Incident Book* (Oxford University Press, Oxford, 1986) 52. This volume henceforth *IB*.

## Notes for Chapter 5

1. Carol Ann Duffy, *Selected Poems* (London: Penguin, 1994) 43. Unless otherwise stated all page references in the text refer to this volume.

2. M.M. Bakhtin, *The Dialogic Imagination* ed. Michael Holquist, trans. Caryl Emerson and Michael Holquist (Austin: University of Texas Press, 1981) 76. This book henceforth D.I.
3. Linda Hutcheon, *The Politics of Postmodernism* (London: Routledge, 1989) 168. Henceforth Hutcheon.
4. Carol Ann Duffy, *Standing Female Nude* (London: Anvil, 1985) 21.
5. Carol Ann Duffy, *Selling Manhattan* (London: Anvil, 1987) 55.

## Notes for Chapter 6

1. Blake Morrison and Andrew Motion, "Introduction" to *The Penguin Book of Contemporary British Poetry* (Harmondsworth: Penguin Books, 1982) 11–20.
2. Alan Jenkins, *Greenheart* (London: Chatto and Windus, 1990) 53–64.
3. Frank O'Hara, "Personism: A Manifesto" in *The Collected Poems of Frank O'Hara* (New York: Knopf, 1971) 498–499.
4. Andrew Motion, *Dangerous Play, Poems 1974–1984* (Harmondsworth: Penguin Books, 1985). Henceforth Motion.
5. Ross Chambers, *Story and Situation: Narrative Seduction and the Power of Fiction* (Minneapolis: University of Minnesota Press, 1984) 214.
6. Jackie Kay, *The Adoption Papers* (Newcastle Upon Tyne: Bloodaxe, 1991) 8–34.
7. George Szirtes, *Metro* (Oxford: Oxford University Press, 1988) 15–46.
8. Jo Shapcott, *Electroplating the Baby* (Newcastle Upon Tyne: Bloodaxe, 1988) 54–62. This sequence is discussed in my concluding chapter.
9. Matthew Sweeney, *Blue Shoes* (London: Secker and Warburg, 1989) 17. Henceforth Shoes.
10. Matthew Sweeney, *Cacti* (London: Secker and Warburg, 1992) 16.
11. Simon Armitage, *Zoom* (Newcastle Upon Tyne: Bloodaxe, 1989) 74. Henceforth Zoom.
12. Simon Armitage, *Kid* (London: Faber, 1992). Henceforth Kid.
13. Glyn Maxwell, *Tale of the Mayor's Son* (Newcastle Upon Tyne: Bloodaxe, 1990) 96–111.
14. Glyn Maxwell, *Out of the Rain* (Newcastle Upon Tyne: Bloodaxe, 1992) 42–62.
15. Paul Durcan, *A Snail in my Prime: New and Selected Poems* (London: Harvill, 1993) 238. All references to Durcan are to this volume.

## Notes for Chapter 7

1. *The New Poetry* ed. Michael Hulse, David Kennedy and David Morley (Newcastle: Bloodaxe, 1993).
2. Viktor Shklovsky, *Mayakovsky and his Circle* (London: Pluto, 1974) 114.
3. Charles Tomlinson, *Selected Poems 1951–1974* (Oxford: Oxford University Press, 1978) 85–86.
4. W.S. Graham, *Implements in their Places* (London: Faber, 1977) 11. All references are to this volume.
5. Tony Bennett, *Formalism and Marxism* (London: Methuen, 1979) 54. All references are to this volume.

6.  *Poetry of the Committed Individual* ed. Jon Silkin (Harmondsworth: Penguin, 1973).
7.  Jon Silkin, *Selected Poems* (London: Routledge, 1980) 83–84.

## Notes for Chapter 8

1.  Edwin Morgan, *Themes on a Variation* (Manchester: Carcanet, 1988). Henceforth *Themes*.
2.  Edwin Morgan, *Poems of Thirty Years* (Manchester: Carcanet, 1982).
3.  Edwin Morgan, *Collected Poems* (Manchester: Carcanet, 1990). Unless otherwise stated all the page numbers in the text refer to this volume.
4.  Edwin Morgan, *Selected Poems* (Manchester: Carcanet, 1985). Henceforth *Selected*.
5.  The most important books of translations are *Poems from Eugenio Montale* (Reading, Berkshire: University of Reading School of Art, 1959); and *Wi the Haill Voice: Poems by Mayakovsky* (Oxford: Carcanet, 1972). *Rites of Passage: Translations* (Manchester: Carcanet, 1975) is a selection.
6.  Edwin Morgan, *Essays* (Cheadle, Cheshire: Carcanet, 1975).
7.  Edwin Morgan, *From Glasgow to Saturn* (Cheadle, Cheshire: Carcanet, 1973). Collected in *Poems of Thirty Years*.
8.  Michael Schmidt, "Edwin Morgan," *An Introduction to Fifty Modern British Poets* (London: Pan Books, 1979) 317.
9.  Edwin Morgan's note on his poem "Seven Headlines" in Emmett Williams, *An Anthology of Concrete Poetry* (New York: Something Else Press, 1967). The book is unpaginated, but organised alphabetically according to the names of contributors.
10. A "translation" of the poem by Heather Bremer which first appeared in the *TLS* on 3 February 1966, incorporating two corrections by Morgan that appeared on 10 February. See Geoffrey Summerfield (ed.) *Worlds: Seven Modern Poets* (Harmondsworth: Penguin, 1974) 275–277. This book also includes a selection of poems by Morgan and a note by him on the origins of and motives for his writing.
11. Marshall Walker, *Edwin Morgan: An Interview* (Preston, Lancashire: Akros, 1977) 6. This pamphlet referred to henceforth as *Interview*.
12. See *Essays* 14, 15, 61, 64, 204 and *Interview* 9–12.
13. R.S. Edgecombe, "The Poetry of Edwin Morgan", *Dalhousie Review* 62 (1982–83) 677.
14. But see "The New Divan" and "The Coals".
15. Robin Hamilton, "Edwin Morgan: Translator of Reality," *Science and Psychodrama: The Poetry of Edwin Morgan and David Black* 35.
16. Kevin McCarra, "Morgan's 'Cinquevalli'", *Scottish Literary Journal* 12 (1985) 70.
17. Roland Barthes, "The Photographic Message", *Image-Music-Text* (Glasgow: Collins, 1977) 15–31.
18. Terry Eagleton, *Literary Theory: An Introduction* (Oxford: Basi Blackwell, 1983) 4.
19. Andrew Crozier, "Thrills and Frills: poetry as figures of empirical lyricism" in *Society and Literature 1945–1970* ed. Alan Sinfield (London: Methuen, 1983) 220–221.

## Notes for Chapter 9

1.  Ian Hamilton, "Four Conversations," *The London Magazine* Vol 4 No 6 (1964) 79. This interview henceforth referred to as "Conversations".
2.  Christopher Middleton, *Selected Writings* (Manchester: Carcanet, 1989) 20–21. Unless otherwise stated all the page numbers in the text refer to this volume.
3.  Christopher Middleton, *Bolshevism in Art and Other Expository Writings* (Manchester: Carcanet, 1978) 223. This volume henceforth referred to as *Bolshevism*.
4.  Christopher Middleton, *Poems* (London: The Fortune Press, 1944) and *Nocturne in Eden* (London: The Fortune Press, 1945).
5.  Christopher Middleton, *Pataxanadu* (Manchester: Carcanet, 1977).
6.  Stan Smith, *Inviolable Voice* (Dublin: Gill and Macmillan, 1982) 231–234.
7.  Christopher Middleton, "For Marton, Erwin, and Miklos" in *The Pursuit of the Kingfisher (essays)* (Manchester: Carcanet, 1983) 42–50. This volume henceforth referred to as *Kingfisher*.
8.  Martin Heidegger, *Being and Time* (Oxford: Blackwell, 1980) 174. This volume henceforth referred to as *Heidegger*.
9.  T.S. Eliot, *The Complete Poems and Plays* (London: Faber, 1969) 23.
10. Roger Waterhouse, *A Heidegger Critique* (Brighton: Harvester, 1981) 174.
11. See John Osborne, "Modernism" *Bete Noire* 4 (1987) 77–78.
12. Michael Schmidt, *An Introduction to Fifty Modern British Poets* (London: Pan Books, 1979) 354–355. This volume henceforth referred to as Schmidt.
13. Christopher Middleton (translator), *Selected Poems* by Friedrich Holderlin and Edward Morike (Chicago and London: University of Chicago Press, 1972) 93.
14. Christopher Middleton, *torse 3* (London: Longmans, 1962) printed as epigraph before the start of pagination.
15. Paul de Man, "Heidegger's Exegeses of Holderlin", in *Blindness and Insight* (London: Methuen, 1983) 253.

## Notes for Chapter 10

1.  Roy Fisher, *Poems 1955–1980* (Oxford, 1980). Henceforth referred to as *Poems*.
2.  Donald Davie, "Roy Fisher: An Appreciation", in *Thomas Hardy and British Poetry* (London: Routledge, 1973), 152–172, henceforth referred to as Davie. Eric Mottram, "Roy Fisher's Work", *Stand* Vol. II (1969–1970) No. 1, 9–18, henceforth referred to as Mottram. See also Deborah Mitchell, "Modes of Realism: Roy Fisher and Elaine Feinstein", in *British Poetry Since 1970*, ed. Peter Jones and Michael Schmidt (Manchester: Caracanet, 1980), 125–130; and J.D. Needham, "Some Aspects of the Poetry of Roy Fisher", *Poetry Nation* 5, Vol. IIIi (1975) 74–87.
3.  Jed Rasula and Mike Erwin, "An Interview With Roy Fisher", in *Nineteen Poems and an Interview* (Pensnett, Staffordshire, 1975), 12–38. The

interview was conducted on 19 November 1973 and is henceforth referred to as "Interview".

4. Charles Baudelaire, *Oeuvres Complètes* Vol. III, *Petits Poèmes en Prose* (Paris: Louis Conard, 1917) 107–112.
5. Philip Gardner, "A City of the Mind", *TLS* March 20, 1981, 314.
6. Roy Fisher, *Consolidated Comedies* (Durham: Pig Press, 1981).

**Notes for Chapter 11**

1. Tim Longville and Andrew Crozier eds., *A Various Art* (Manchester: Carcanet, 1987). All references to Prynne and Crozier are to this volume. Henceforth Various.
2. Gillian Allnutt, Fred D'Aguiar, Ken Edwards and Eric Mottram eds., *the new british poetry* (London: Paladin, 1988). Henceforth nbp.
3. Andrew Crozier, "Thrills and Frills: poetry as figures of empirical lyricism" in Alan Sinfield ed. *Society and Literature 1945–1970* (London: Methuen, 1983) 223.
4. Simon Armitage, *Zoom* (Newcastle Upon Tyne: Bloodaxe, 1989) 80.
5. Simon Armitage, *Book of Matches* (London: Faber, 1993).
6. Edwin Morgan, "A Sequence for Veronica Forrest-Thomson", *Poems of Thirty Years* (Manchester: Carcanet, 1982) 374.
7. Veronica Forrest-Thomson, *Collected Poems and Translations* (London: Allardyce, Barnett, 1990) 22. Unless otherwise stated all the page numbers in the text refer to this volume.
8. Ludwig Wittgenstein, *Philosophical Investigations* (Oxford: Blackwell, 1968) 193–229. This volume henceforth *PI*.
9. Victor Shklovsky, "Art as Technique" in *Russian Formalist Criticism – Four Essays* trans. and ed. Lee T. Lemon and Marion J. Reis (Lincoln: University of Nebraska Press, 1965) 12.
10. Veronica Forrest-Thomson, *Poetic Artifice* (Manchester: Manchester University Press, 1978) 53. This volume henceforth *Artifice*.
11. Ludwig Wittgenstein, *Zettel* (Oxford: Blackwell, 1967) 113. This volume henceforth Zettel.
12. James Keery, "A Unique Voice, Veronica Forrest-Thomson, *Collected Poems and Translations*", *PN Review* Vol. 17 Number 4 (1991) 86. See also Keery's essay "Blossoming Synecdoches: A Study of Veronica Forrest-Thomson", *Bete Noire* Issue Ten/Eleven (Autumn 1990/Spring 1991) 109–122 – this is especially good on *Poetic Artifice*.
13. Denise Riley, *Mop Mop Georgette: New and Selected Poems 1986–1993* (Cambridge: Reality Street, 1993) 54. All references to Riley are to this volume.

**Notes for Chapter 12**

1. See John Osborne, "The Incredulous Eye: Craig Raine and Post-Modernist Aesthetics", *Stone Ferry Review* Number Two, Winter 1978, 51–65.
2. Blake Morrison and Andrew Motion, "Introduction" to *The Penguin Book of Contemporary British Poetry* (Harmondsworth, 1982) 20.
3. Blake Morrison, *Seamus Heaney* (London: Methuen, 1982).

4. Michael Schmidt, *An Introduction to Fifty British Poets, 1300–1900* (London: Pan, 1979) 398.

5. Seamus Heaney, *New Selected Poems 1966–1987* (London: Faber and Faber, 1990) 1. Henceforth *NSP*.

6. Seamus Heaney, *Seeing Things* (London: Faber and Faber, 1991) 16–18.

7. Seamus Heaney, *Preoccupations: Selected Prose 1968–1978* (London: Faber and Faber, 1980) 57–58.

8. Ciaran Carson quoted in Edna Longley, "*North*: 'Inner Emigré' or 'Artful Voyeur'?" in *The Art of Seamus Heaney* ed. Tony Curtis (Bridgend: Poetry Wales Press, 1982) 78.

9. John Ashbery, ed. *The Best American Poetry 1988* (New York: Macmillan, 1988).

10. Donald Hall, ed. *The Best American Poetry 1989* (New York: Macmillan, 1989).

11. Martin Booth, *British Poetry 1964–1984* (London: Routledge and Kegan Paul, 1985) 250.

12. John Ashbery, *Selected Poems* (London: Paladin, 1987) 196–212. Unless otherwise stated, all quotations from Ashbery are from this volume.

13. John Ash, *Disbelief* (Manchester: Carcanet, 1987) 68–70. This volume henceforth *D*.

14. Piotr Sommer, "John Ashbery in Warsaw", *Quarto* No. 17, May 1981, 14.

15. David Kalstone, *Five Temperaments* (Oxford: Oxford University Press, 1977) 171.

16. John Ashbery, "Hunger and Love in their Variations", in *Kitaj: Paintings, Drawings, Pastels* (London: Thames and Hudson, 1983) 11.

17. John Ash, *The Branching Stairs* (Manchester: Carcanet, 1984) 39. This book henceforth *BS*.

18. John Ash, *The Goodbyes* (Manchester: Carcanet, 1982) 48. Henceforth *G*.

19. John Ash, "John Ashbery in Conversation", *P.N. Review* No. 46 Vol. 12 Number 2, 1985, 34.

20. John Ash, "Reading Music: Part 1", *P.N. Review* No. 50, Vol. 12 Number 6, 1986, 47.

21. Peter Ackroyd, *The Diversions of Purley* (London: Hamish Hamilton, 1987).

22. Peter Ackroyd, *T.S. Eliot* (London: Hamish Hamilton, 1984).

23. Peter Ackroyd, *Hawksmoor* (London: Hamish Hamilton, 1985).

24. John Ashbery, *As We Know* (Manchester: Carcanet, 1979) 3–68.

25. David Lehman, "The Pleasures of Poetry", *New York Times Magazine* December 16, 1984, Section 6, 92.

26. Peter Didsbury, *The Butchers of Hull* (Newcastle Upon Tyne: Bloodaxe, 1982) 42–43.

27. Peter Didsbury, *The Classical Farm* (Newcastle Upon Tyne: Bloodaxe, 1987) 20–21.

28. Christopher Middleton, *Bolshevism in Art* (Manchester: Carcanet, 1978) 214. Henceforth *Bolshevism*.

29. Christopher Middleton, *Selected Writings* (Manchester: Carcanet, 1989) 129.

30. Jean-Francois Lyotard, *The Postmodern Condition: A Report on Knowledge* (Manchester: Manchester University Press, 1984) 77. This book henceforth Lyotard.
31. John Ashbery, *Flow Chart* (Manchester: Carcanet, 1991).
32. Helen Dunmore, *New and Selected Poems* (Newcastle upon Tyne: Bloodaxe).
33. John Ash, "A Classic Post-Modernist", *Atlantic review* Number Two, Autumn 1979, 39–50. Henceforth "R.F.".
34. Roy Fisher, *Poems 1955–1980* (Oxford: Oxford University Press, 1980) 102–104.
35. John Ash, *The Burnt Pages* (Manchester: Carcanet, 1991). Henceforth *BP*.
36. Ian McMillan, *Selected Poems* (Manchester: Carcanet, 1987) 76–77.

## Notes for Chapter 13

1. Linda France, ed. *Sixty Women Poets* (Newcastle Upon Tyne: Bloodaxe, 1993).
2. Andrew Motion, *Dangerous Play, Poems 1974–1984* (Harmondsworth: Penguin Books, 1985) 12–13.
3. Selima Hill, *The Accumulation of Small Acts of Kindness* (London: Chatto and Windus, 1989).
4. Margaret Whitford, *Luce Irigaray: Philosophy in the Feminine* (London: Routledge, 1991) 42.
5. Jo Shapcott, *Electroplating the Baby* (Newcastle Upon Tyne: Bloodaxe, 1988) 54–62.
6. Jackie Kay, *The Adoption Papers* (Newcastle Upon Tyne: Bloodaxe, 1991) 8–34.
7. George Szirtes, *Metro* (Oxford: Oxford University Press, 1988) 15–46.
8. Kerryn Goldsworthy, "Interview with Angela Carter", *Meanjin*, 1985, 4 (1), 5.
9. Jo Shapcott, *Electroplating the Baby* (Newcastle Upon Tyne: Bloodaxe, 1988) 11.
10. John Ash, *The Goodbyes* (Manchester: Carcanet, 1982) 11–12.
11. Jo Shapcott, *Phrase Book* (Oxford: Oxford University Press, 1992) 12–13.
12. Stephen Knight, *Flowering Limbs* (Newcastle: Bloodaxe, 1993) 46–47.
13. Charles Simic, *Charon's Cosmology* (New York: Braziller, 1977) 29.
14. John Mole, *Passing Judgements* (Bristol: Bristol Classical Press, 1989) 32.
15. Sean O'Brien, *HMS Glasshouse* (Oxford: Oxford University Press, 1991) 3–4.
16. Blake Morrison and Andrew Motion, "Introduction" to *The Penguin Book of Contemporary British Poetry* (Harmondsworth: Penguin Books, 1982) 20.
17. John Ashbery, ed. *The Best American Poetry 1988* (New York: Macmillan, 1988).
18. Glyn Maxwell, *Tale of the Mayor's Son* (Newcastle Upon Tyne: Bloodaxe, 1990) 96–111.

19.   Simon Armitage, *Book of Matches* (London: Faber, 1993).
20.   Simon Armitage, *Zoom* (Newcastle Upon Tyne: Bloodaxe, 1989).
21.   Simon Armitage, *Kid* (London: Faber, 1992).
22.   Carol Ann Duffy, *Mean Time* (London: Anvil, 1993).
23.   Viktor Shklovsky, *Mayakovsky and his Circle* (London: Pluto, 1974)
      114.

# Index